Beyond Wolves

Beyond Wolves

The Politics of Wolf Recovery and Management

Martin A. Nie

University of Minnesota Press

Minneapolis

London

An earlier version of chapter 2 appeared as "The Sociopolitical Dimensions of Wolf Management and Restoration in the United States," *Human Ecology Review* 8, no. 1 (2001): 1–12. Copyright 2001 *Human Ecology Review;* reprinted by permission.

Published by the University of Minnesota Press
111 Third Avenue South, Suite 290
Minneapolis, MN 55401-2520
http://www.upress.umn.edu

Library of Congress Cataloging-in-Publication Data

Nie, Martin A.
 Beyond wolves : the politics of wolf recovery and management / Martin A. Nie.
  p.   cm.
 Includes bibliographical references (p.   ) and index.
 ISBN 0-8166-3977-9 (HC : alk. paper) — ISBN 0-8166-3978-7 (PB : alk. paper)
 1. Wolves—Reintroduction—Political aspects—United States.
 2. Wildlife management—Political aspects—United States.   I. Title.
 QL737.C22 N53 2003
 333.95'9773'0973—dc21   2002152215

Printed in the United States of America on acid-free paper

The University of Minnesota is an equal-opportunity educator and employer.

To Vanessa and Joe

Contents

Preface

Those who have followed the story of wolf recovery and management in recent years surely recognize that it goes well beyond wolves. Take one public comment hearing held in Duluth, Minnesota, for example. The U.S. Fish and Wildlife Service (FWS) invited public comment specifically targeted to its proposed plan to downlist and delist the wolf from the Endangered Species Act (ESA) list in parts of the country. Opening the microphones to a crowded room, three serious FWS officials sat for two and a half hours "soliciting public comment." Of course, the comments went well beyond wolves, and they usually had nothing to do with the FWS's proposed plan. The crowd heard stories of federal government conspiracy and urban out-of-touch "wolf lovers," and both praise and vilification of the ESA. Farmers and ranchers proposed "getting wolves out of farm country." An equal number of citizens proposed "getting farms out of wild country." According to one outraged farmer, we ought to reintroduce rats to the homes of wolf lovers and then restrict them from protecting their children from attack. Another speaker informed the crowd in no uncertain terms that he really did not care about the cows, sheep, or turkeys at risk: "No one's self-interest is paramount over the survival of a species." As the logic goes, you don't care about my future, why should I care about yours?

There were also moments of courage, often words spoken by people with complex feelings and a desire to "just move on." A Chippewa farmer informed the crowd that she would cry if the wolf was again unfairly persecuted, but her family and its livestock also suffered greatly because of Minnesota's growing wolf population. She talked of an indigenous knowledge and of complex ecological relationships. One young college student bravely declared, "I am a wolf lover," but then went on to tell about her roots in a Minnesota farm family. She knows both sides, she said, and then ended perfectly a rather ugly evening on a beautiful and more promising note of empathy and common ground.

This public comment meeting should teach us at least a couple of things. First, this debate will continue to be about much more than just wolves, and for good reason. Second, the future of the wolf should be vigorously debated in an arena as inclusive, representative, and democratic as possible.

In this book I cover the ground between the leap from this public comment meeting to this observation and recommendation. The impetus for this project came about as I moved from the Southwest to northern Minnesota. During my last months in northern Arizona, Mexican wolves were being released into wild but politically hostile territory. The amount of controversy that these relatively few wolves caused in the region was not a big surprise. After all, I had recently witnessed the acrimony over the Grand Staircase–Escalante National Monument and the Mexican spotted owl, among other environmental controversies. What surprised me was not the antiwolf rhetoric, but how quickly this program was faltering on the ground. Soon after I left Flagstaff, wolves were quickly being illegally killed.

Northern Minnesota soon provided me a different type of wolf story. As the public comment session attests, more than a few themes and conflicts are found in both places; the historic war on the wolf happened throughout the United States. Still, when wolves eat livestock, people get angry. But I also quickly noted how different the story was in Minnesota. The typical wolf story in the newspaper in Duluth is one of an angry farmer whose prize bull was eaten, or of a shaken property owner whose dog was killed by wolves. They were angry or scared indeed, but their response and the context in which they spoke was somehow different. The response usually goes something like, "I don't mind having wolves around, but I want to kill the wolf that just killed my dog." This is anecdotal to be sure, but the fact remains that northern Minnesota manages to live with roughly 2,500 wolves, and the Southwest struggles over the 65 that have been released. I wanted to find out more, and this complicated social and political story is the result.

I would like to say a word about my target audience. I believe this book should be of some value to all those involved in wolf management and policy in one capacity or another. I believe, as do others writing about the "human dimensions" of natural resource and wildlife policy, that understanding political context is critically important for successful policymaking and its implementation. In large part, those people most involved in the wolf debate and those interviewed during the wolf policy project helped determine the direction in which this research would flow. In many places I have pursued questions and issues that these participants told me were most important to their future and the future of the wolf. I hope that this book can help us better understand the wolf debate in a more inclusive way, and somehow help us resolve or work through future conflict.

The book is also written for students of public policy and environmental studies. I hope it is used as a case study and supplement in such courses as environmental politics and policy, natural resource policy and management, public policy, and environmental studies. It applies a number of subjects and useful concepts from political science and public policy to the study of natural resources, wildlife, and wolves. It also examines issues and debates that go beyond disciplinary and management boundaries, such as the use of stakeholders in environmental decision making and management, contending environmental approaches and strategies, struggles over political compromise, and human values and political power in the policymaking process. Many studies have placed wolves in their larger ecological context, but this book tries to place them in our larger democratic process, a task that is no less confusing or important.

Let me also be straightforward about where I stand in this debate, because readers deserve to know a little about who is doing the analysis and interpretation. I strongly believe in the words written by Lois Crisler from Alaska's Brooks Range in the 1950s: "Wilderness without its animals is dead—dead scenery. Animals without wilderness are a closed book."[1] I also agree with writer and wilderness advocate Rick Bass: "My affinity, my allegiance, is with complete landscapes, with wild places. I'd rather try to protect an undesignated wilderness area—a landscape's wild qualities, which comprises millions of variables—than spend energy on lobbying for the return of some single species—a grizzly, a caribou, a wolf."[2] I also believe that we must find ways to allow wolves, wilderness, and sustainable communities to flourish. My personal politics aside, I have tried, above all, to fairly represent the array of values and viewpoints heard in this debate.

There are countless individuals who have been of great help to me and the wolf policy project, including Ed Bangs, Karlyn Atkinson Berg, Dick and Mary Bishop, Greg Bos, Toby Boudreau, Pete Buist, Kimberly Byrd, Robert McGreggor Cawley, Barb Cestero, John Coady, Jim Cross, Jake Cummins, Peter David, Karen Deatherage, Kristin DeBoer, Mike Doogan, Bonnie Drummond, Rob Edward, Gerry Ring Erickson, Nina Fascione, Hank Fischer, Mike Fleagle, Michael Furtman, David Gaillard, Craig Gardner, Craig Grau, Gordon Haber, Jim Hammill, Cathie Harms, Jeff Hughes, Mark Johnson, Paul Joslin, Randy Jurewicz, Michele Keck, Robert Keiter, Pete Kelly, Sarah Leonard, William Mangun, James Marcotte, Mark McNay, David Mech, Craig Medred, SuzAnne Miller, Stanley Ned, Mark Neuzil, David Parsons, Jim Peterson, Dan Pletscher, Doug Pope, Michael Robinson, John Schoen, Bob Skinner, Chris Smith, Doug Smith, Susan Todd, Tom Toman, Pam Troxell, David Tyler, Vic Van Ballenberghe, David van den Berg, Becky Weed, George Wuerthner, Adrian Wydeven, and Heidi Youmans. Reviewers of the manuscript were also very helpful, and the thorough editing by Mary Keirstead is much appreciated. Ralph Maughan's online *Wildlife Report* (www.forwolves.org/ralph/index.html) and the Center for the Rocky Mountain West's *Headwaters News* (www.headwatersnews.org) provided an excellent way to stay up-to-date with wolf and environmental news in the Northern Rockies. My friend Jacqueline Vaughn Switzer provided support and insight, and research and writing by those such as Tim Clark, Stephen Kellert, Deborah Stone, and Steven Yaffee have proven indispensable from the beginning of the project.

Various organizations have also been of particular assistance, including the Alaska Outdoor Council, Alaska Wilderness Recreation and Tourism Association, Alaska Wildlife Alliance, American Farm Bureau Federation, Center for Biological Diversity, Central Rockies Wolf Project, Coalition to Restore the Eastern Wolf, Defenders of Wildlife, Foundation for Research on Economics and the Environment, Friends of Animals, Greater Yellowstone Coalition, Great Lakes Indian Fish and Wildlife Commission, International Wolf Center, Izaak Walton League, Maine Wolf Coalition, Midwest Wolf Stewards, Minnesota Deer Hunters Association, Minnesota State Cattlemen's Association, Montana Farm Bureau

Federation, Montana Stockgrowers Association, Montana Wildlife Federation, National Audubon Society, Northern Rockies Conservation Cooperative, Predator Conservation Alliance, Rocky Mountain Elk Foundation, RESTORE: The North Woods, Sinapu, Sonoran Institute, Tanana Chiefs Conference, Thirteen Mile Lamb and Wool Company, and Timber Wolf Alliance. I also want to thank personnel in the U.S. Fish and Wildlife Service and those working in various state wildlife agencies, especially those in Alaska's Department of Fish and Game. The Environment and Natural Resources Institute at the University of Alaska, Anchorage, and the Mountain Research Center at Montana State University provided significant institutional support while I conducted interviews and fieldwork in Alaska and the Northern Rockies region.

I am indebted to the dozens of individuals who were interviewed or discussed wolf politics with me. Many of these people donated a significant part of their day and have in turn provided the project an important voice and grounding. And thank you for the free coffee. Generous grant support from the Office of the Vice President for Research and Dean of the Graduate School of the University of Minnesota provided me the opportunity to carry out this research. Research assistance by the University of Minnesota Duluth has also been significant.

Finally, I would like to thank my family and friends. Booker T. has always kept my feet warm and the door open. Vanessa, my loving wife and best friend, has given me more support than I could ever imagine—thank you.

Introduction

It is ordered, that there should be 10 shillings a piece allowed for such wolves as are killed.

Wolf legislation in the Colony of Massachusetts Bay, 1637

The reintroduction of the wolf is an extraordinary statement for the American people. It enables us to come close to restoring, in one specific area, conditions resembling what Lewis and Clark would have seen as they made their way across the West in 1803–07. It reconnects our historical linkage with the wilderness that is so central to our national character. It admits to past errors and asserts our willingness to correct them. It offers a new vision of a developed society living in harmony with its magnificent wilderness endowment.

Secretary of the Interior Bruce Babbitt, on the reintroduction of wolves into Yellowstone National Park, 1995

By quietly walking on their own, or with helicopters, biologists, and the media in a maelstrom of controversy, wolves are returning to old American landscapes. Their story of persecution and recovery will be one of the most important told of American wildlife and the history of American environmentalism. For this reason the story of their return has been told often and well. This book examines the issues that those most involved in wolf recovery and management often tell me go "beyond wolves."

Although the science of the wolf—its ecological needs, the prey on which it depends, mating behavior, social characteristics—is relatively well understood and the stuff of television documentaries, the socio-political context that wolves ultimately find themselves in is still largely one of public bewilderment or dismay. While details of a wolf-moose battle are sometimes more appreciated than a rundown of livestock industry campaign contributions, the latter may prove to be just as important to the survival of the wolf. By examining the sociopolitical aspects of our relationship with *Canis lupus*, we can more fully grasp a number of important issues that transcend wolves. In this book I explore these issues with one eye while keeping the other eye specifically focused on wolf recovery and management in the United States. The book does not try to duplicate what has already been done so well by others.[1] It is not a comprehensive account of wolf history nor does it provide a detailed study of one particular case of wolf reintroduction. Instead, it takes off from the historical and popular works and places the story in its larger context of politics, management, and conflict resolution.

During the early stages of research for this project, it quickly became apparent that wolves continue to be an important symbol and barometer for a host of different political, social, cultural, and economic issues. Whether during a formal interview or informally over a cup of coffee, most of my discussions about wolves quickly became discussions of something else entirely. Many of these did focus specifically on wolves—livestock depredation concerns, threats to human safety, declining moose, deer, and elk populations—but many of these discussions were only tangentially related to this symbolic predator. Sometimes I had to remind myself that the discussion actually began as one about wolves. I think this says more about the subject matter than it does about my interviewing skills. Ranchers, or their representative organizations, would tell me how elite urban "enviros" are simply using the Endangered Species Act (ESA) as a tool to lock out ranchers and extractive industries from the public domain. They would accentuate the importance of more local control, custom, culture, private property rights, and the need for "sound science" in wildlife management. Environmentalists, on the other hand, were quick to remind me that wolves are an example of how ranching dominance in the West is no longer unchallenged and that the public will no longer remain silent or be intimidated by the Western cowboy culture. They, of course, also emphasized the importance of "sound science" in the wolf debate. Talks with state wildlife managers would become talks about budgets, boondoggles, and state wildlife commissions; talks with hunters, about custom and culture; with state and local politicos, about federal arrogance, intrusiveness, and unfunded (wolf) mandates; and so on. What quickly became apparent is how wolves are so often entangled in a number of larger and more daunting political and cultural debates.

Wolves are an important indicator species both biologically and politically. Their return provides an opportunity for the country to assess where we are and in what direction we want to proceed. Wolves have forced us to take stock and ask some challenging questions on a number of different levels, some cultural, some deeply personal, and others that are pure politics and political strategy. Do we value wolves, biodiversity, and evolution? Do we value the wilderness or habitat they will need to persist without constant human manipulation and interference? If so, are we willing to back off a little to ensure this protection? Are we willing to coexist with a species that cannot be consumed or turned into profit? Are wolves merely another commodity, one more thing that Americans want but are not willing to make sacrifices for?[2] And on the political front, how should wolf policy and management decisions be made and by whom? Can the states or a smaller unit of government effectively safeguard biodiversity and the nation's collective wildlife legacy? Who are the "stakeholders" here? And once invited to the decision-making process, what role should they play?

In asking these and other questions, this book examines issues that affect wolves, to be sure, but also other carnivores, wildlife, biodiversity, and the continuing struggle over wilderness preservation in the United States. The wolf debate is an important case to learn from because it is often a microcosm of how the natural resource policy and management process works (or does not work) in this country. The following policy-related questions are explored in the book's chapters:

- What policy players and interests are involved in wolf policymaking and management? In what type of political conflict are they engaged? What values are embedded in the wolf policymaking process? And finally, what power and position do these players have, and what role are they likely to play in the future? (chapter 1)
- Why is the debate over wolf recovery so controversial and acrimonious? How has the wolf debate (the "wolf problem") been defined? Who cares? (chapter 2)

- What are the contexts in which wolves are being reintroduced and managed? What are the policy implications of these contexts? What do these contexts mean for future wolf management by states? (chapter 3)
- How should decisions regarding wolf policy and management be made? Who are the stakeholders, and what role do they have in decision making? What role should they have? (chapter 4)

By asking these questions, I hope that the wolf debate of the future can become smarter, more positive, vision-oriented, public, and democratic.

As writer Barry Lopez so poignantly explains, the story of wolves and men has always been tied to landscape, culture, and historical context. The wolf, says Lopez, exerts a powerful influence on the human imagination: "It takes your stare and turns it back on you."[3] Lopez's important work broadened a rather myopic understanding of wolves to show how differently they are perceived in different times and spaces by those such as native Alaskans, biologists, hunters, and trappers. The wolf in American history cannot be understood outside of its larger context, including manifest destiny, the sanctity of private property, and the perceived need to tame the western frontier and its wilderness. In assessing the unprecedented slaughter of wolves in frontier America, Lopez singles out the latter as the root cause: "The hatred has religious roots: the wolf was the Devil in disguise. And it has secular roots: wolves killed stock and made men poor. At a more general level it had to do, historically, with feelings about wilderness. What men said about the one, they generally meant about the other. To celebrate wilderness was to celebrate the wolf; to want an end to wilderness and all it stood for was to want the wolf's head."[4]

The abomination and violence migrating settlers displayed in ridding the frontier of wolves are instructive here. Wilderness and the animals in it were interpreted as obstacles to progress. The wolf became not only an object of pathological animosity but also a scapegoat for larger sociocultural and economic hardships. The symbolic importance of the wolf was also often place specific: the wolf is wise (Irish folktale), the wolf is ferocious (a Pennsylvania legend), the wolf is foolish (German folktale), the wolf is friendly (Japanese folktale). Other examples are the stories of "Peter and the Wolf," "The Three Little Pigs," and "Little Red Riding Hood," and stories about werewolves.[5] These culturally imposed traits were often context specific as well; thus, humans-as-hunters often saw wolves as symbolizing skill, intelligence, teamwork, and courage. Farmers, on the other hand, often saw wolves as symbolizing danger and posing a sinister threat to their livelihoods and well-being.

The wolf continues to symbolize larger cultural values, beliefs, and fears. Values and context can change, however. While a deeply seated animosity toward the wolf remains strong among some Americans, for others, the wolf and its restoration now symbolize a last chance to atone and make amends for past destruction of wildlife and wilderness. New generations are interpreting the wolf and other large carnivores with a different set of environmental values and in an altogether different historical and political context.[6]

From a political and public policy standpoint, what makes the case of wolf recovery so incredibly complex is the political context in which it is taking place. Context is the key to understanding the wolf's history, and it will be everything in its future. Wolf bounties were paid in the historical context of manifest destiny. Wolves are returning in a political environment that is more multifaceted and socially complicated. For better or worse, questions and issues such as the proper relationship between science and advocacy; finding a workable balance between federal and state wildlife responsibilities; the use of "stakeholders," collaboration, and public participation in environmental decision making; the struggles and transformation of rural communities; and an important visionary shift toward the proactive in the American conservation community will continue to affect wolves and other wildlife in the twenty-first century.

Wolf recovery is but one chapter in a much longer story about the loss and recovery of American wildlife and its habitat.[7] While threats to both have never been so serious, efforts to halt their destruction have provided a different type of environmental story. Species are being lost at unprecedented rates, but at the same time many people are heartened by stories of second chances and rebirth. White-tailed deer, beaver, black bear, and wild turkey have returned to much of the East. The presence of moose in New England, sea otters in California, and bald eagles throughout much of their previous range provides reasons for hope. Wildlife is dependent on the land it needs to survive. Therefore, its story has usually been told in its larger historical and ecological context of frontier logging, grazing, predator control, fire suppression, and economic development.

Interwoven throughout this new story of wolf recovery is a larger narrative speaking of a possible and even larger ecological restoration.

From one side of the debate, the "rewilding" of New England, maintaining or creating biological corridors for wildlife movement, returning landscapes to their pre-Columbian character, often using fire to do so, and allowing natural processes to continue to carve their will on both the land and its creatures provide the larger context in which wolves are making their return. From another standpoint, however, wolves are situated in quite a different sort of narrative. This "rewilding," critics point out, has taken place because rural communities could not subsist with traditional ways of living with the land. Hence, while some see this rewilding and the wolf's place in it as important symbols of natural rebirth and rejuvenation, others see them as symbols of cultural decline, disempowerment, misplaced priorities, and rural community instability. In a way, then, wolves are a cultural Rorschach test, revealing our cultural preferences, biases, fears, and aspirations.

A Sociopolitical GIS

While our mind's eye is quick to place the wolf within its wilderness environment—perched atop craggy peaks in Idaho's Sawtooth Mountains, in winter-white spruce-fir woods, in a remote southwest arroyo—they are often found in less-than-wild places. Wolves can be found in a variety of environs, from the picturesque wilderness to the less frequently envisaged farmyard. While wolves will need wilderness in the future, if necessary, these habitat generalists can survive with less. If there is any consensus within the wolf policy community, it is that the greatest determinant of wolf success or failure—past, present, and future—is how humans choose to live, or not live, with them. Thus, the story of wolf management and reintroduction is essentially as much about a social question as about a biological one.

While the natural landscapes to which wolves are returning are often bruised, crowded, and frayed, the political and managerial landscape that wolves will traverse is daunting and complex. Take, for example, a dispersing wolf in Minnesota heading from the northeast corner of the state to northern Wisconsin or the Upper Peninsula of Michigan. During this journey, the wolf would likely find itself on national forest lands, officially designated wilderness, state forest lands, state park lands, a variety of private lands, tribal lands, and possibly in different wolf management zones, some protective, some not so. The sociopolitical landscapes in which wolves are making their return are often as varied as their physical environments. Different state and regional contexts, histories, and trends can be as important to wolves as that of ungulate numbers and prey densities. Wolves in the greater Yellowstone National Park ecosystem, for instance, find themselves in an environment dominated by public land and public land agencies. It is an American Serengeti no doubt, but one with thousands of cattle hugging the park's boundary. If wolves find their way back to Maine, on the other hand, they will be managed in a state with a paucity of public land, and one in which the largest landowners are private timber and paper corporations, not the federal government. Simplified, it is a story of bureaucratic politics, environmentalists, and ranchers in the Yellowstone area; it will be one of bureaucratic politics, environmentalists, and multinational timber companies in Maine. These differences are hardly trivial. They affect everything from grassroots strategy to formal policy implementation.

So wolves are making their return in varied and complex political environments. Wolves are thus often entangled in complex storylines, replete with cows, condos, the cowboy caucus, the Old and New West, animal rights extremists, multiple-(ab)use, wise use, game farms, black helicopters, the United Nations, wilderness and national park designation, roadless areas, ecosystem management, regional animosity, the northern spotted owl, the Mexican spotted owl, dams and salmon, grizzlies, deconstructionist wilderness philosophy, and so forth and so on.

The GIS—geographical information system—has become a standard item in many scientific and conservation toolboxes these days. This technology enables users to map a number of important wolf-related variables such as prey density, ungulate distribution, public and private land composition, road density, wilderness and roadless areas, and other important factors. Equally important to the future of the wolf is mapping the cultural, economic, and sociopolitical factors relevant to successful wolf recovery.[8] Such contextual mapping would provide important information—the least obstructed pathways—toward wolf recovery and successful human-wolf interactions. Such factors as state and regional subcultures, partisanship patterns, styles of governance, interest group power, demographic trends, public opinion, urban-rural makeup and conflict, and other variables could be transposed onto the various ecological factors important to wolf recovery. In the end, these social and political factors—always in flux, and unlike ecological factors, always talking back—will ultimately determine the "cultural carrying capacity" necessary for wolf recovery.

Wolf Restoration and Management in the United States

Alaska

For analytical purposes, it would be wonderful if we were able to use the case of wolves in Alaska as a policy-based control group. If we could only somehow contrast the political machinations in the lower forty-eight to a purer story of wolves in a more or less untouched wilderness environment. Of course no such control group exists, if one ever did. The story of wolves in Alaska is as political and contentious as they come. Although wolves in Alaska have never reached the status of threatened or endangered under the ESA, the question of how they should be managed, or whether they should be managed at all, has long been debated by those inside and outside the state. Current estimations put the number of wolves in Alaska between six and eight thousand, the largest population in the United States.

Before 1989 there was no limit on the number of wolves that could be hunted in Alaska. While headlines about wolf reintroduction have been common in the lower forty-eight, issues of wolf control by the Alaskan government, and the public hunting and trapping of wolves have long mired this case in conflict.[9] Hunters, trappers, and other interests in the state often see wolves as a threat to game species and believe that wolves are largely responsible for various declines in moose and caribou populations. Accordingly, they have advocated "intensive management" and wolf control programs administered by Alaska's Department of Fish and Game (ADFG) and Board of Game, as well as various public hunting and trapping measures. In addition to public hunting and trapping, the state has used aerial wolf control as a management tool and allowed private hunters to kill wolves by "land and shoot," the practice of spotting wolves from a plane and then shooting them from the ground.

The public hunting and trapping of wolves, together with wolf control efforts by the state, have generated lots of acrimony and have raised a number of serious questions about future state wolf management elsewhere. While biologists and wildlife managers argued over predator-prey dynamics, wolf advocates were busy filing lawsuits and threatening national boycotts if the state of Alaska did not mend its ways. While the state had been the first to use citizen stakeholders in devising an acceptable state wolf management plan, ultimately the Alaskan public was asked to decide the fate of Alaska's wolves by ballot initiative. In 1996, nearly 60 percent of Alaskan voters prohibited same-day airborne hunting of wolves by the public while also prohibiting the state from using aircraft in government wolf-control programs except in the case of a biological emergency. Settling little, in 1999–2000 the Alaska legislature used its state constitutional power to reverse these decisions and reinstate these practices, while also introducing a state constitutional amendment prohibiting all future wildlife policymaking by the initiative process. Despite these legislative decisions, Alaskan residents voted in the 2000 election to reinstate the ban on public same-day airborne wolf hunting and rejected the amendment prohibiting "ballot box biology."

When wolves are delisted from the ESA list, management authority goes from the U.S. Fish and Wildlife Service (FWS) to the appropriate state wildlife agency. Alaska provides a vivid reminder that controversy does not end once wolves are finally delisted. In a way, it only begins. The question of how we ought to manage wolves once they are delisted will be as controversial as the debate over reintroduction. As wildlife biologist Bruce Hampton said of wolf politics in Alaska before the initiative, "But given the emotional debate that wolf control has elicited during the past forty-odd years, even a public vote may not permanently resolve the controversy between hunters and environmentalists [and] in a more ominous regard, it may portend the fate that awaits other areas where wolf recovery is only just beginning."[10]

Lake Superior Region

Outside of Alaska, northern Minnesota is the only place in the United States where a wolf population has continually persisted since European settlement. With an important flow of wolves from Canada, gray wolves in Minnesota have recently repopulated adjacent areas. Wolves are managed within the ecological boundaries of this region, variously called the upper Midwest, the western Great Lakes states, and the north woods. Using a GIS, those interested in identifying boundaries other than the political could map the number of wolf packs and the dispersal of wolves to provide a useful way of thinking about this region. Because of the ecological and demographic character of Minnesota, Wisconsin, and Michigan, wolves are currently most populous in the northern portions of these three states and are managed to keep them there.[11] Scientists estimate that there are roughly 2,500 wolves in the state of Minnesota, and from this population (the largest outside of Alaska), wolves have dispersed into northern Wisconsin and the Upper Peninsula of Michigan.

Wolves were once numerous throughout this region. Human persecution, federal and state bounties, loss of habitat and prey (bison, elk, deer, moose, caribou, and beaver), and other factors led to a drastic reduction of wolf numbers. Elimination of the wolf from all of Wisconsin and Michigan (except Isle Royale) and most of Minnesota was complete by 1960. It was not until federal protection was granted with the Endangered Species Act of 1973 that wolves began their successful recovery in the upper Midwest. Following the directives of the ESA, the *Recovery Plan for the Eastern Timber Wolf* was written by the FWS and approved in 1978. Later revised in 1992, the recovery plan identified conservation and management actions needed to establish a viable wolf population that would no longer need ESA protection. The successful population of wolves in Minnesota is the basis of wolf recovery in the region. Both downlisting wolves from endangered to threatened status and delisting the wolf from the endangered species list ultimately depend on the wolf population segment in Minnesota. In other words, if the FWS is not certain that wolves in Minnesota can be adequately managed and protected to ensure their long-term viability, wolf management in Wisconsin and Michigan would also be affected.

New England

Outside of Minnesota, northern Wisconsin, and the Upper Peninsula of Michigan, the *Eastern Timber Wolf Recovery Plan* identified three areas deserving investigation as to whether wolves could be successfully reintroduced, based on human population densities, amount of public land, and favorable input from the states that were identified in the original version of the plan.[12] These areas are (1) eastern Maine, consisting of about 2,500 square miles that are largely uninhabited; (2) northwestern Maine and adjacent New Hampshire, an area consisting of more than 11,300 square miles, most of which is privately owned other than Baxter

State Park; and (3) the Adirondack Forest Preserve Area in northern New York, consisting of approximately 9,375 square miles and having relatively low human density.

According to the plan, the eastern timber wolf would be officially recovered once two distinct wolf populations were established, one in Minnesota and one elsewhere. With federal protection in place, wolves from Minnesota were quickly dispersing into Wisconsin and the Upper Peninsula. Because of this success, the FWS did not put priority on northeastern wolf recovery, and instead focused on wolf recovery in the western Great Lakes region. Believing that wolves have an ecological and cultural role to play in the great north woods of the Northeast, Defenders of Wildlife, a nonprofit environmental organization based in Washington, D.C., and other nongovernmental organizations began conducting the work necessary to assess the biological and social feasibility of northeastern wolf recovery.

Among other issues, including a debate over the taxonomic status of eastern canids and what type of wolf used to occupy the region, the means by which wolf restoration would take place is among the most significant questions regarding northeastern wolf restoration. While some believe that a "natural" migration-based recovery bodes best for the wolf and human-wolf relations, others believe that an organized reintroduction (translocation) holds more promise and might be the only way wolves will get on the ground in the Northeast. Wolf advocates in the region also have the advantage of learning from other wolf restoration programs; while the Yellowstone translocation program has been biologically successful, it has been politically controversial to say the least. Conversely, the natural migration of Minnesota wolves into northern Wisconsin and the Upper Peninsula of Michigan has been relatively quiet with relatively high levels of public support or acquiescence. Questions of where wolves should be restored and how to restore them are interrelated. While some believe the Adirondack region and much of New England provide suitable habitat and enough prey, natural wolf migration from Ontario and Quebec is largely precluded because of urban development, dangerous roads, agricultural lands, the unprotected status of Canadian wolves, the Saint Lawrence Seaway, and other challenging obstacles.

It was once a creative jab by sardonic western political representatives to propose sending wolves to the East, and especially to New York, an important symbol of eastern colonial power and intrusive liberalism according to some influential western political representatives. After a non-western congressional member voted for western wilderness designation, predator reintroduction, or some type of public land management reform, it was commonplace to hear western representatives propose the same type of policies be implemented in the "out-of-touch East." Little did these western representatives know how seriously their proposals would one day be taken.

The possibility of reintroducing wolves into the Adirondack Park has been seriously examined from both an ecological and social perspective. The park comprises six million acres, many of which have been protected since the early twentieth century by the state's constitution mandating they be kept "forever wild." Although public and private lands are intermingled within the boundary of the park, taken as a whole it is still one of the wildest reserves east of the Mississippi. Yet, wolves from Ontario and Quebec cannot so easily repopulate this region as they do farther west. While Ontario's Algonquin Provincial Park to the north has several packs of wolves, the Saint Lawrence Seaway (kept open by icebreakers year-round) is thought by some to present too great an obstacle for dispersing wolves; thus, the natural migration between populations that is so important to wolves in Minnesota and the upper Midwest may not be possible in the Adirondacks.[13] Nevertheless, many wolf advocates in the Northeast believe that taken together, the Adirondacks and parts of northern New Hampshire, Vermont, and Maine have enough suitable wolf habitat for possible reintroduction or natural recovery from wild wolves to the north.

Northern Rockies

Nowhere in the country has the story of wolf recovery been so closely followed as that in Yellowstone National Park and the Northern Rockies. The *Northern Rocky Mountain Wolf Recovery Plan* was written by the FWS following the finding of a small litter of wolf pups in Glacier National Park in 1986.[14] The recovery plan identified northwestern Montana, central Idaho, and the greater Yellowstone area as recovery areas, and established a biological goal of at least ten breeding pairs of wolves in each of these three areas for three successive years. Naturally recolonizing wolves in northwestern Montana remained listed as endangered, providing the greatest degree of protection. Wolves were caught in Alberta, Canada, and released into central Idaho and Yellowstone in 1995 and 1996. They were designated as "nonessential, experimental populations," as allowed under revisions made to the ESA in 1982, as a way to give both the government and local landowners more flexibility in managing (troublemaking) wolves. Section 10(j) of the ESA authorizes the secretary of the interior to identify and release an experimental population that is "wholly separate geographically" from nonexperimental populations of the same species. Each member of an experimental population is to be managed as a threatened (rather than an endangered) species. The secretary is also authorized to designate experimental populations as "nonessential" if they are determined to be not essential for the continued existence of the species. Section 10(j) has been used as a way to address various local concerns, such as livestock depredation issues and fears of restricted land use.

This reintroduction effort was fraught with controversy and litigation from its beginning. Suits by the Mountain States Legal Foundation on behalf of those such as the American Farm Bureau Federation, as well as by some environmental organizations opposing the compromising nature of the experimental designation, clouded the Yellowstone and central Idaho reintroduction programs in uncertainty until the United States Court of Appeals for the Tenth Circuit finally ruled that experimental wolves could stay. The court ruled that although a few lone naturally dispersing wolves had been sighted in the Yellowstone area in the past, this did not preclude the FWS from reintroducing additional wolves under the experimental rule (the Mountain States Legal Foundation strategically argued that the flexible management allowed under the experimental designation would endanger naturally recolonized wolves, which have greater protection under the ESA). Because of the Idaho state legislature's vehement opposition to wolf reintroduction, the Nez Perce Tribe has played a key management, monitoring, and educational role in Idaho's wolf recovery. Defenders of Wildlife has also played an important role in this region, as they have throughout the country, financially compensating ranchers who have lost cattle and livestock to wolf depredation.

The conflict over wolves and ranching is as paramount in the Northern Rockies as was the conflict over owls and the timber industry in the Pacific Northwest. And like the case of birds and trees farther west, the story is far from finished. A grand vision like this in such a highly symbolic natural environment—the nation's first national park and one of the most intact ecosystems left in the world—raised the stakes and stature of the wolf reintroduction debate. Only at the surface is the debate about wolves and potential livestock depredation. At its core are issues of deeper and more symbolic social significance.

Southwest

Perhaps the most historically symbolic act of all regarding wolf recovery and conservation in the United States was provided by Aldo Leopold half a century ago. In his 1949 *A Sand County Almanac* Leopold tells the following story of shooting a wolf in the Apache National Forest while working for the U.S. Forest Service (USFS) in the Southwest:

> In those days we had never heard of passing up a chance to kill a wolf. In a second we were pumping lead into the pack, but with more excitement than accuracy: how to aim a steep downhill shot is always confusing. When our rifles were empty, the old wolf was down, and a pup was dragging a leg into impassable slide-rocks. We reached the old wolf in time to watch a fierce green fire dying in her eyes. I realized then, and have known ever since, that there was something new to me in those eyes—something known only to her and to the mountain. I was young then, and full of trigger-itch; I thought that because fewer wolves meant more deer, that no wolves would mean hunters' paradise. But after seeing the green fire die, I sensed that neither the wolf nor the mountain agreed with such a view.[15]

Leopold's deeply personal tale of the Mexican wolf is well known and often told as evidence that how one sees the mountain and the wolf can change. Perhaps we as a nation are now collectively experiencing Leopold's epiphany. Leopold's recognition of the wolf's place on the mountain was atypical—not only did the fierce green fire of this wolf fade, but so did the entire subspecies north of the Mexican border. Fifty years later, however, the fierce green fire has returned to the Southwest. After years of tireless work by wildlife professionals and citizen activists, culminating, fittingly, with Leopold's granddaughter helping carry a wolf to its acclimation pen, the Mexican wolf is slowly returning to the American Southwest.[16]

The Mexican wolf *(Canis lupus baileyi)* was extirpated from the wild in the United States by the mid-1900s, and is considered the most endangered wolf subspecies in the world. The FWS adopted a recovery plan for the Mexican wolf in 1982.[17] This plan called for a captive breeding program followed by the reintroduction of these captive-born Mexican wolves into the Blue Range Wolf Recovery Area (BRWRA) west of the Arizona–New Mexico border. Reintroduction of Mexican wolves was approved by Secretary of the Interior Bruce Babbitt in 1997. Under the approved plan, captive-raised Mexican wolves were released into the Apache National Forest in eastern Arizona and allowed to recolonize the BRWRA in order to meet the recovery criteria of more than one hundred free-ranging Mexican wolves.[18] Similar to wolves in Yellowstone and central Idaho, Mexican wolves were reintroduced as a nonessential, experimental population under provisions of section 10(j) of the ESA.

The recovery program in the Southwest has been no easier than that farther north. While the Southwest has substantial amounts of public land and federally designated wilderness areas, the area is also heavily grazed by livestock. Despite another Defenders of Wildlife livestock compensation program in place, the New Mexico Farm and Livestock Bureau filed suit claiming irreparable damage from actual or potential livestock losses. The suit also questioned the genetic purity of the reintroduced wolves. In 1999, the U.S. District Court for the District of New Mexico ruled against the Farm Bureau on all counts. Nevertheless, human-caused mortality has been a significant factor in the Southwest, a number of wolves having been killed since the reintroduction program began.

Southeast

Wolf recovery in the Southeast has taken place in quite a different ecological and political context than that farther west. The red wolf (Canis rufus) was one of the first endangered species to attract recovery attention after the 1973 ESA was passed, and its reintroduction was the first of a species that was officially extinct in the wild in the United States. Red wolves were once common throughout the Deep South and once ranged as far north as Pennsylvania and as far west as Illinois, Missouri, Oklahoma, and central Texas. With red wolves clearly in danger of becoming extinct, the FWS captured the region's remaining red wolves in 1975. By this time, there were only a few wild red wolves left isolated among the refineries and oil fields of coastal Texas and Louisiana. These animals were bred in captivity, and although they were declared extinct

in the wild, there were enough captive wolves alive to begin a reintroduction program as outlined in the *Red Wolf Recovery Plan*.[19]
The question of where to reintroduce wolves in the Southeast was
answered when the FWS received 120,000 acres on a peninsula west of
the North Carolina Outer Banks. Captive animals were released into
the new Alligator River National Wildlife Refuge in northeastern North
Carolina in 1987 and were designated as "nonessential, experimental."
The FWS hoped that the remote location and inhospitable environment
of the refuge (in an area with a small, nonranching rural population,
and next to a military bombing range, much of the refuge is freshwater
bog and has junglelike terrain surrounded by water on three sides) would
allow wolves to fare better than they had in the previous, failed reintroduction in the Great Smoky Mountains on the Kentucky-Tennessee
border. A small number of wolves have also been released as propaga-
tion experiments in Pocosin Lakes National Wildlife Refuge in northeastern North Carolina, and on coastal islands of South Carolina, Mississippi, and Florida.

The red wolf program has faced numerous challenges and raises important questions regarding wolf and carnivore conservation in the
eastern United States. First is the issue of hybridization. Many wildlife
scientists question the purity of red wolves and their classification as a
separate species. The removal of wolves from the wild and the subsequent captive breeding program were precipitated by the declining red
wolf population's interbreeding with coyotes. The scientific debate over
red wolf genetics carries significant policy implications because the ESA
does not provide protection for hybrid species. Furthermore, because
this is the only wild red wolf population in the world, there is an acute
fear of jeopardizing this rare population. Captive breeding, moreover, is
only a palliative, a way of buying time until the harder and more culturally rooted questions are confronted.[20] Red wolf habitat, or the lack
thereof, is therefore the major issue in the Southeast. Wolves are not allowed to leave the confines of the refuge, so there is an added layer of
human management in this program. According to the FWS, complete
species recovery permitting delisting will probably never be achieved
for the red wolf.[21]

In addition to these serious challenges, the FWS has faced various
legal hurdles, including a recent, unsuccessful suit filed by two North
Carolina counties and landowners challenging the FWS's legal right to

regulate the killing or trapping of endangered red wolves on private property. As they are elsewhere, perceived threats to custom, culture, and traditional land use are also important components of the red wolf debate. Several local hunters, for example, see both the refuge and red wolves as a threat to traditional ways of hunting with dogs.

Future Wolf Recovery and Management

In addition to these programs, other wolf recovery projects are at different stages of conceptualization and planning. The FWS, Defenders of Wildlife, and other conservation organizations have explored them in varying detail, sometimes assessing both their biological and social feasibility. Defenders, one of the most important players in wolf politics throughout the country, recommends wolf reintroduction in a variety of ecological regions where the animals once naturally occurred.[22] All of these regions have different sets of ecological and political variables that are being considered by activists, wildlife managers, and political decision makers. In Washington State, for example, wolves have been spotted in North Cascades National Park and the Ross Lake National Recreation Area, and in other areas as well. Wolves have also made the journey from central Idaho to eastern Oregon, and in the process have forced the FWS to answer questions regarding natural dispersal out of the Northern Rockies.

In some places, natural dispersal and natural wolf recovery are more difficult to imagine. Development in western Washington, for instance, will likely preclude a natural recovery of wolves in the Olympic Peninsula (within Olympic National Park and Olympic National Forest). If wolves are to return to the peninsula, it will most likely be through a federal reintroduction program. Similarly, there is some debate as to how wolves could naturally recolonize the Southern Rockies. While there are millions of acres of suitable wolf habitat in Colorado (one biological study estimates that Colorado alone could support over 1,100 wolves), Utah, and New Mexico, some believe that there is little chance that wolves in the Northern Rockies could successfully run a gauntlet of roads and tempting livestock on their way south.[23]

Although wolves are now on the ground in various parts of the country, conflict and controversy are far from finished. At this writing, debate is centered on questions related to where wolves are best maintained and how to manage them most effectively. Because of increases in gray

wolf numbers, expansion of the species' occupied range, and the progress made under various gray wolf recovery plans, the FWS has proposed changing the classification of the gray wolf under the ESA. If successful, wolves would be downlisted from endangered to threatened in
some regions, and delisted in some others. The FWS is again emphasizing Section 4(d) of the ESA, a provision in the act allowing for special
regulations and flexibility in managing threatened (not endangered)
species and subspecies. These special rules relax normal ESA restrictions and provide the FWS more freedom in managing conflict among
humans and wolves. The FWS would also like to delist wolves in states
and regions where there currently are no wolves, in effect ruling that
much of the nation is unsuitable for future wolf recovery (including
California, Nevada, Appalachia, and most of the lower Midwest, Southeast, and Mid-Atlantic regions).

The FWS's proposal is just the beginning of a new phase of the debate over wolf recovery. There are just as much passion and politics in
the debate over how wolves should be managed as there were over natural recovery and reintroduction. Issues pertaining to the public hunting and trapping of wolves, the use of snares and snow machines to kill
wolves, aerial (helicopter) wolf control by state wildlife agencies, and a
host of other issues are likely in store for the future. While we learned a
lot about ourselves and our politics in reintroducing wolves to places
such as Yellowstone, we are about to learn much more.

A Politics Model of Wolf Policy

The "politics model" of public policy fully embraces the symbolism,
multiple meanings, and cultural complexity of controversial policy issues.[24] For purposes here, it provides the most realistic and accurate
way to explore wolf politics and policy from the ground up. Both support for and opposition to wolf restoration are better understood using
a political framework acknowledging the importance of cultural history and political symbolism—two key components in the art of political decision making.

Wolf politics and policy will confound even the most sophisticated
techno-rational approaches to policy analysis. The rationality model
has often been applied to environmental and natural resource policy.
That is, if we could just get politics out of public policy, we would have
both better environmental legislation and better implementation of

these public laws. In other words, "the rationality project" often sees politics as being messy and chaotic and presenting menacing obstacles to rational and scientific public policymaking. Those immersed in wolf politics and policy, however much they may pine for more rational, scientific, and orderly policymaking, will recognize that the rationality model is overly simplistic. This rationality project, according to political scientist Deborah Stone, not only misses the point of politics but also "grossly distorts political life" (17).

The politics model recognizes the following important features of public policy:

- Community and competing conceptions of the public interest
- That groups and organizations, as opposed to individuals, are the basic building blocks of politics
- Culture, influence, and socialization
- The role of history and loyalty in politics
- Myths and images
- Cooperation, coordination, coalition-building, and strategic alliances
- Information as interpretive, imperfect, framed, and strategically withheld
- That the essence of policymaking is the struggle over ideas—the "very stuff of politics" (32)

Stone, whose work is central here, contends that "people fight about ideas, fight for them, and fight against them. Political conflict is never simply over material conditions and choices, but over what is legitimate. The passion in politics comes from conflicting senses of fairness, justice, rightness, and goodness. . . . Political fights are conducted with money, with rules, with votes, and with favors, to be sure, but they are conducted above all with words and ideas" (32–34). Choosing from an array of controversial policy issues, Stone shows that there are often multiple understandings of what appears to be a single concept. Moreover, these understandings become manipulated as part of political strategy. And from a practical standpoint, "revealing the hidden arguments embedded in each concept illuminates, and may help resolve, the surface conflicts" (11). These ideas and competing visions of the public interest are at the heart of wolf politics and policy. They are inevitably about political meaning, and as Stone concludes, "science cannot settle questions of meaning" (376). While science can certainly answer a question such as how much livestock depredation can be expected from a recovered wolf population in a national forest area, it cannot answer the normative question of whether wolves or cows *should* be in this national forest.

The political and policy analysis found here emphasizes the importance of political context, political culture, social construction, competing narratives, political power, value conflict, problem definition, the policy story, political systems, policy players, and competing conceptions of the public interest.[25] All of these factors are interwoven and analyzed throughout the book. Multiple subjective wolf stories are told by a dizzying number of interests in an incredibly complicated political environment. But this complexity is to be expected, according to policy analysts Randall Clemons and Mark McBeth: "The policy process is complex, messy, and indeterminate, and centers on value conflict. One must learn the ideas behind the process, as well as the process."[26] As such, "postpositivism suggests that the role of the analyst is not to find the truth, but rather to be suspicious and distrustful of all policy claims and ultimately to provide access and explanation of data to all parties, to empower the public to understand analyses, and to promote political issues into serious public discussions. In short, this view of analysis seeks to turn the expert policy analyst into the democratic facilitator."[27] This approach is especially useful when analyzing such a controversial, value-laden, and highly symbolic case like wolf recovery and management, and is particularly effective with so-called wicked policy problems.[28] And wolf politics certainly fits this category.

The Wolf Policy Project

The wolf policy project was conducted from 1999 to 2002. The research design was qualitative and inductive. Extensive in-depth personal interviews with key stakeholders in wolf policy and management throughout the country provided the project with an important grounding in real-world concerns and concrete issues of significance. Prominent environmentalists, wolf advocates, wildlife managers, biologists, political representatives, tribal representatives, journalists, ranchers, hunters, trappers, and dozens of other important stakeholders were interviewed. Personal interviews and fieldwork were conducted in south-central and interior Alaska, northern Minnesota, northern Wisconsin, central Idaho, western Montana, Washington State, and Colorado. A number of tele-

Wolf recovery and management as value-based political conflict
• Policy subsystem and advocacy coalition framework (and deep/ policy–core values) • Kellert's value typology • Political power • Competing values, ethics, and conceptions of the public interest • Political use and limitations of science
The wolf as symbol, surrogate, and policy problem
• Multiple sociopolitical dimensions • Strategic problem definition and issue framing • Social construction • Implications for conflict resolution
Wolves and the politics of place
• Historical, cultural, political economic, and management contexts • Complex and multifaceted • Political subcultures and state/regional variation • Policy implications (state wolf management)
The use of stakeholders and public participation
• Expanding or limiting the scope of conflict • Importance of process (how decisions are made) • Professional and organizational values • Value representation (and the lack thereof) • Promising framework for future political conflict

Figure 1. A politics model of wolf recovery

phone interviews were also conducted. Lasting from one to three hours, these sixty-three interviews ranged from a formal semistructured design to more free-flowing conversation.

This extensive fieldwork and interviewing determined the direction in which the research would flow. I pursued questions, conflicts, and issues that participants told me were central to the debate over wolf recovery and management. A qualitative-style "grounded theory" analytical approach was utilized and is especially evident in chapters 1 through 3.[29] This inductive approach, popular in sociology and anthropology, ties concepts directly to empirical observations. A number of themes, issues, and concepts were identified in the initial round of interviews and research. These themes, issues, and concepts were then "tested" in subsequent interviews and research. The data gathering and analysis steps were repeated several times. Ideas taken from interviews, fieldwork, or other sources were constantly analyzed and tested in the "real world." With time and each iteration, it became apparent that some themes, issues, and concepts are perceived to be more relevant than others. It are these that are discussed in the following chapters.

While I interviewed key biologists, wildlife managers, interest groups, and decision makers, I also made a special attempt to talk to people that are often most personally affected by wolf policy and management decisions. For example, interviews and fieldwork were conducted in McGrath, Alaska, a small fly-in bush community in the south-central interior part of the state. McGrath has been in the midst of wolf controversy for some time, and I wanted to hear from people who are really affected by policy and management decisions. In addition to these interviews, I analyzed documents (draft and final environmental impact statements, public opinion polls, transcripts from official proceedings, official public comments), observed stakeholder sessions, and attended key meetings and public hearings throughout the project.

Many of the participants I interviewed play an indispensable role in wolf management and the wolf policy debate. Refocusing our attention on "the human envelope" of species recovery has practical benefits. This network of people and organizations is critical to a recovery program—"for if the organization is not handled well, the species will not be handled well."[30] It is therefore necessary to move away from a predominately scientific-technical approach to one with politics and policy front and center. In doing so, the issues become more complex and multifaceted, but at the same time numerous opportunities often present themselves. Tim Clark, who has long examined the human dimensions of endangered species recovery, summarizes:

Shifting focus to the human envelope of species recovery is a big step toward opening up constructive new avenues to tackle problems. Reconstructing the recovery process around a policy-oriented approach—as we might call the focus on the human envelope—can help guard against oversimplifying problems, ignoring contexts, and demonizing opponents.... Knowing about the policy process opens up many opportunities to improve decision and policy making.[31]

According to Clark, among others, lip service has been given to "human dimensions," "biopolitics," and "socioeconomic considerations." What is needed, however, is a policy-oriented view that goes deeper. Says Clark,

Of the myriad problems cited by critics of current efforts to conserve endangered species, few are biological. Nearly all relate to human systems and the dynamic patterns of interaction among people, worldviews, interests, values, organizational structures and cultures, processes of decisionmaking, and many other aspects of human society. These human components undeniably constitute the contexts and conditions of species losses. Yet in past approaches to conservation that focused narrowly on science or particular organizations, they have rarely been acknowledged or identified, let alone explored, understood, or resolved.[32]

The debate over wolf recovery and management in the United States is best understood as a value-based political conflict that transcends issues strictly pertaining to science, biology, and techno-rational approaches to problem solving. As such, chapter 1 references two helpful theoretical frameworks to examine the conflict between the most prominent players and interests in wolf politics. The policy subsystem and "advocacy coalition framework" are used to describe and explain the thinking, strategy, and behavior of various players and interests involved in the debate.[33] This is followed by a discussion of the myriad human values about wolves, wildlife, and the natural world.[34] Various conflicts and tensions among stakeholders, managers, and advocacy coalitions are examined, including conflict between scientist and stakeholder, the contested role of science and politics in wolf management, values and political power (ranching in the West), differences between public and wildlife agency values, hunting and animal welfare-rights interests, and the different philosophical approaches to wildlife management.

Also in chapter 1, some of the more important players in wolf politics such as wolf biologists, state wildlife agencies, and hunting groups are examined. Their interests and the conflicts between them are placed within a larger discussion of human values about wildlife, biodiversity, and the natural world. The issues and conflicts among these participants will likely dominate the wolf debate of the future. And they once again illustrate how this debate goes beyond wolves.

Chapter 2 documents how the debate over wolf management and reintroduction is often as much about an array of sociopolitical issues as it is about wolf behavior and potential livestock depredation. Drawing on the experiences of various wolf programs throughout the nation, this chapter explores "symbol and surrogate issues" such as the following: land use and the politics of ecosystem management, different levels of support for natural wolf recovery versus reintroduction, wolves and the political struggle over wilderness preservation, The Wildlands Project and large-scale carnivore conservation efforts, the role of conservation biology in political decision making, the use and future of the ESA, the politics of ESA implementation, rural culture, concerns, and interests, and tribal participation and management authority. These "symbol and surrogate" issues are often the reason why the debate over wolf recovery and management is so controversial and acrimonious. The chapter ends with a discussion of how these sociopolitical issues affect political decision making and prospects for conflict resolution. The discussion also illustrates the importance of problem definition in the policymaking process. Participants in the debate have attempted to strategically define "the wolf policy problem" and frame the issue in such a way as to mobilize their values and interests and advance their conception of the public interest.

Chapter 3 examines the importance of place in wolf policy and management. The chapter places this value-based conflict and these symbol and surrogate issues in their larger political setting. Wolf politics in Minnesota, the Northern Rockies, and the Southwest are used for cases and examples. Historical, cultural, political-economic, and management contexts are considered. A number of contextual factors are discussed in this framework including the western frontier, the cultural transition from "old West" to "new West," ranching and rural economies, public opinion, political-institutional structure and support, agency funding and budgetary incentives, and the use of state wildlife commissions to make wildlife policy. Policy implications are discussed in each subsection.

Chapter 4 examines the important use of public participation and stakeholder-based collaborative conservation in wolf decision making and management. The Minnesota Wolf Roundtable, Wisconsin's Wolf Management and Advisory Committee, the Adirondack Wolf Citizen's Advisory Committee, and the history of using, and not using, stakeholders in Alaska wolf management are examined. These cases raise a number of important issues and questions regarding the use of public participation, stakeholders, and collaboration in natural resource and wildlife management. What are the challenges of policy and interest-based collaboration? How do we seek local perspectives and use local knowledge? Who is a legitimate "stakeholder," and how much authority should stakeholders be given? What role should First Nations play in these processes? And what is the proper role of Congress and state legislatures in this new management paradigm? These and other issues are explored using these four cases as examples. Wolves are making their return while traditional natural resource and wildlife management paradigms are being challenged throughout the country. The importance of this paradigm shift as it relates to wildlife policy and management in general, and wolves in particular, cannot be stated strongly enough. This chapter provides a few more important cases with which to evaluate these important trends. It is in this chapter that I make the case for a stakeholder-based approach to future wolf political conflict. A well-structured stakeholder framework can offer a constructive way of dealing with value-based political conflict, symbol and surrogate issues, and the politics of place.

The book concludes with a review of some of the essential wolf-related policy and management issues that I believe should be addressed in the future. Instead of finishing with the one right political assessment, I put forth a more democratic approach. It is based on the core assertion made in this book that wolf policy and management are, above all, value-based political issues that should be debated in an inclusive, fair, and more representative democratic arena.

CHAPTER ONE

Wolf Recovery and Management as Value-Based Political Conflict

> There are some who can live without wild things, and some who
> cannot.
>
> Aldo Leopold, *A Sand County Almanac,* 1949

There are deeply rooted moral conflicts over wolf recovery. Wolves present difficult ethical and moral challenges, ones that go well beyond science, biology, and technical wildlife management. This value-based political conflict is over a deeply symbolic animal and is taking place in a controversial political and cultural setting. A policy-oriented approach has much to offer the debate, especially if it is contextual and places human values and ethics at the center of its analysis. It is also important for those engaged in the debate to acknowledge its value-based character. The policy implications of not doing so are serious and will become only more so in the future.

The values and human dimensions of this debate will seriously challenge any attempt at conflict resolution. The "deep core" values held by some groups and interests are non-negotiable. Thus, many interests may not collaborate or be willing to compromise in the future. They will be heading to the courtroom, not to the collaborative roundtable. In doing so, however, these groups risk having no voice in the decision-making process. On the other hand, some of these values are not necessarily mutually exclusive. Many of the apparent value conflicts between stakeholders are not zero-sum games but are instead tensions that can and should be balanced. Furthermore, many of these interests are willing to compromise and make important concessions. As I discuss in chapter 4, process is essential to constructive dialogue and compromise. Problem solving is much more likely if the decision-making process is perceived as being fair. While these values will test a collaborative approach to problem solving, it still offers a promising way to deal with these value-based political conflicts.

Those most involved in wolf policymaking are well aware of the importance of values and political power in the wolf debate. Take the debate over possibly reintroducing wolves into the Olympic National Park in Washington State. While a full range of human values are in perpetual tension, in this case, the value that mattered most was that held by former Washington Senator Slade Gorton, an elected and powerful political representative. According to Senator Gorton, most people on the peninsula oppose reintroduction, and "if they're opposed to it, I'm opposed to it, and I will prevent it from happening."[1] These words were hardly empty rhetoric. Senator Gorton, chair of the Senate committee that would authorize the reintroduction money, made good on his pledge. The Olympic program had been stalled and would remain so, according to some state politicos, until he was defeated or retired from the Senate (he was defeated in 2000). There is nothing new in this story. Those involved in environmental, natural resource, and wildlife policymaking would only expand the list of key congressional committees and the powerful names often involved and the cases in which their power and positions were exercised most skillfully.

The question of who participates in the political system is among the most important we can ask. The late political scientist E. E. Schattschneider captured the basic pattern of politics:

> The first proposition is that the outcome of every conflict is determined by the *extent* to which the audience becomes involved in it. That is, the outcome of all conflict is determined by the *scope* of its contagion. The number of people involved in any conflict determines what happens; every change in the number of participants, every increase or reduction in the number of participants affects the result."[2]

Furthermore, said Schattschneider, the scope and bias of the pressure system reveal that some groups do better than others, that "[t]he flaw in the pluralist heaven is that the heavenly chorus sings with a strong upper-class accent."[3] Schattschneider's work is as relevant today as it was forty years ago. In the realm of wolf and wildlife politics, the values and interests that are "mobilized" will undoubtedly affect the content of public policy.

The Wolf Policy Subsystem

Research on policy subsystems and advocacy coalitions provides a useful framework for better understanding the players of the wolf policymaking process and the conflict between them. As any casual observer of the American political scene can attest, groups matter. Those concerned with environmental protection are among the most attuned to how the balance and power of a state's interest groups can fundamentally affect everything from mining reform (e.g., Anaconda Copper Company in Montana's history) to clean air (e.g., coal industry in West Virginia). Despite popular misconceptions, from both the political left and right, most states are not dominated by any one industry or single interest. While the situation is far from a pluralistic ideal of public and private interest group balance, countervailing power, and fair competition, there are numerous groups (although private as opposed to public-oriented) active at the state level of governance, each with varying amounts of political power, access, and influence.[4]

Understanding public policy is largely an exercise in understanding the players involved in the policymaking process, from problem definition through implementation. Policy professionals have long tried to accurately describe and explain who is involved in such processes and why inequities in participation matter. What is known about the policymaking arena is that previous conceptions of who is involved in various policy areas were overly constricted.[5] The iron triangle of public policy— relatively exclusive relationships among a bureaucratic agency, an interest group, and a congressional committee—is often helpful but incomplete. Instead, the policy process regarding carnivore conservation is best understood as a "policy subsystem" within an "advocacy coalition framework."[6] This does not mean, however, that iron triangles and more exclusive forms of decision making do not exist in other areas of natural resource and wildlife policy. As I discuss later, state wildlife management, as opposed to federal wolf reintroduction, has historically been characterized by more exclusive decision-making patterns.

According to political scientists Paul Sabatier and Hank Jenkins-Smith, the concept of the policy subsystem—the "interaction of actors from different institutions who follow and seek to influence governmental decisions in a policy area"—broadens the notion of the iron triangle to include an array of actors, both public and private, at various levels of government, including journalists, researchers, policy analysts, and others.[7] Actors in this subsystem include both policy brokers—those seeking mediation and compromise—and advocacy coalitions. Advocacy coalitions, in short, seek to translate their beliefs into public policies.

Information, according to this model, is not only used instrumentally but is also limited by a hierarchical system of values and beliefs. Each advocacy coalition has both deep (normative) core values and near (policy) core values. At the belief system's "normative core" are deeply personal values and beliefs that are highly resistant to change, "essentially akin to a religious conversion."[8] For some animal rights advocates, for example, the public taking (hunting or trapping) of wolves after ESA delisting is antithetical to everything they stand for and believe in. Many of them find it simply unacceptable to support such behavior given their deeply rooted personal values.

These deep normative core beliefs also inform us about the role and strategic use of science in the debate over wolf management and restoration. "Objective," peer-reviewed, quality research remains a valuable commodity in the debate, and it is often used instrumentally as a political strategy and a means of further entrenchment. Once something has been accepted as a core belief, it becomes resistant to change, even in the face of contradictory empirical evidence. Scientific information and evidence supporting a political position become important currency in many policy circles. Pro-wolf groups in Maine, for example, use scientific studies to quell public concern over a potential decline in moose and deer numbers if wolves return to their state. There is little likelihood that these groups, or their organized opposition, will use such scientific findings when they do not bolster their own policy position.

Near (policy) core values also prove important in wolf restoration. These values refer in part to fundamental policy positions concerning the basic political strategies for achieving deep core values. While these values are also difficult to change once fixed, they can be changed in some situations. Policy core values are often related to questions concerning the "hows" of public policy—strategy and approach. In other words, there are important tactical differences in how to effectively forward a policy: government versus market approaches, the proper role of the federal government, economic incentives, coercion, education, and others.[9] While participants may share similar deep core values and beliefs, they often differ on how such values and beliefs can be most effectively advanced. Deep core values can also preclude some types of approaches. For example, a group that interprets its cause in absolute and moralistic terms would likely favor adversarial litigation or one-sided legislative initiatives rather than an approach requiring compromise or mediation.[10]

As I will discuss in the following chapter, in the case of wolf restoration in Yellowstone and Idaho, influential environmental organizations were deeply divided on both deep and policy core values. An analysis that applies the framework of policy subsystems, advocacy coalitions, and deep core and policy core values thus provides a useful way of understanding the political and legal machinations behind the reintroduction debate. To answer the question of why pro-wolf organizations would initially file a lawsuit against reintroduction, one needs a requisite understanding of the deep core and policy core values of these organizations. Many groups could simply not condone, on either ethical or strategic grounds, the designation of Yellowstone wolves as a nonessential, experimental population.

These deep core and policy values found within advocacy coalitions are the essential components of "policy-oriented learning," or the way in which advocacy coalitions use feedback from their own actions as a way to support their own goals and the techniques to help achieve them.[11] In other words, scientific information and knowledge are often used in a strategic and politicized manner. In an area rich in science, like wildlife policy, scientific information and analysis will usually be employed "as a post hoc defense of core beliefs."[12] Because of Minnesota's unique wolf situation, for example, the state is setting important political precedents for other wolf programs and reintroduction efforts, thus, providing opportunities for this type of policy-oriented learning to occur. Competing advocacy coalitions look to Minnesota for cases and evidence that support their position. Furthermore, because wolves in this state are among the most studied in the world, wildlife biologists have a unique understanding of this important population. This knowledge is especially significant in the case of predator-prey relations between wolves and ungulates in the region.

One of the most important arguments against reintroduction or increasing wolf numbers is that it will dramatically affect a hunter's chances of killing moose, deer, and other ungulates. From Alaska to Maine, the same concerns have arisen time and again among hunters, trappers, and organized sporting associations. To quell these fears, wolf advocates throughout the country often cite wolf-prey statistics and trends in Minnesota as an example of the exaggerated nature of most claims about plummeting deer, elk, and moose numbers. The Maine Wolf Coalition, for example, points out that during the past two decades, both wolf and white-tailed deer populations have increased significantly in Minnesota. The Coalition also notes that Minnesota's registered deer harvest increased from a low of 36,000 animals in 1976 to a high of 229,000 animals in 1992, and that the state ranks first in the nation in the number of trophy buck entries in the Boone and Crockett Club's "Records of North American Big Game." This relationship between wolves and game in Minnesota will continue to be an important element in future reintroduction dialogue and informational campaigns.

While the theory of the policy subsystem and advocacy coalition broadens our understanding of who participates in public policymaking, it would be naive to believe that political power is no longer an important factor. The complicated story of political power and ranching is discussed later, but it is only one part of a much larger picture. The issue involves not just the political, cultural, and economic power of the western livestock industry but all the economic special interests that feel threatened by wolves, endangered species, and the legislation protecting them: timber companies, oil and gas interests, real estate developers, the industrial recreation industry, and others. Campaign finance data, obtained from the Center for Responsive Politics, show which western representatives benefit most from various resource industries. But we cannot know with any certainty whether such financing leads a representative to vote in a particular way, or whether this financing has been won by previous legislative behavior. In other words, the road from campaign financing to voting behavior can be a murky one.

Framing the issue this way misses the point, however. Campaign financing is dominated by private interests having a large stake in economic growth and development. As usual, environmental interest groups were absent from the list of top overall contributors in the 2000 election cycle. Whether this is unacceptable because these economic interests may be representing the national public interest is not the point. What is important is the simple fact that there are some values and interests that are more dominant than others in public policymaking.

Human Values toward Wolves and Wildlife

Stephen Kellert, a professor at the Yale School of Forestry and Environmental Studies, has provided a useful conceptual framework and value typology that can be used to better understand the range of public values and attitudes toward wolves, wildlife, and the natural world.[13] A consistent problem, according to Kellert, "has been the underestimation of the significance of these variations among critical social groups essential to species recovery [and] the limited use of this information to clarify values among opposing groups, to educate varying constituencies, and to work toward the resolution of conflicts."[14] Kellert's value typology has been applied to the study of numerous species in a variety of cultures and contexts. These values and beliefs toward the natural world have been hypothesized as being "universal dispositions" and basic human tendencies rooted in the biological character of the human species.[15] These basic values are "depicted as inborn biological tendencies ... greatly influenced by learning, culture and experience" (*Value of Life,* 7).

Whatever the "biophilic" roots of such values, Kellert's framework provides a useful way of organizing the stakeholder values inherent in wolf politics. According to Kellert,

> The goal of endangered species protection and recovery clearly depends on an adequate understanding of the basic values, motivations, and interests of all stakeholders. Most endangered species programs, however, fail to consider the wide diversity of values held by competing constituencies in an endangered species dispute. . . . A consistent problem in many endangered species programs is an underestimation of key value differences among critical stakeholders and an inadequate incorporation of this information in the design and implementation of recovery efforts. (*Value of Life,* 176–77)

There are nine basic values toward wildlife according to Kellert's typology: utilitarian, naturalistic, ecologistic-scientific, aesthetic, symbolic, dominionistic, humanistic, moralistic, and negativistic. These "terms are just labels of convenience, ... not terminological straightjackets" (*Value of Life*, 10). The following is a description of Kellert's typology and a brief look at the values that are often embedded in wolf politics. A few contemporary examples are also placed into his framework to illustrate policy implications. Many of these values, and conflicts between them, reappear in the following pages. They were also regularly expressed in stakeholder interviews.

Utilitarian. According to Kellert, "The utilitarian value emphasizes the many ways humans derive material benefit from the diversity of life ... the conventional idea of utilitarianism used here reflects the traditional notion of material benefit derived from exploiting nature to satisfy various human needs and desires" (*Value of Life*, 10). This value forms the bedrock of many of our natural resource and wildlife agencies. From Gifford Pinchot's conception of wise use, meaning the "greatest good for the greatest number over the longest time," to the argument of preserving natural resources and biodiversity for their economic and medicinal benefits, utilitarian values are preeminent in most natural resource and wildlife policy debates. While the utilitarian-based arguments against wolf recovery (from livestock depredation costs to perceived threats to private property) need not be repeated here, there are also utilitarian arguments for wolf recovery.

Environmentalists and pro-wolf advocates, while possessing an array of values toward wildlife, certainly understand how important this value (and the bottom line) is in the political arena. While the wolf's symbolic and moralistic importance moves many, these values are impossible to accurately quantify and do not fit neatly into traditional cost-benefit analyses. As a result, scientists, wolf managers, and pro-wolf forces have often attempted to sell wolves in terms of their utilitarian value, or at least with the argument that the economic benefits will outweigh their costs. The wolf recovery program in the Northern Rockies, for example, estimated in its Final Environmental Impact Statement (FEIS) that the presence of a recovered wolf population in the greater Yellowstone area could generate as much as $23 million in tourism-related economic activity.[16] Many wolf advocates in Alaska, moreover, often talk of the eco-tourism–related benefits resulting from the famous wolves of Denali National Park. The eco-tourism potential of wolves is pointed to in other regions as well. One often-cited economic study, for instance, documented the economic impact of the International Wolf Center (a wolf-based "ecocenter") on the local community of Ely, Minnesota. This study found that the Center draws almost fifty thousand visitors annually and generates about $3 million in annual economic activity, with as many as sixty-six new jobs associated with it.[17]

Naturalistic. The naturalistic value, says Kellert, "emphasizes the many satisfactions people obtain from the direct experience of nature and wildlife [and] reflects the pleasure we get from exploring and discovering nature's complexity and variety" (*Value of Life*, 11–12). This value is often expressed through various types of formal and informal recreation, like hiking, backpacking, birding, fishing, hunting, and whale-watching. Consider, for example, the "wolf-jams" (traffic jams caused by wolf watchers) in Yellowstone National Park and other types of wolf-related tourism.[18] As I drove through the Lamar Valley after a round of interviews in the Yellowstone area, the highway shoulder was busy by four in the morning with people eagerly awaiting their chance to see the famed Yellowstone wolves. Since 1963, moreover, more than sixty-five thousand people have attended the famous "wolf howl" at Ontario's Algonquin Provincial Park.

Ecologistic-Scientific. Kellert maintains that despite differences in approach, both the ecologistic and scientific perspectives converge "in their assumption that through systematic exploration of the biophysical elements of nature, living diversity can be comprehended and sometimes controlled" (*Value of Life*, 13). From recognizing the interdependency of natural processes, and Aldo Leopold's famous assertion that the first rule of intelligent tinkering is to keep all the pieces, to the belief that most of the natural world can be effectively and scientifically managed and controlled, the ecologistic-scientific value is deeply seated in wolf and wildlife management. Sometimes so deeply rooted is this value that some people simply cannot understand or fully appreciate other values toward the natural world: they are "unfounded," "irrational," and "not supported by the literature." But this value has also helped reinvent the wolf, from nothing more than a varmint to an "apex predator" playing an indispensable role in complex ecosystems. Scientists have also shown that there is an ecological price to pay for what we do to wolves, from the increase in ungulate and coyote populations to the alarming decrease in native flora.

Aesthetic. Nature and living diversity, according to Kellert, "also exert an extraordinary aesthetic impact on people [and] each aesthetic experience evokes a strong, primarily emotional, register in most people, provoking feelings of intense pleasure, even awe, at the physical splendor of the natural world" (*Value of Life,* 14–15). Humans, for example, regularly show a favoritism for scenes and constructs depicting the natural world rather than a human-made one (art by public opinion). This value, moreover, often transcends culture. People throughout the world find beauty (the Grand Canyon) and horror (rats and spiders) in the same things. The popularity of the wolf due to its aesthetic quality is hard to miss. It is evident that in parts of Minnesota, for instance, the wolf has become an important symbol of the state's character and identity—what makes Minnesota unique, wild, and northern. Though environmental retail marketing is behind much of the wolf phenomenon—from wolf trinkets to the best-selling wolf photographs by Jim Brandenburg—the aesthetic quality of the wolf is clearly evident.[19] "Charismatic megafauna" like the wolf often benefit from this human value. Would the public show the same degree of interest in restoring hyenas if they were native to North America? Aesthetic values often accentuate animals such a wolves, bears, lions, deer, antelopes, and cranes. The political ramifications stemming from this value are also important, for it is much easier to galvanize public support for these species than it is for less charismatic ones.

Symbolic. Kellert says that "the symbolic value reflects the human tendency to use nature for communication and thought . . . through story, fantasy, and dream, the natural world offers raw material for building our species' seemingly unique and arguably most treasured of capacities: the ability to use language to exchange information among ourselves" (*Value of Life,* 17–18). We also often impart humanlike qualities to many species like the wolf. One rancher in Wyoming, for example, told me that she admires wolves because of their humanlike qualities, including a commitment to family, discipline, and cooperation. And, as I will discuss in chapter 2, the wolf is a potent symbol for many people of the intrinsic value of wilderness, biodiversity, and the natural world.

Dominionistic. The "continuing desire to exercise mastery over nature" stems from the physical and mental challenges presented by nature and wildlife, thus "testing and refining people's capacities for enduring, even mastering, the chore of survival in the face of worthy opposition" (*Value of Life,* 20–21). The dominionistic value can encourage an excessive suppression of nature and wildlife but can also lead to mental and physical competence and feelings of self-reliance. Utilitarian and dominionistic values were at the core of manifest destiny and western settlement, as I will discuss in chapter 3. Consider, moreover, the variety of natural challenges posed to the contemporary small-scale family rancher—draught, disease, fire, bears, lions, and now wolves, to name a few. For many western ranchers, a clear line separates the "window westerner" from those who make a tough living from a hard and unforgiving land. The implications resulting from this value are quite serious. According to one wolf biologist, the cultural belief that humans should dominate, control, and manage other species for human benefit makes it difficult for people to embrace the idea of protecting biological diversity. "The question 'what good are they' is often invoked," he says.

Humanistic. Wildlife and nature, says Kellert, also provide people with "an avenue for expressing and developing the emotional capacities for attachment, bonding, intimacy, and companionship [and] these abilities are nurtured through close association with single species and individual animals, often culturally significant vertebrates and especially domesticated animals that become part of the human household" (*Value of Life,* 21). Humans often develop emotional capacities for attachment, bonding, intimacy, and companionship with animals and sacred places. Wolves are affected by this value because they resemble and sometimes behave like the family dog, and no dog lover likes to imagine their pet being poisoned, trapped, or shot. The wolf-dog hybrid is another manifestation of this value. Many people feel such a strong kinship to wolves that they misguidedly try to keep a wolf or a wolf-dog hybrid as a family pet.

Moralistic. This value refers to the unifying structure, basic symmetry and design, and purpose underlying the natural world. The moralistic value, says Kellert, "flows from discerning a basic kinship binding all life together, and an ethic emerges directing humans to minimize harm to other creatures viewed as fundamentally like ourselves—particularly species characterized by the seeming capacities for sentience, reasoning, and directed self-action" (*Value of Life,* 23). Examples of this value at work include those interests and individuals concerned with the ethical treatment of animals and nature, those believing that there is a right and wrong way to treat the nonhuman world, and the belief among many indigenous peoples that the natural world is a living organism deserving respect and reciprocity. For the Nez Perce of Idaho, for example, the wolf is a spiritual totem, and since it has been gone, an important link in their sacred circle has been missing. Bringing the wolf back to Idaho, then, is not only a scientific and management challenge but a way of marrying that science to tradition. For the Ojibwe, moreover, the wolf is seen as a brother and a guide to heaven who also taught Nana-bush—son of mortal woman and the West Wind—how to hunt.

Negativistic. This value refers to the way some animals and landscapes provoke negative and anxious feelings in many people and cultures. Says Kellert, "Snakes, spiders, sharks, scorpions, large predators, strong winds, stagnant swamps, dark caves—all can precipitate acute passions and avoidance responses in many people. And once aroused, these feelings are hard to extinguish" (*Value of Life,* 24–25). This important value can logically lead to both self-preserving and functional behavior and to irrational and extremely cruel actions toward the nonhuman world. Author Barry Lopez documents these negative feelings among a few individuals and the extreme cruelty with which wolves have been historically treated. According to Lopez, "They were few in number but their voices, screaming for the wolf's head, were often the loudest, the ones that set the tone at a grange meeting and precipitated the wolf's extirpation in the lower forty-eight states."[20] We treated wolves differently than we treated other predators, says Lopez:

> But the wolf is fundamentally different because the history of killing wolves shows far less restraint and far more perversity. A lot of people didn't just kill wolves; they tortured them. They set wolves on fire and tore their jaws out and cut their Achilles tendons and turned dogs loose on them. They poisoned them with strychnine, arsenic, and cyanide, on such a scale that *millions* of other animals . . . were killed incidentally in the process.[21]

Lopez reminds us that even in the 1970s, people in Minnesota choked wolves to death in snares as a way to show their contempt for the wolf's designation as an endangered species. Negativistic behavior toward wolves is well documented and requires little elaboration here. Human-caused wolf mortality remains the gravest threat to wolf recovery and long-term persistence. Some Americans continue to hate and fear the wolf, and a few of these people act on their beliefs. Recall the number of Mexican wolves that have been illegally shot and killed since they were first reintroduced in the Southwest. And in Minnesota, while only a small proportion of residents report ever killing a wolf, a large proportion of farmers (21 percent) and especially northern residents (48 percent) report knowing someone who presumably has.[22]

As can be seen from these few examples, Kellert's typology offers a useful conceptual map to better understand the fundamental values that are deeply embedded in wolf politics. It also illustrates how the ubiquitous effort by all interests in the wolf debate to provide more information to the public as a way to win adherents is clearly not enough. This is not to suggest that environmental-biodiversity education is not important, but that, as Kellert notes, it must contain a mix of cognitive, affective, and value-based learning. Any group or interest that thinks that it can flood the public with what they consider the "right information" and automatically win the public's support is mistaken. In the political process, information is not necessarily a means to enlightenment but is instead a tool to use to get what one wants.

These values should also be understood in the context of stakeholder politics (see chapter 4). As Julia Wondolleck and Steven Yaffee note in their comprehensive assessment of collaboration in natural resource management, not all issues are amenable to a collaborative solution: "Where fundamental value differences exist among the stakeholders and collaboration involves compromising those values, a negotiated approach may not be appropriate. Where an organization wants to establish a precedent or influence policies broader than the situation at hand, going to court or lobbying the legislature might be more effective."[23] These authors make a distinction between fundamental value differences and preferences. With the latter, collaboration can still provide a useful and promising way of solving problems. Wolf control following delisting from the ESA provides one example. Some groups and interests will not give any ground when it comes to the public hunting and trapping of wolves, from airborne methods to the use of snares. Instead, they will likely utilize more adversarial methods of conflict resolution.

Cases of Value-Based Political Conflict and Tension

This section explores a few cases to illustrate how many of these values and their representative interests are rooted in wolf policy and management. Many of these values and the conflicts between them will characterize the wolf debate of the future. These examples also show that the wolf debate is value-based and political, and one that must be waged in a more democratic context.

Conflict and Tension between Scientist and Stakeholder

Gone are the days in which scientists were given the only word in natural resource and wildlife management. Ecologists have exhaustively documented how our most pressing environmental problems are fraught with uncertainty and complexity. Contrast, for instance, the relatively simple paradigm of how to eradicate the nation of wolves versus the intimidating social and scientific context in which the field of conservation biology now operates. This "postnormal" scientific paradigm, according to Thomas Prugh, Robert Costanza, and Herman Daly, is inherently more political and cultural than scientific in orientation: "Where once science was a source of authoritative advice on how to extract and use resources more rapidly...now science must become just one partner in a broad-based decision-making process that involves anybody with a stake in the outcome...essentially everyone is a stakeholder."[24] Accordingly, they conclude that the "peer community" must be widened to include other types of expertise and those with a stake in the outcome.

Although much is still to be learned about the wolf, an impressive amount of information has been collected and analyzed by some of the world's most respected wildlife biologists. With such knowledge, along with the significant strides made in wildlife monitoring and management, some scientists believe that they should have primary responsibility for managing wolves.[25] Others, however, noting the significant sociopolitical, economic, and cultural elements of human-wolf relations, as well as the lack of consensus in many areas of wolf and wildlife science, believe that the public, in one form or another, should have the preeminent role in setting objectives, guidelines, and overall management parameters.

Minnesota's wolf roundtable plan presents an excellent example of the antagonism between scientific values and concerns and the management recommendations reached through stakeholder consensus and compromise. What happens when the public, as represented by the roundtable, advocates more wolves than many scientists and managers want or think they can effectively manage? The roundtable recommended that wolves in Minnesota be allowed to continue to naturally expand their range in the state, and to assure their continued survival, they set the minimum statewide winter population goal at 1,600 wolves with no maximum goal or ceiling. The numbers recommended by the roundtable were above those stated in the 1992 *Recovery Plan for the Eastern Timber Wolf,* which placed optimal populations in the 1,250 to 1,400 range in wilderness and semi-wilderness locales. The plan justified these recommendations as a way to ensure wolf survival in the state, produce enough dispersers to help repopulate adjacent states, and minimize human-wolf conflict.

One of the most consequential developments in the story of Minnesota wolf management has been the disparity between scientific and public management of the state's wolves. Wolf biologist and expert L. David Mech, for example, an ardent and long-time wolf advocate and chair of the World Conservation Union's (formerly IUCN) Wolf Specialist Group, feared that the roundtable management recommendations would likely lead to increased livestock depredation, exacerbated human-wolf conflicts (especially as they disperse outside of the northern wilderness zone into agricultural areas), and a possible public backlash.[26] Mech was also concerned that once wolf numbers got as high as those recommended by the roundtable, attempts at controlling wolf populations would become more difficult, time-consuming, and expensive, if even possible.

Mech is critical of various interest groups having such an important voice in the management of Minnesota's wolf population. Not only does he believe that biologists should be making these decisions rather than stakeholders, but he worries that decision makers in other wolf reintroduction projects are watching the Minnesota situation, and "if they see that, once wolves are re-introduced, management of the animals is essentially taken out of the hands of professionals, they will be much less likely to conduct the introductions."[27] Mech believes that wolf reintroduction is contingent on proving to local communities, the public, and policymakers that the animal can be successfully and scientifically managed, and if management is taken away from the wildlife professional and given to special interests in whatever guise, global wolf restoration will be halted. Furthermore, says Mech, provision for strict population control was the premise to wolf restoration in the Northern Rockies, the Southwest, and North Carolina. For Mech and others, wolf recovery means wolf management.

Although Mech is a well-respected authority in the wolf science and policy community, many stakeholders are skeptical of what they see as a rather simple dichotomy between the "scientific" and "nonscientific" approach to wolf management. Some stakeholders see Mech as an expert to be sure, but one with as many values and ethical inclinations as anyone involved in the wolf debate.

Not all scientists agree of course on the proper role of public participation in policymaking and management. One prominent wildlife biologist, for example, sees little conflict between the scientist and stakeholder. He believes that wolf biologists and scientists in general can influence the decision-making process by informing the stakeholders and the public that "if you do X, Y will be the outcome." It is then up to the public to decide whether they can accept this anticipated result. This biologist is enthusiastic about community-based decision making as well as the use of stakeholders in various state wolf management plans. As long as decisions are made within the parameters of national goals, he believes that this new wave of conservation is a wonderful way of solving problems.

Wildlife biologist Vic Van Ballenberghe of Alaska draws a parallel to a doctor-client relationship. Many wolf conflicts in Alaska revolve around issues pertaining to wolf predation on moose and caribou. Many interests in the state, from urban hunters to moose-dependent bush communities, plead for increased wolf control as a way to help recover declining ungulate populations (real or perceived). Biologists like Van Ballenberghe are often asked to assess the science and biology of a particular case. Similar to a medical doctor, he proceeds cautiously before he recommends surgery (wolf control) for his client (decision maker or stakeholder). After all, surgery could unnecessarily cost a lot of money and even result in death. He first wants to understand the nature of the problem; thus, he orders some diagnostic tests to identify possible causes. Once the cause is evident, treatment is prescribed after the risks and benefits are explained to the client. The client would then probably seek a second opinion. At the very least, this client would want to be sure that the medical advice given was science-based. Of course the client is then free to make a decision based on this medical advice and other nonmedical factors. According to Van Ballenberghe, wildlife management is not much different: "It is a mix of science and non-science issues. Management actions must first have a sound scientific base. Public policy decisions by the Board of Game and the governor may then include other considerations, but the science base cannot be ignored without risking failure." He is critical of some wolf control efforts in Alaska for these very reasons. It is analogous, he says, to a medical doctor prescribing treatment (wolf control) before doing the necessary diagnostic tests (predator-prey research).

Many questions and conflicts related to elite versus majoritarian decision making are debated in other regions over different animals. Conflicts are bound to escalate given the growing number of states using public referenda and initiatives as a way of managing wildlife.[28] As of 1996, there had been more than twenty ballot measures in various states (mostly in the West) that asked voters to make some decision related to wildlife management.[29] In 1996, for example, citizens in Washington State banned bear hunting with hounds, and bait-and-hound hunting of bobcat, cougar, and lynx. This type of majoritarian decision making often pits urban (with more voting power) versus rural constituencies. And swings of public sentiment scare wildlife professionals such as Mech, who says:

> It is ironic that this simple majority-rule type of wildlife management is basically the same approach that extirpated carnivores many years ago. Although there were no actual referendums at that time, there were bureaucrats acting contrary to scientific opinion but bending to the public will.... The lesson to be learned is that public sentiment is fickle. If major carnivore management decisions are determined by public mood rather than by the knowledge of professionals, we could end up with California full of carnivores and North Dakota with none.[30]

The proper role of science is often a subtle theme in other wildlife and natural resource management issues and debates.[31] Analyzing the politics of ecosystem management in greater Yellowstone, political scientists R. McGreggor Cawley and John Freemuth found that science is a key component in the competing "scripts" on how to best manage the greater Yellowstone ecosystem.[32] The "tree farm" script is organized around a combination of natural science and scientific management principles, while the "mother earth" script is organized around the science of ecology and its key principles of ecosystems and diversity. But science and management are asked to answer different questions. Cawley and Freemuth provide the following example:

> Scientific observation remains more or less content with the conclusion that a 16-ounce container has 8 ounces of fluid in it. From a management perspective, however, the crucial question may be whether the container

is half full or half empty. This question determines the appropriate course of action—whether more fluid is needed, as it were. The problem, of course, is that half full and half empty are value judgments derived from the interests of people. As such, they are open to negotiation at any given moment, and over time, unless we assume that values and interests remain constant. Scientists, and managers who center decisions solely on science, do not have any special position in negotiations over value questions.[33]

There is also no consensus among wolf stakeholders on the appropriate place and legitimacy of "scientific management." For some animal rights and welfare interests, scientific wolf management means wolf control, either through government trapping or a public take, or by some other means, often experimental in nature. Scientific management, they say, may sound value-free, but its emphasis on managing wolves rather than managing humans is steeped in questionable values and ethics toward the nonhuman world. This sort of criticism by the animal rights and welfare contingent angers those such as Mech, who believes that wherever we have wolves, we must also have management. Mech, who has long been vilified by wolf opponents for his pro-wolf policy positions is now being attacked by what he calls "wolf protectionists." He thinks strategically about future wolf recovery throughout the world and believes that we could have more wolves in far more places if pro-wolf interests could understand and accept the necessity of wolf control.[34] The political implications resulting from the power and misconceptions of animal rights groups are serious, says Mech. First, because some people oppose control, they are in effect opposing wolf restoration. And second, the anti-wolf public intensifies its opposition toward wolves in part in response to the extremism of the other side. As a result, says Mech, some public officials who may like the idea of wolf recovery will oppose it because of the zealotry of some pro-wolf forces.

Scientific Values in the Policymaking Process

Since Rachel Carson's *Silent Spring* was first published, the line between scientist and advocate has sometimes been blurred. The backlash to Carson's research and writing by the chemical industry is an example of how the values of science can differ in important ways from the values of profit and politics. Carson was not only a well-respected scientist but also a brave woman who dared speak truth to entrenched power. She acted on her science and her conscience and did so at her personal and professional peril. Carson has not been the last person to act in such ways in the face of political and industry harassment. Scientists and natural resource and wildlife managers in agencies such as the U.S. Forest Service, FWS, and various state agencies have blown whistles while attempting to steer their agencies in what they see as a more public-interested direction. These stories are an important reminder of where the values of science and ecology often fit in political hierarchies and policymaking processes.

Writer Todd Wilkinson documents the stories of various "combat scientists" in *Science under Siege: The Politicians' War on Nature and Truth* (a book recommended by a prominent wolf biologist). According to Wilkinson, federal workers inspired by the spirit of Carson are fighting for good science and its honest and earnest use. Risking their careers and livelihoods, says Wilkinson, "they have taken on corrupt politicians and bureaucrats wedded to logging and mining companies, industrial polluters, the livestock industry, water developers, and energy conglomerates that have left ecological destruction in their wake."[35] Wilkinson illustrates where solid science fits or does not fit into the game of power and industry politics.

While what constitutes the most valid and reliable science is often up for debate, Wilkinson's work does show that there is often a clear line separating the public and private when it comes to natural resource and wildlife policy. While conceptions of the public dominate our popular understanding—that public taxes support public institutions that supposedly conduct public science in the public interest that should then be used in public policymaking—Wilkinson's work documents a system in which scientists doing politically unpopular work often face ostracism, harassment, and intimidation. His findings also foreshadow where wolf biology and science may fit into the future political puzzle of state wolf management, and the formidable obstacles facing public-interested science, public opinion, and the implementation of enacted legislation such as the ESA. The Western States Coalition (formerly the Cowboy Caucus), real estate developers, the livestock industry, industrial tourism interests, politically manipulated budgets, the "purging" of agencies of potential "troublemakers," private interests sponsoring their own "science," and an array of other daunting challenges may lie in wait.

This sort of conflict has been especially prevalent, or at least more transparent, in the Mexican wolf recovery program. Many wolf advocates believe that David Parsons, a wildlife biologist and the former leader of the Mexican Wolf Recovery Program for the FWS, was given an early retirement due to his steadfast support of sound biological science in the face of heavy political and livestock industry pressure. Parsons had always believed that the Gila-Leopold wilderness complex in New Mexico provided the most suitable habitat for wolves and would provide the greatest opportunity for successful wolf recovery by minimizing the chances of livestock depredation. Nevertheless, political pressure from New Mexico resulted in wolves being released into Arizona's Blue Range (with more roads and more livestock) rather than New Mexico's wilderness. In the middle of negotiations over possibly expanding the possible release sites to include areas in the Gila-Leopold complex, Parsons was provided an early retirement by the FWS. The timing of Parsons's departure is a clear indicator to many conservationists and wolf advocates of where sound science and biology—the essence of the ESA—now fit into the culture of the FWS.

Many wildlife biologists believe that it is not an issue of politics versus sound science but rather one of sound science being legislatively mandated by the ESA, a law passed by Congress and upheld by the courts. Many wildlife biologists see themselves as doing what is required by law: conducting thorough biological assessments and making science-based recommendations. For them, the ESA is clear in what is required, and they expect those involved to honor the legitimacy of this public law made in a democratic context. Asked what a political environment most conducive to successful wolf management would look like, one prominent wolf biologist answered, "an environment where government agencies were allowed to carry out legislative mandates without intimidation or threats of harm or political retaliation."

The perception held among some stakeholders that wolf biologists sometimes appear to be politically aloof and above the fray can be partially explained by this perspective. Some scientists are skeptical of public input when that input is a contest of who can yell the loudest and complain the most. Locals opposing wolf reintroduction are mistaken, says one wolf biologist, if they believe these issues are decided by how many people complain at public hearings. The ESA is a legislative man-

date, he says, that has already been debated in a more inclusive democratic forum.

The tension between science and politics is not as simple as it first
appears. Not all scientists, nor wildlife biologists, agree on what constitutes sound science or the public interest. One of the most vocal critics
of western wolf reintroduction from a scientific point of view, for example, argues that federal wildlife managers in the Northern Rockies have
played fast and loose with biological science. Wildlife ecologist Charles
Kay has long complained that the recovery plan for wolves in the Northern Rockies is predicated on a political, not a biological, interpretation
of what constitutes a minimum viable wolf population. He says that he
is committed "to science being used responsibly in policy debates, something I have not seen with wolf recovery. My analysis indicates that the
federal government and other wolf advocates have taken liberties with
the truth and with science."[36]

In the Northern Rockies, wolves will be delisted from the ESA when
at least ten breeding packs have been maintained for at least three successive years in all three (Yellowstone, central Idaho, and northwest
Montana) recovery areas. Assuming that on average there are ten wolves
in each pack, there would be one hundred wolves in each recovery area
and at least three hundred wolves in all. But Kay questions how the government arrived at these figures: "Because the [FWS] developed its 10
wolf packs, 100 wolf recovery goals with little, or no, supporting scientific evidence, all the government's recent wolf recovery reports, wolf
population models, and studies regarding possible impact on big game
hunting are arbitrary and capricious. They represent not science but a
masterful job of deception."[37]

Kay contends that the FWS developed its goal of ten wolf packs and
one hundred wolves because it was more politically acceptable than a
larger viable population number. The federal government, maintains
Kay, proposed one hundred wolves knowing full well that this number
would not be enough to meet minimum size requirements for a viable
population. Kay lashes out at environmentalists as well. While they have
argued for large minimum viable populations for many species, such as
the northern spotted owl, they have not done so for wolves in the Northern Rockies. In explaining why, Kay presents a hypothetical look into
the future: "Wolves arrive and increase to 100. The government moves
to delist. Environmentalists sue and win. The wolf population is allowed

to reach 1500 or more. Environmentalists are happy, the federal agencies are happy, and the public, only too late, realizes what has happened."[38] While these comments, made in 1993, are directed at the estimated impact of reintroduced wolves on big game populations, Kay continues to lambaste the program for "hidden agendas," and still sees the debate over wolf reintroduction as having nothing to do with wolves "and everything to do with values and whose view will control the future of the West."[39]

Values and Political Power: Ranching in the West

From the big "group of ten" environmental organizations and the American Farm Bureau inside the Beltway, to the more regional or state-based groups spread throughout the country, the debate over wolves is often one of competing interest groups struggling over different ideas and conceptions of what constitutes the public interest. Political scientists have long debated the meaning and importance of such groups in the American political process. Pluralists have seen the interest-group system as being not only inevitable in a democratic society but also positively and inherently democratic. Critics, from a variety of different political and ideological positions, challenge this rosy picture with a more skeptical line of inquiry. They most often ask in what way is political, cultural, and economic power embedded in the political and decision-making process, and how does this affect the framing, formation, and implementation of public policy. While some scholars emphasize the fluidity, fairness, and competitive nature of interest-group politics, others criticize a system that is often exclusive, unfair, and unjust and dominated by relatively few privileged groups and interests. The question of political power—who has it and who cares—must be at least part of our inquiry into the wolf policymaking process. If we are to explore the values and players of wolf policy—from the legislative conference committee and courtroom to the collaborative roundtable—we must also investigate this important question of political and cultural power.

As discussed throughout this book, in many cases the most powerful interest opposing wolf recovery has been the western ranching industry. In whatever voice, from the American Farm Bureau Federation to the National Cattlemen's Association, ranching interests have been a dominant player in the wolf policy debate. In seventeen western states, livestock grazing is allowed on 254 million acres of federal lands. On these public lands—an area equal to California, Oregon, Washington, and Idaho combined—roughly 26,300 ranchers graze 3.2 million cattle.[40] Grazing occurs on all types of private and public lands, including lands managed by the Bureau of Land Management (BLM), U.S. Forest Service, National Park Service, and FWS. One study reports that 94 percent of BLM lands in sixteen western states are grazed, and 35 percent of federal wilderness areas have active livestock grazing allotments.[41]

Public rangeland policy is most often characterized as being distributive in a relatively closed process with a small number of players involved.[42] The iron triangle, or protective subgovernment, is the term often used to describe this area of public policymaking. The BLM, groups such as the National Cattlemen's Association, and key western political representatives sitting on important natural resource committees are usually subsystem participants (or according to one's politics, "the usual suspects").

Anyone doubting the power and influence of this subgovernment should review President Clinton's first year in office. Among other natural resource policy reforms in Clinton's first proposed budget was a proposal to raise public land grazing fees. This proposal, advocated by environmental organizations and Secretary of the Interior Bruce Babbitt, ignited the western cowboy caucus. Western senators (mostly Republicans), representing a relatively small percentage of Americans, charged Clinton with the usual "crimes against the West": threats to Western customs and culture, local economic hardship and dislocation, federal aggrandizement and bureaucratic paternalism, eastern and outsider arrogance, and other often repeated rhetorical themes. Filibusters and political maneuvering by western senators temporarily blocked this reform, and the 1994 congressional elections putting Republicans in control of both the House and Senate finally put an end to such naive (in hindsight, of course) executive tampering.

According to political scientist Christopher McGrory Klyza, this story illustrates not only the importance of powerful groups in public land policymaking but also how the history of past policy can shed valuable light on the more recent. Klyza maintains that public land policies are best understood by examining them as part of a "policy regime" that becomes (1) embedded within the state, then (2) a privileged idea constraining state actors, and finally (3) an institutionalized idea that becomes difficult to dislodge, despite efforts to do so. In Klyza's analysis, some policy ideas and patterns become privileged. The privileged idea and pattern of grazing policy, says Klyza, are interest-group liberalism and agency capture: "In summary, passage of the Taylor Grazing Act resulted in policies that were controlled by the regulated interest group and the local elites that comprised the livestock industry, establishing a captured policy regime justified by the privileged idea of interest-group liberalism."[43] Despite federal ownership, says Klyza, these lands were managed as if they were private property.

The western range has of course been controversial turf for some time. Wolves are but one part of a much larger and acrimonious debate over public lands ranching. Debra Donahue, a law professor at the University of Wyoming, raised the stakes and the sophistication of the debate in her controversial 1999 book *The Western Range Revisited: Removing Livestock from Public Lands to Conserve Native Biodiversity*. Donahue provides an all-out assault on the western ranching industry and romantic perceptions of it. She begins her case with the following indictment:

> In this "romantic view," ranchers are "cowboys," who are seen as synonymous with the American West. Yet ranchers have never filled the boots of the mythical cowboy—the independent, freedom-loving, self-reliant figure of the open range. The public land ranchers of today are something of a paradox. Their numbers are few, but their political power is substantial. They act like they own the range when, in fact, their toehold on it is but a revocable "privilege." They pride themselves on their self-reliance and rail against government meddling in their affairs, while availing themselves of every government benefit and fighting to maintain a grazing fee that fails to recoup even the government's administrative costs. They replace their own cowboys with new-fangled balers and four-wheelers and snowmobiles and yet appeal to public sentiment and nostalgia to help preserve their traditional way of life. Arguing that the economy of their local community depends on their staying in business, they "moonlight" to make ends meet. The animals they raise on the range deplete the very capital on which their, and the animals', living depends. They call themselves the "original conservationists," but they have a rifle slung behind the seat of their pickups for picking off coyotes and other "varmints." They poison prairie dogs and willows and sagebrush and replace native meadows with water-guzzling alfalfa.[44]

Challenges such as this do not go unnoticed in the West, and especially in places like Wyoming. Following publication of Donahue's meticulously cited scientific and legal challenge, the University of Wyoming and its College of Law were seriously challenged by the state's ranching industry and their state political representatives. Republican Jim Twiford, president of the Wyoming State Senate, told the *Casper Star Tribune* that "we've got some unlicensed, unbridled folks running over there that ought to be smarter than to be biting the hand that's feeding them."[45] Twiford also drafted a bill, which was later pulled, to close the University of Wyoming College of Law. Influential ranchers are cutting off contributions to the university and are asking the school to do a better job of weeding out "troublemakers." The president of the Wyoming Stock Growers sent a letter to university trustees stating that the school needed to "do a better job screening applicants for different positions to adequately ensure that the majority of professors and instructors represent the ideals and views of Wyoming's people."[46] This political response to Donahue's book only adds credibility to parts of her critique, especially regarding what she sees as a disproportionate amount of political and cultural influence wielded by a small but powerful segment of the American West. Donahue builds on the work of other scholars who have long studied the entrenched political power, at both the federal and state levels, of the less than thirty thousand ranchers holding BLM grazing permits.[47]

The political influence of the ranching industry is also due in part to the agency structure of the BLM. Unlike the U.S. Forest Service or Environmental Protection Agency, with regional offices dispersed throughout the country, the BLM is more state- and local-based, making the agency more susceptible to state and local political and economic pressures. The influence of western stockgrowers on the BLM is often traced to the agency's use of grazing advisory boards established under the Taylor Grazing Act of 1934. These boards have been seen as particularly dominated by local elite interests. Environmentalists also complain that grazing is given preferential treatment by other federal agencies as well. Grazing, for example, is allowed on a number of national wildlife refuges administered by the FWS and in more than twelve units of the national park system, including Grand Teton National Park.

Most disconcerting for some is the control exerted by ranchers and ranching associations over Wildlife Services (formerly known as Animal Damage Control), the federal agency responsible for managing and killing species that are perceived as a threat to livestock, such as wolves, bears, mountain lions, and coyotes. From 1937 through 1983, the Department of Agriculture's Animal Damage Control Program had the dubious honor of killing approximately 26,000 bears, 500,000 bobcats,

3.7 million coyotes, 50,000 red wolves, 1,600 gray wolves, and 8,000 mountain lions.[48] The majority of the western livestock protection program is funded with federal and state tax dollars.

For critics of the ranching industry, the program is but one additional example of how much political protection ranchers have always enjoyed without paying the associated costs. The Montana-based Predator Conservation Alliance, a staunch critic of Wildlife Services, says that "public money is being spent to kill publicly owned wildlife, often on public lands, at the request of a small percentage of private livestock producers, who are neither required to change their management practices to reduce livestock/predator conflicts nor directly pay for this government 'service.'"[49]

Wolf advocates also point out that the control methods used by Wildlife Services can be indiscriminate and lethal to nondepredating wolves. A few wolves in the Northern Rockies, they point out, have been killed by the Services' widespread use of M-44, a spring-loaded bait laced with sodium cyanide. Congressional debate over the agency's future is becoming an annual occurrence as well.[50] An amendment that would have drastically cut the agency's budget was added to the FY 2000 agriculture appropriations bill in the House of Representatives. Although the amendment initially passed, it was overturned the following day with heavy pressure from the American Farm Bureau, western representatives, and other ranching interests.

Generalizing about wolves and ranchers can be problematic, however. It is important to distinguish between the absentee corporate ranching outfit and the smaller-scale family-based ranch. One heralded in-depth investigative report by the San Jose Mercury News found the differences between the two striking. Investigators reviewed more than 26,000 federal billing records and found corporations, millionaires, and "Rolex ranchers" dominating the public's range. The report uncovered "the extent to which wealthy hobby ranchers, agribusiness giants and corporations—far more than hardscrabble families portrayed in John Wayne movies—benefit from federal grazing subsidies."[51] For example, the top 10 percent of grazing permit holders control 65 percent of all livestock on BLM property.

What is perhaps most striking is the contrast painted between corporate ranching interests, like Anheuser-Busch Inc., hotel mogul Barron Hilton, and french-fry billionaire J. R. Simplot, and struggling family ranchers, like Hugh B. McKeen of Catron County, New Mexico, who runs about 145 cattle on the Gila National Forest and cleared $12,000 from his family's livestock business. As in farming with its chasm between the family and corporate farm, the ranching industry is undergoing the same type of economic concentration: more cows on public lands are being managed by fewer ranchers. These trends only compound the difficulties of managing wolves and endangered species on public lands throughout the West. Imagine the challenges facing the modern-day family rancher: drought, mountains of debt, low beef prices, crashing Asian markets, finicky American consumers, and now wolves. To make matters even more frustrating, the family rancher finds himself battling perceptions of the welfare Rolex rancher, his fate (and grazing fees) lumped together with others found on the Fortune 500 list.

Whatever political power the western livestock industry may have, it should be properly understood in its larger historical and cultural context. The only species that carries more symbolic baggage than the wolf is the western rancher. The imagery evoked by ranchers needs no elaboration; they are seen as the very essence of the West, or what the West once was or should be again. Like the wolf, however, they have recently undergone serious demythologizing. For critics, the difference between the small-scale, rugged, individualistic, and self-reliant western rancher and the wolf is that only one exists. Again illustrating how policy is often more influenced by fiction than science, the future of the wolf in the West will continue to be entangled in this divisive cultural debate. In talking wolves, one inevitably treks into a political and cultural minefield, loaded with explosive issues pertaining to custom, lifestyle, culture, community stability, and the fate of the rural West.

In the West the wolf once again finds itself introduced not only to a physical landscape but also into a larger cultural context. Wolves have returned during the quarrelsome transition from old West to new (see chapter 3). In this context, public lands ranching is often defended because it is seen as providing an important economic base to local rural communities, because it is a way of life worthy of preservation for its own sake, and, finally, because it is a way to preserve the West's last open spaces. If wolves are perceived as a threat to the commodity on which this defense is based, they will be opposed. For critics of the ranching industry like Donahue, however, these assumptions and arguments have no basis in fact and pose a real danger to the health and future of the western environment and its biodiversity.

As for wolves, the significance of this relationship between values and political power cannot be emphasized enough. It adds a commonsensical explanation of why the return of wolves to the West has been so much more caustic than in places such as the upper Midwest. According to a prominent wolf scientist and manager in Wisconsin, for example, one of the main reasons that the return of wolves to Wisconsin has been less controversial is the absence of public land ranching in the state.

Competing values and conceptions of the public interest are at work here. And while there are an array of human values toward the natural world, some of these values have more political influence and clout than others. An earlier study conducted by Kellert shows that the values of livestock operators differ from the general public in important ways. Contrasting the results of a national survey of American attitudes toward animals, wildlife, and natural habitat with randomly selected members of the National Cattlemen's Association (NCA) and American Sheep Producers Council, Kellert found that livestock producers had extremely high utilitarian and dominionistic scores, and the lowest moralistic scores of any activity group. The livestock group also had quite low humanistic and comparatively high negativistic scores, and moderately high naturalistic and ecologistic scores.[52]

Public and Institutional Values toward Wildlife

While the values and attitudes of the general public and those held by interest groups and invited stakeholders are critical in wolf policymaking, the explicit and implicit values of implementing wildlife agencies are equally as important to the future of wolf recovery. The organizational culture of state wildlife agencies, including state wildlife commissions and federal agencies like the Department of Agriculture's Wildlife Services, will play an integral role in future wolf management following ESA delisting. The personal and professional values within an organization influence the levels of support for various programs and can be used to better understand organizational behavior.

The organizational culture of state wildlife agencies has been described in colorful ways. One assessment describes wildlife professionals as a cohesive culture entrenching themselves defensively like a herd of musk ox whenever challenged.[53] Some observers have also noted that this entrenchment and the protection of traditional management styles are especially evident in the face of complex sociopolitical challenges posed by the human dimensions of wildlife management.[54]

Similar to the American forestry profession, the wildlife professional subculture is largely based on the Progressive Era ideals of utilitarianism, scientific-technical expertise, bureaucratic management, and Pinchotian wise use. Many wildlife professionals, unlike an increasingly urbanized American public possessing an array of nonutilitarian wildlife values, have rural community roots and utilitarian agricultural values. The effect, according to one critical assessment, is the formation of "a defensive, Bastille-mentality that views itself and dissenting publics as a contest of right and wrong, the informed vs. the uninformed, the rational vs. the emotional."[55] Bruce Gill of the Colorado Division of Wildlife similarly proclaims that "despite growing public support for wildlife protection and ambivalence, if not opposition, to utilitarianism, wildlifers still preach and practice the utilitarian gospel of 19th-century Prussian forestry."[56] State wildlife agencies have an incentive to rechannel funds back into fish and game programs, since this is where most of their budgets originate. Gill observes that though perhaps unintentional, license fees effectively married public wildlife agencies to special interests. Says Gill, "It was an unholy marriage because it blurred the essential distinction between public interest and special interest and inevitably eroded both scientific credibility and public trust."[57]

There are institutional incentives at work, but there are also important personal and professional values at play as well, and these values and worldviews are often different from those of the general public. In Utah (a state in proximity to wolves within the greater Yellowstone ecosystem), for example, approximately 80 percent of wildlife managers within the Utah Division of Wildlife Resources (DWR) adhere to a utilitarian value orientation supporting the management of wildlife resources as a commodity (this research found a more "holistic utilitarianism" than is discussed in this chapter, showing, for example, that these utilitarians also strongly support the preservation of the biological health of wildlife populations as one of the primary goals of wildlife management).[58] Compare this utilitarian score to a recent survey done in the state showing that 36 percent of wildlife stakeholders have exclusively nonconsumptive interests in wildlife, while 8 percent have strong non-recreational wildlife interests. The number of nonconsumptive users is also increasing in Utah.[59]

This research also shows how multidimensional and complex the story of values, political power, and management authority can be. For example, while DWR managers felt that more authority should be given to wildlife professionals in all types of wildlife management decisions, this "desire for more professional authority is likely due to managers wanting to protect the interests of the 'silent majority' from domination by special interests in wildlife management decision-making."[60] Although this reasoning by wildlife managers wanting to do the "public's work" may be admirable, the important differences between public and agency values should not be underestimated, especially when an agency is given increased managerial flexibility, as was done for the FWS with the experimental designation of wolves. This research also suggests that the stories told by Wilkinson about the ostracism of scientists doing politically unpopular work, and by environmentalists about Parsons's early retirement from the Mexican Wolf Recovery Program may not be isolated anomalies.

As mentioned earlier, the policy implications resulting from these differences between public versus agency values are illustrated by the unprecedented use of state ballot initiatives about wildlife management. If the public or a committed interest group believes that the values and resulting policies of a state wildlife agency are out of step with the public's values, then wildlife policymaking by the initiative process is not far behind. Tom Beck, a bear biologist for the Colorado Division of Wildlife, for example, believes that it was this chain of events that led to Colorado's controversial passage in 1992 of Amendment 10 banning spring black bear hunting and the use of trailing hounds and bait piles.[61] According to Beck, both the culture of the division and its commission was seriously out of step with the state's public opinion regarding black bear hunting, and as a consequence, the division had its management guidelines set by an exasperated public.

The role of science and the agricultural model of wildlife management is important here. First, says Beck, supporters of status quo wildlife management "rally to their hallowed icon—science [yet] the greatest flaw in our profession is the failure to acknowledge the limited role of biological science in most of our actions, as we mostly deal with conflicts of values and the human spirit."[62] Second, the agricultural model of wildlife and natural resource management is characterized by single-factor maximization of harvests. We thus "harvest" deer and elk, manage wetlands as "production units" for waterfowl, and focus on "getting out the cut." Beck says that allegiance to the agricultural model has also led to the belief among many managers that the population of a species is all that counts in wildlife management. Allegiance to the model is "another false paean of the wildlife profession" according to Beck.[63] Focusing solely on population, demographics, and animal production, says Beck, "may work for soybeans, but in a nation that, at least verbally, strongly supports animal welfare issues, it not only does not work, it is misguided."[64]

Scientific reductionism and the agricultural model will likely affect wolf management in the future as well. Wildlife agencies must recognize that scientific management, by itself, will be inadequate when dealing with value-based decisions and issues of social significance. Moreover, if states decide to forge ahead with a public "harvest" of wolves and defend such management solely in terms of viable wolf populations and do not address issues pertaining to individual animal welfare, they should also be prepared for more criticism and more wildlife policymaking by the electorate.

Consumptive and Nonconsumptive Values

Next to that of livestock depredation, questions pertaining to the effect of wolves on ungulate prey populations such as deer, elk, moose, and caribou have continually emerged as major issues in all wolf programs. Historically, some hunters have feared that ungulate populations will decline as the numbers of wolves in an area increase. Many wolf recovery and management programs throughout the country have become a forum on hunting and hunters. Friends of the Yellowstone Elk Herd, for example, are concerned that wolves are decimating the famous elk of northern Yellowstone, while many biologists believe that the elk are still overpopulating and wreaking ecological damage in this important ecosystem. Some outfitters and guides are worried about their future, complaining that wolves have caused severe declines in ungulate numbers or are moving them to places they have not been before, thus making them harder to hunt. Hunters in North Carolina opposed red wolf recovery because of the perceived threat to local hunting customs and culture. Among other things, they were concerned about further restrictions being placed on hunters within the Alligator National Wildlife Refuge, such as not being able to hunt with dogs. And in Alaska, the debate over hunting wolves to control their effect on moose and caribou populations has become one of the most contentious issues in the history of American wildlife management.

The political force of hunters goes well beyond their numbers and financial contributions to state wildlife agencies. It is a power rich in custom, culture, and tradition. Any perceived threat to a state's game population is therefore often attacked as a threat to a sacrosanct cultural lifeway. Says Stan Meyer, chairman of Montana's Fish, Wildlife and Parks Commission, "For me and for tens of thousands of other Montanans hunting is not sport, it's not recreation, it's not business; a hunter is what I am. It's part of my lifestyle; it's part of my culture.... When we feel that that lifestyle is being threatened, that we're in the cusp of losing something of our heritage, something that causes us to live, we're scared."[65]

Meyer believes that Montana's urban-rural divide will likely characterize future conflict in the state. He, as do many others in the debate, frames the issue as one pitting local hunters who have long supported professional wildlife management through fees and excise taxes versus a more numerous urbanized public. Predator management is a political issue, he says: "It's coming down to who can send the most e-mails. And I know who can send the most e-mails and it ain't Montana hunters and trappers. It's out-of-staters, and this is the difficult thing to deal with."[66] Of course, this commissioner is not the first to note the importance of numbers when it comes to making public policy. One of the first commentators on American political culture, French observer Alexis de Tocqueville, saw a system dangerously susceptible to a "tyranny of the majority." Given the concept of "majority rule" and "supremacy of the people," says hunting advocate and historian John Reiger, "The sportsmen minority, therefore, is quite correct in seeing its position as precarious."[67]

In the Northern Rockies, outfitters have been among the most vocal critics of wolf reintroduction. They similarly frame the debate as an extreme fringe of urban environmentalists attacking their traditional way of life and livelihoods. According to Scott Farr of the Idaho Outfitters and Guides Association, there has never been a more critical issue for the existence of outfitters than wolf reintroduction. He believes that wolf population goals must be commensurate with maintaining current ungulate populations in the region. If this and other goals cannot be accomplished, says Farr, "then wolf reintroduction should not have taken place as it shows a complete disregard for residents of this state, and we suggest that a movement get underway to eliminate this intrusion in our way of life. The avenues aren't clear at this time, but I assure you the will of the sportsmen, outfitters, ranchers, and residents of Idaho to protect our way of life will prevail."[68]

Similar to how wolves have become an important symbol to many ranchers of all of the disparate challenges they face, wolves have been added to a larger pile of unresolved issues and controversies pertaining to hunting. Some prominent members of the hunting community in the Northern Rockies believe that this type of response among outfitters is due to the changing paradigm of wildlife management. Where once the state of Montana de facto guaranteed the right of outfitters to use and make a living from the wildlife "resource," they no longer enjoy such unchallenged support. They no longer have a guaranteed right to the resource and must now accept a redistribution among all predators within an ecosystem.

While hunting organizations will certainly play a significant role in the future of wolf policy and management, they are participating during an especially fractious time. Game farming and the use of ATVs to hunt are but two cases in which hunters fail to speak with a unified voice. Pigeonholing hunters can be as difficult and foolhardy as stereotyping "the environmentalist." After all, the chasm separating some anti-wolf guiding outfits from groups like the Montana Wildlife Federation and the Izaak Walton League is as wide as that separating the Sierra Club from the Earth Liberation Front. Some of the most ardent wolf and wilderness advocates hunt, and hunters have been among the most effective defenders of wilderness and wildlife in American history.

As discussed earlier, science is an important currency in the wolf debate. It has been an especially important factor in the debate over predicting and assessing the impact of wolves on ungulate populations and the possibility of a public wolf harvest after ESA delisting. And like most debates about hunting, it is a heavy mix of both science and ethics. Michael Furtman of Minnesota's Izaak Walton League, a disenchanted member of the Minnesota wolf roundtable, contends that not only did the roundtable become a forum on hunting, but that both hunting interests and animal rights groups ignored biological fact for political gain. According to Furtman, the animal rights contingent claimed that any type of public taking would endanger wolves, despite scientific evidence revealing that even a 30 percent harvest of wolves would not threaten the population, because of their high reproductive rates. On the other end, says Furtman, the two pro-hunting groups clung to outdated myths that wolves are severely depressing the state's deer population, despite the fact that deer, wolves, and hunter harvest levels all increased throughout the 1980s and 1990s (until the severe winter of 1995–96 caused the deer herd to decline). Says Furtman, "While I fully expected the animal rights groups to ignore biology and embrace emotionalism, it was disturbing to me, as a deer hunter, to see these two hunting groups eschew scientific wildlife management, which we so often claim as the birth child of the hunting community. We forever rail at the animal rights group to stick with biology, but at least these two organizations of hunters failed that same mandate. We can't have it both ways." Furtman also sees the demands made by some hunting organizations in the state as being unfounded. Most hunters abandoned the notion of predator control for barely noticeable gains in game populations decades ago, says Furtman: "Grouse hunters don't demand the removal of goshawks to bolster bird populations. Anglers don't demand the gill netting of large pike or muskies to save smaller gamefish, or the shooting of osprey or bald eagles."

The issue of hunting and trapping wolves—a public take—after they become delisted is perhaps the most divisive and potentially explosive issue in the entire wolf debate. It engenders the type of emotions and deep core values that make conflict resolution nearly impossible to achieve. Some environmental and pro-wolf groups are so opposed to the idea that they will not sit down at any stakeholding table that dares discuss the issue. Others see it as a slippery slope, especially when managed by a state wildlife agency they do not trust. Some see it as a dangerous path that has been traveled before, one that led to bounties, poisons, and eventually wolf eradication. Others, however, believe that managing wolves as a game species, as are mountain lions and black bears, will lead to the long-term viability of this animal.

Some animal rights and welfare interests feel so strongly about a public take and wolf control in general that they oppose wolf recovery in some parts of the country.[69] As noted earlier, this opposition angers those such as wolf biologist David Mech, who believes that we could have increased wolf populations in more places if these interests could accept the necessity of wolf control. The basis of this disagreement can be partially understood by how deep core values manifest themselves in the debate. Animal rights and welfare interests often focus on the individual animal, so practices such as snaring are sometimes seen as cruel and inhumane. Many hunters and wildlife biologists, on the other hand, often focus on the population of a species, not the individual animal. Reiger summarizes, "How the surplus dies, whether by so-called 'natural' causes or by 'unnatural' ones (i.e., human predation), is unimportant, for nature reverses the sacred tenet of American culture: the species is everything and the individual nothing."[70]

Given this level of controversy, Minnesota has gone ahead with devising a state wolf management plan while postponing addressing the issue of a public take for at least five years. The Minnesota wolf roundtable delayed making this decision knowing full well how sharply this issue divides Minnesotans and that it would likely preclude consensus. Recent polls suggest that close to half (49 percent) of statewide residents agree that "hunting and trapping of wolves should be allowed to cut the current wolf population and reduce areas where wolves currently are located." Similar to urban-rural splits in other wolf areas of the country, support for a public take increases in areas outside of the Twin Cities metropolitan area. While 39 percent of metropolitan-area residents agree with such action, 62 percent of residents in the rest of the state do.[71] More focused and longitudinal surveying by Kellert also shows, however, that while most Americans accept hunting for meat, most do not accept hunting mammals for recreation/sport or trophy hunting.[72]

As I will discuss in chapter 4, Alaska provides a number of important policy lessons here. From national boycotts over wolf control to state proposals for culling wolf numbers by use of aerial machine gun, Alaskan wolf management provides a case study in adversarial state environmental politics.[73] The Alaskan situation has also been colored with subcultural symbolism and resentment from the beginning of the controversy. Whether in response to "outside meddling" (resolutions calling for the relocation of Alaskan wolves to the lower forty-eight states are quite commonplace) or to support charges of urban and federal domination, many of the state's politicos have used the "custom and culture" argument as a way to defend the state's wolf control tactics and management practices.

The controversy surrounding wolf control in Alaska is also a telling example of how important hunting and trapping organizations can prove to be in the wildlife policymaking process. Despite the complexities inherent in the predator-prey relationship, many hunters and trappers in Alaska have called for massive reductions in the wolf population because of declines in moose and caribou numbers. In response, many wolf advocates and independent scientists have made the case that the state's Department of Fish and Game is operating not on principles of sound science and wildlife management but to appease their most economically important constituency: hunters and trappers.

Independent and controversial wildlife biologist Gordon Haber, who has long studied wolves in Alaska's Denali National Park, is one of the most vocal critics of the "farming" approach to wildlife management, the belief that virtually all major wildlife populations can and should be harvested and that many of them can be harvested to their full reproductive potential. Haber is critical of the science forwarded by many wolf biologists and wildlife agencies showing that northern wolf populations can be harvested at high annual rates without significant impact. He has long disagreed with Mech and others who believe that wolf control is usually warranted and necessary.[74] While much of Haber's criticism of Alaska's wolf management is based on scientific disagreement, his defense of wolves goes well beyond biology. Because of the wolf's high intelligence, expressiveness, and sophisticated social bonds, there is an important ethical component to wolf management. Haber says,

> The same extraordinary sentience that is so integral to their basic biology also provides an ethical reason for not allowing them to be harvested and for considering remedial short-term control only in the rarest of circumstances, when there are solid, irrefutable biological and cost-benefit arguments and no other reasonable alternatives. To treat them otherwise is wrong. Such higher standing is now generally accorded to other creatures of obvious high sentience, including whales, dolphins, gorillas, and chimpanzees, and it is time to extend it fully to wolves.[75]

Haber not only recognizes the values inherent in such a position but urges other scientists to do the same:

> I recognize that my strong opposition to the way wolves are managed in Alaska and elsewhere involves more than pure biology. I receive frequent criticism for this position from my peers. Nevertheless, Aldo Leopold did not hesitate to venture into such areas of overlap between biology and ethics, to distinguish between right and wrong in advocating improved management of natural systems. Other wildlife scientists who regard his ideals as a guiding light for the profession should not hesitate to do the same.[76]

Alaska's wolf management is but one example used by many groups to show how entrenched the hunting paradigm is in many state wildlife agencies. Again, it is not just a question of what values are involved in the wolf policy debate, but of where these values are located and what power they wield in the decision-making process. Some animal rights and welfare interests argue that there is a serious dichotomy between the institutional values of state fish and game departments and that of the general public. They say that the public is increasingly opposed to the needless killing of animals, including trophy hunting, recreational trapping, and bear baiting. These interests may utilize the initiative process when they feel that their values and the values of the general public are not well-represented by state fish and game departments or state wildlife commissions. Wayne Pacelle, senior vice president of the Humane Society of the United States (HSUS), says, "To the extent that the states placate hunters and ignore the wishes of non-hunters, there will be increasing numbers of wildlife policy questions settled by politicians and voters."[77] As evidence of this disconnect, Pacelle points to the rise in statewide ballot initiatives restricting hunting or trapping practices. According to Pacelle, while from 1940 to 1990 American voters approved only one such initiative, from 1990 to 1998, voters sided with animal protection advocates in ten of thirteen ballot races addressing specific hunting and trapping practices.[78]

Pacelle, like other animal rights and welfare advocates, is unmoved by the "biology knows best" and "viable population" stand on wildlife management; that is, he believes that some practices are not necessarily right just because they do not threaten the viability of a population. He says, "These voices fundamentally misunderstand public attitudes and the role of science in policy making. Biology does not give us answers. It gives us options. Society's ethical standards ultimately shape the rules governing hunting programs. A practice that is sustainable is not necessarily ethically defensible."[79] Baiting ducks and jack-lighting deer may be done sustainably, he says, but they are both considered unethical and inappropriate.

Managing Wolves or Managing Humans

Conflict between hunters and animal rights and welfare interests over the issue of wolf management and possible public hunting or trapping of wolves will become only more evident and embittered in the future. There is perhaps no better example of core values being pitted against one another and projected onto a highly symbolic animal. Whether at the hands of the public or the professional wildlife manager, the issue of wolf control will go beyond the killing of wolves. What is at stake is no less than the meaning of nature and our role in it. Difficult issues pertaining to wildlife management in particular and to the humans-nature relationship in general will be debated by the various sides, as they have with different species in other places.

For example, Jan Dizard critically examined the sharply divergent beliefs and images of nature as they played out during a controversial "deer reduction program" at the Quabbin Reservoir in western Massachusetts.[80] The themes discussed in Dizard's important book were among the most prevalent in my stakeholder interviews. In Massachusetts, debate centered on the question of whether the managing agency should allow hunters into an area traditionally closed to hunting as a way of reducing an abundant deer population that was believed to be damaging the forest. A philosophical fault line quickly appeared and separated the various interests. On one side were those opposed to the hunt. These people emphasized that nature (and the reservoir) can achieve balance, harmony, and equilibrium if we humans step back and give it a chance. It is only once we relent that "nature will take care." In other words, the best management is no management at all. This side is of course skeptical of what it sees as an intrusive, myopic, reductionist, and often arrogant scientific management paradigm. Managers were perceived not only as addicted to meddling but "as the handmaidens of a culture whose appetites knew no bounds."[81] Dizard says,

The real fight was over symbolic turf. People had projected onto the Quabbin the qualities they longed for nature to possess. For people who believe deeply, *and with good reason,* that "nature knows best," one more turn of the interventionist screw, especially one that threatens to open a reserve to the violence of hunting, is sacrilege. Animal rights advocates may fear the loss of a few hundred deer, but the bulk of the critics feared a far larger loss—the loss of one more place where an embattled vision of harmony and unity had stood a chance and might have become a beacon. There is no possibility of compromise, and no consolation, when the stakes are that high.[82]

On the other side were those in favor of the hunt as a way to meet the reservoir's management objectives, among them a safe watershed and forest diversity. Within this worldview, we have an obligation to intervene and manage nature on a regular basis. Dizard, clearly in the pro-management camp, makes his case:

Choices such as these are morally troubling. It would be comforting to be freed of the burden of having to make them. Those who hold that nature, left to itself, balances out deer, geese, and seals with supplies of fish, trees, water, and bacteria seem to occupy a moral high ground. But it is a high ground of their own creation, fabricated out of a particular set of beliefs about nature and its processes. Theirs is a morally simplified world, like the world of the laissez-faire economist. It is a world freed of the troubling need to take responsibility for outcomes.

Unfortunately, this is not the world we actually inhabit. The world we inhabit is a world we have had a large hand in making . . . we cannot now walk away from this history. We cannot start afresh. There are no clean slates. We have, I am afraid, no alternative but to face squarely the need to manage and to accept the burden of making choices.[83]

There is every reason to believe that such philosophical division found at the Quabbin (between hunters and animal rights and welfare interests, and between those favoring proactive management and those advocating a hands-off approach) will also characterize the wolf debate of the future. Stakeholders in the wolf debate often fall into one of these two camps. Many hunters and wildlife biologists promote the necessity of wolf control and hands-on wildlife management. If a moose population declines, for example, they want wildlife managers to do something about it, and in some cases this may mean killing wolves. Many wolf advocates reject this paradigm and recommend "letting nature run wild" (the official motto of the Alaska Wildlife Alliance), at least in some places.

They are not only skeptical of the scientific basis of such wildlife man-agement but also of the special interests for whom it is being done. Oth-ers simply want parts of their state safe for wolves and other wildlife, places where human wants are not primary.

Minnesota's expanding wolf population provides but one example of this divide. According to Mech, there is no wolf population anywhere in the world as large as Minnesota's that is not subject to harvesting or at-tempted population control.[84] This population could be controlled in two ways, and both involve killing wolves and therefore conflict among humans: one way is to control the population's expansion (the zone management plan discussed earlier), the other is to reduce the popula-tion. Mech sees the latter as being unlikely. Each of Minnesota's esti-mated 350 to 400 packs produces an average of five to six pups each year. He estimates that to reduce the Minnesota population would re-quire killing 1,000 to 2,000 wolves each year, because that is the popula-tion's potential annual increase.[85] Given the remote likelihood of this killing taking place, it is now up to Minnesotans to decide how much former range wolves can take back. The state appears divided between those who favor wolf recolonization of all of Minnesota and those who want to restrict them to nonagricultural areas. Yet, in reality, wolves them-selves may determine their range. Bob Ream explains: "With poisoning of protected animals no longer legal . . . there seems to be little humans can do to control the Minnesota wolf population. Thus, it might be the wolf, rather than the public, that will decide how much of the state it will re-occupy."[86]

Whatever path we choose, the "burden of making choices" will in-creasingly fall on us as more wolf populations fully recover and wolves leave places such as Yellowstone and northern Minnesota, looking for new territory. These choices, moreover, will become starker as wolves recover in a more populated and developed country. As I discuss in the next chapter, various voices and interests have already placed wolf recov-ery in one of these larger narratives. The "wolves in wilderness" theme, for example, presupposes a certain naturalness that clearly runs con-trary to more management-intensive plans. Some hunters in Alaska, on the other hand, have a hard time swallowing the "natural balance" argu-ment made by some pro-wolf forces. They want abundant moose and caribou populations and want wolves managed to meet this goal. Similar controversies are on the horizon, including the very goals of wolf management, and the question of who exactly will be doing the managing and on whose behalf.

Conclusion

There are deeply rooted moral conflicts over wolf recovery. Wolves, as do other carnivores and wildlife, present difficult ethical and moral challenges, ones that go well beyond science, biology, and "objective" wildlife management.[87] The ethical quandaries underpinning the wolf debate will become only more evident in the future. Take, for example, future conflict over a public wolf harvest. Or what about killing coyotes in the Southeast to protect a tenuous red wolf population too susceptible to hybridization? Both cases boil down to competing morals, ethics, and values, and we must begin to seriously address each.

This chapter uses two popular frameworks to better understand and further examine the ethics, values, power, and players of wolf policy and management. The policy subsystem and advocacy coalition framework is a useful way of conceptualizing the deep and policy core values embraced by those in the wolf debate. The system is more open and fluid than that of many political iron triangles. Nevertheless, political, economic, and cultural power remains a key component. Kellert's value typology is also useful in exploring the values that many individuals and groups in the wolf debate embrace and activate. But while the public possesses an array of values toward wolves and other wildlife, not all groups have the same amount of political influence. Important conflicts also result from these different values and perceptions, a few of which have been examined here. It is this type of value-based conflict that will likely characterize the wolf debate of the future.

CHAPTER TWO

The Wolf as Symbol, Surrogate, and
Policy Problem

On May 18, 2000, Michael Simpson, a Republican representative from the second district of Idaho, introduced the Protecting America's Wolves Act (PAWS). While wolf-related bills are not uncommon in Congress, this one differed in one important way: it proposed the reintroduction of the eastern timber wolf into the Catskill Mountains of New York State. Simpson's bill would direct the secretary of the interior to reintroduce Canadian wolves into an area that is approximately one hundred miles northwest of New York City. These wolves would be protected under the ESA as fully endangered and not designated an experimental population. As fitting, of course, the designation of critical habitat in the Catskills would also be required under the bill, as well as the necessary studies on reducing road densities and providing for wolf dispersal corridors. Simpson said, "There is a tremendous support for reintroduction of wolves in the United States. Eighty percent of New Yorkers say they are in favor of wolf reintroduction, according to Defenders of Wildlife. Preservation of a species should not be just a western issue. If we are serious about conservation, reintroduction needs to be a nationwide effort."[1]

Simpson's bill is one example of the political and cultural dimensions of the wolf policy debate. Having had wolves reintroduced into his district a few years earlier, Simpson, as do several other Western representatives, place wolves in a more inclusive story. In some situations wolves provide the latest opportunity to stoke old fires and controversies, but in others they symbolize something far greater and more portentous.

Drawing on the experiences of various wolf programs throughout the country, in this chapter I explore the debate's sociopolitical dimensions. The following "symbol and surrogate" issues are examined: (1) land use and the politics of ecosystem management, (2) the government's role in wolf recovery, (3) the role of conservation biology, (4) wilderness preservation and large-scale land conservation strategies, (5) the future of the ESA, (6) implementing the ESA and debate over environmental compromise and capitulation, (7) the future of rural places, and (8) tribal participation and management authority. The chapter ends with a brief discussion of how these sociopolitical dimensions affect political decision makers, conflict resolution, and those responsible for policy implementation. I also answer the question of why the debate over wolf recovery has been so controversial and acrimonious. These symbol and surrogate issues often compound the value-based conflicts discussed in the previous chapter.

As is the case with a number of other natural resource issues and debates, wolf politics and policy are often about much more than just wolves. The struggle over wolf recovery and carnivore conservation is often a surrogate for broader cultural conflicts. According to Steven Primm and Tim Clark, carnivore conservation is much more than a biological problem:

> Conservation of large carnivores is also linked inextricably to several broader issues. The U.S. Endangered Species Act (ESA), ecosystem management, use of western public lands, and other contentious issues all manifest themselves in the issue of carnivore conservation. Wrangling over carnivore conservation is also often a "surrogate" for broader cultural conflicts: preservation versus use of resources, recreation-based economies versus extraction-dependent economies, urban versus rural values, and states' rights versus federalism.[2]

In *The Wisdom of the Spotted Owl: Policy Lessons for a New Century,* Steven Yaffee documents how the spotted owl controversy in the Pacific Northwest transcended the overly simplistic "jobs versus owls" dichotomy to include a number of more complex sociopolitical and bureaucratic dimensions. According to Yaffee, "Just as children and owls strongly reflect the environment in which they live, policy and management decisions are shaped by their sociopolitical context. To understand why things are the way they are, professionals and organizations need to understand this context. To ensure that good technical ideas are implemented effectively, they need to be able to deal with, and influence, this sociopolitical environment."[3] Furthermore, says Yaffee, in the case of the northern spotted owl, as in other endangered species issues, what often appear to be simple conflicts are instead multidimensional ones with serious consequences for public policy and natural resource management. Yaffee notes that the sociopolitical context of endangered species issues is vitally important, "making them much more important and symbolic, and more difficult to resolve, than they would be otherwise."[4] These issues have serious implications for wildlife agency organizational and professional behavior, and Yaffee urges organizations and professionals to consider more seriously the sociopolitical dimensions of endangered species management.

In Washington State, Yaffee's research on the northern spotted owl is as apropos now as it was in 1994. According to one wolf advocate in the state, "residual resentment" and hostility on the Olympic Peninsula because of the spotted owl controversy have tainted the debate over possibly reintroducing wolves in Olympic National Park. Town hall meetings were held to gather input from peninsula residents, and these meetings revealed that the debate over wolves cannot be easily separated from other issues such as owls, perceptions of federal intrusiveness, and the still lingering resentment among some residents about the creation of the park in the first place. This "residual resentment" was confirmed by a public attitudes study conducted by the Olympic Natural Resources Center, a branch of the University of Washington. According to Director John Calhoun, the memory of the northern spotted owl controversy is fresh in residents' minds, and they do not want to encourage any activity by the federal government that might further restrict logging or other uses of the land: "They no longer trust the park right next to them, they don't trust the Forest Service, they don't trust Fish and Wildlife, they don't trust anybody having to do with the federal government."[5]

As in the case of the northern spotted owl, there is a range of important policy issues that are sometimes only tangentially related to wolf management and restoration. David Mech, a prominent wolf research biologist who has studied wolves since 1958, reminds us that "wolf management has developed a sociopolitical dimension that extends beyond the primary biological concerns."[6] In many cases, wolves serve as a surrogate for wider conflict, and in others, they serve as an important symbol. As Peter Steinhart notes in closing his popular and comprehensive assessment of the historical human-wolf relationship, "We cannot help viewing wolves in symbolic terms, but symbols change. The wolf was once widely seen as a symbol of the depravity of wildness; it is now to many a symbol of the nobility of nature. Largely by the use of symbols, we nearly eradicated the wolf. Largely by manipulating symbols, we may yet save it."[7] Symbols also play an important role in the politics model of wolf recovery. Symbolic representations are, says Deborah Stone, "the essence of problem definition in politics."[8] They are collectively created, help shape our perceptions, suspend skepticism, and are important means of political influence and control.[9]

The Wolf Policy "Problem": The Politics of Problem Definition

Problem definition is an important part of policy studies. How an issue or conflict becomes "framed" and socially constructed is critical because it alters the way we think, talk, and approach the issue.[10] Problem definition determines what issues get on the governmental agenda, and how they will be acted on—if acted on at all. The late political scientist E. E. Schattschneider put it well: "Political conflict is not like an intercollegiate debate in which the opponents agree in advance on a definition of issues. As a matter of fact, the definition of the alternatives is the supreme instrument of power."[11] The process is a contested one, with competing individuals, interests, and organizations trying to sell their preferred definition of the problem. The defining process occurs in a number of ways, but each has major implications for an issue's political standing, perceptions of its legitimacy, and the types of policy solutions that are advanced. As David Rochefort and Roger Cobb say, "By dramatizing or downplaying the problem and by declaring what is at stake, these descriptions help to push an issue onto the front burners of policymaking or result in officials' stubborn inaction and neglect."[12]

Competing interests fully understand that how an issue becomes framed and a problem defined favors some players and solutions over others. Janet Weiss says that problem definition relies on "a package of concepts, symbols, and theories" that energize and empower some interests while silencing others.[13] In Stone's politics model, "problem definition in the polis is always strategic, designed to call in reinforcements for one's own side in a conflict.... strategic problem definition usually means portraying a problem so that one's favored course of action appears to be in the broad public interest" (*Policy Paradox,* 154). These problems "are created in the minds of citizens by other citizens, leaders, organizations, and government agencies, as an essential part of political maneuvering" (155). The language and symbols used in problem definition legitimate and mobilize some values while discounting others. Stone refers to Schattschneider in stating that "strategic definition also means manipulating the scope of conflict by making some people seem to be affected by it and others not. Certain symbols such as individualism, freedom, privacy, private enterprise, localism, and states' rights, are calculated to restrict the scope of conflict, while others, such as equality, justice, and civil rights, are calculated to expand it" (155).

Wolf politics in Alaska shows how problem definition is used by policy participants. Some of those groups and individuals favoring wolf control have attempted to wash those groups opposing some control measures as being "animal rights extremists." They have attempted to frame the debate as being one of scientific wildlife management versus the out-of-touch emotional animal rights fringe. Some wolf advocates, on the other hand, respond by framing the debate as scientific wildlife management versus a powerful and privileged sport and trophy hunting minority.

Problem definition is an important problem-solving tool as well. One comprehensive assessment of its use with carnivore conservation concludes that "problem definition should be viewed as the key analytic and technical tool for developing effective, practical solutions to carnivore conservation."[14] The importance of problem definition in endangered species management is illustrated by the black-footed ferret recovery program in Wyoming. The black-footed ferret, widely considered the most endangered mammal in the United States, was once thought by many to be extinct. In 1981, however, a small population was discovered in northwestern Wyoming. A captive breeding program was soon initiated, and some ferrets were reintroduced back into the wild in 1991. As allowed under Section 6 of the ESA, the federal government gave Wyoming, specifically the Wyoming Game and Fish Department (WGF), primary responsibility for ferret restoration.

This management program has been extensively studied by Tim Clark, who is highly critical of the way in which WGF defined the ferret problem. According to Clark's analysis, WGF defined the problem in ways that greatly influenced the program's operation. For example, it was defined as a states' rights issue. This definition, says Clark, "figured prominently in the agency's relationships with all other participants and had paramount consequences for how all aspects of the ferret program were structured and carried out."[15] In short, "WGF would run the show, the federal government would pay for it, and all other participants would be subordinate to this arrangement" (142). Closely associated with this states' rights definition, according to Clark, was the agency's bureaucratic management orthodoxy. Because the problem was defined this way, "only a very limited range of structural and operational options was thus deemed plausible, namely, those that maintained or enhanced agency power and constituted the program along bureaucratic lines" (143). Scientific conservatism was another dominant problem definition used by the agency. As such, the program followed the time-honored practice of calling for yet more study and research instead of taking necessary action. Clark says that like most recovery efforts since the ESA, "the ferret program was thus largely cast as a scientific problem. Even though ferret protection had widespread social, economic, and political implications, the language of ferret recovery remained fundamentally scientific and technical" (147). Clark also places this problem definition and "package of ideas" in its larger subcultural setting: "the strength of certain political symbols in Wyoming (and the region)—states' rights, individual and property rights, and scorn for the federal government, environmentalists, and easterners—provided a highly favorable medium for WGF's definition" (157).

Many of Clark's "ferret problem" definitional themes are found in some wolf cases as well. What differs perhaps is the extraordinary symbolic quality of the wolf debate and the sheer number of players involved. And, of course, ferrets do not eat cows, sheep, or elk. Nonetheless, various interests have attempted to define the "wolf problem" in a way that advances their vision of the public interest and their hand in the game. Wolves and wilderness, wolves as a science and management problem, wolves and ecological restoration, wolves as a federal Trojan horse, and wolves and the urban exploitation of rural communities are but a few of the ways in which participants have tried to define the problem. If the public and political decision makers accept that the wolf problem stems from too many cows and not enough wilderness, then both wolves and wilderness go forward. If, on the other hand, the issue is one of federal intrusiveness, then wolves, the ESA, and the FWS are on trial.

Symbol and Surrogate Issues

The following discussion elaborates on these ideas. While not all of these symbol and surrogate issues have been used in problem definition, many of them have, with serious implications for how we approach "the wolf problem."

Land Use and the Politics of Ecosystem Management

Wolves are an important political symbol not only because of what they may do, but because of what some believe they may preclude others from doing. Questions and controversies pertaining to land use dominate the wolf policy debate. Many interests believe that wolf recovery, especially reintroduction in the American West, is a ruse and political ploy for more regulatory federal lands management, thus posing a serious threat to rural communities, extractive industries, and the sanctity of private property and individual freedom. Some fear that traditional uses of public land and private property will be jeopardized by more wolves in more places.

These fears are particularly acute in places with a preponderance of federal land. Nearly 50 percent of Wyoming, 62 percent of Idaho, and 28 percent of Montana (concentrated in the western part of the state) is owned by the federal government. In comparison, little land in the Midwest, South, and East is federally owned (for example, 1.2 percent in Iowa, 3.3 percent in Alabama, and 0.4 percent in Connecticut). Federally designated wilderness is also concentrated in the West, with more than 95 percent of designated wilderness located in the twelve states (excluding Hawaii) fully west of the one-hundredth meridian (99,332,644 out of 103,754,595 acres). Given this ubiquitous federal presence, it is important to distinguish between dimensions of federalism and environmentalism, that is, federal support versus environmental support. Many interests in the rural West are more apprehensive about federal usurpation and its accompanying regulations than they are about wolves and other endangered species.

Nowhere are the divergent meanings and varying social constructions of wolves more apparent than in the greater Yellowstone ecosystem. This important ecosystem has provided the arena in which environmentalists and wise-users debate not only wolf reintroduction but also the future of land use and land-use planning on the public domain, shifts in economic power, the meaning and balance of nature, and the human role in it.[16] Sociologist Matthew Wilson remarks about wolf re-introduction in Yellowstone National Park that "this is not really a story about wolves, but a story about people and their struggle to define the future of land use in the American West.... it is within this highly charged political context that the wolf in Yellowstone must be understood as a symbol, 'a biopolitical pawn' in a much larger conflict currently being waged between the activists of two social movements— environmentalism and wise use."[17] Wilson's assessment is still relevant. One Western Stockgrowers Association official, for example, informed me of three basic "wolf issues" that most concern him: the need for more local control, more respect for private property rights, and the need for and proper use of sound science. This spokesperson simply used wolves as a springboard to launch a more inclusive assault on the environmental agenda. He is critical, for instance, of environmentalists using the "subsidized rancher" argument when they pay nothing for their recreational use of public lands. Declaring that "the best thing for land is the footsteps of its owner," he believes that private property and the threats it faces are a central part of the debate over wolves in the Northern Rockies.

The federal government is the dominant player in the greater Yellowstone ecosystem, owning and managing, on average, over half of the county land base. Because many communities in the area are dependent on extractive economies, federal natural resource management paradigms are not abstract decision-making models but have concrete and economically important implications. Families, homes, schools, and other aspects of these communities are dependent on how these principles are implemented.[18]

The shift from a multiple-use, resource-based paradigm (resourcism) to a more holistic and participatory ecosystem management paradigm is often central in the debate over wolf recovery. Ecosystem management (in theory and sometimes in practice) is a dramatic break from the traditional resource management paradigm ushered in with Gifford Pinchot.[19] Hanna Cortner and Margaret Moote summarize the differences: "Traditional resource management is pragmatic, seeing in nature a collection of resources that can be manipulated and harvested, with humans in control. Ecosystem management, on the other hand, views nature with some reverence and respect for the awesome complexity with which its components are interwoven. Protection of ecosystem attributes and functions, particularly biodiversity, is critical."[20] Ecosystem management accentuates the intrinsic values and natural conditions of the environment, seeks ecological sustainability as a management priority, and is considered more flexible, adaptive, inclusive, participatory, and decentralized than traditional resource management. Furthermore, many of the paradoxes and challenges of wolf policy and management are really those presented by ecosystem management in general (e.g., how do we balance collaborative decision making, political responsiveness, and public accountability?).

Some observers have noted the symbolic importance of wolf reintroduction in the Northern Rockies and see it in its larger context of a changing West. As Robert Keiter and Patrick Holscher observe, "The extractive industries, which have long dominated the federal natural resource management policy agenda, are grudgingly giving ground to a new order sensitive to environmental values and ecological management principles. From this perspective, restoration of the wolf can be viewed as the end of an era of agricultural dominance on the public domain and the ascendancy of ecosystem-oriented resource management policies."[21] Carnivores like the wolf and grizzly bear have also forced us to reconsider the needs and habitat requirements of large species. According to Tim Clark and others examining the Yellowstone experience, "Reintroduced wolves and their offspring in the Yellowstone ecosystem are showing us once more that our national park and other geopolitical boundaries are meaningless in their search for habitat, and these boundaries are insufficient if we want these magnificent carnivores to have populations that are viable for the long term." Carnivores like the wolf, they say, "have forced us to move from ecosystem theory to ecosystem management and conservation."[22]

Participants in the wolf debate see this potential paradigm shift differently. Environmentalists frame their arguments for wolves in the context of natural, healthy, and well-functioning ecosystems. Wolves and other predators are but one part, although an important one, of these larger natural processes. The issue is not just about wolves, but about such things as unchecked deer and elk populations, native flora under pressure from these populations, and other complex biological relationships and ecological cycles we do not yet fully understand. They thus urge public land agencies to move away from a strict utilitarian ("multiple abuse") model toward one with more well-balanced management principles.

One example of this varying interpretation is provided by the debate over managing for the wildlife "resource" versus managing for ecosystem health and biodiversity. For instance, some hunters believe that the key to winning support for wolves among hunters is the ability to maintain an adequate prey base. If deer, elk, and moose numbers get too low, support for wolves and other predators will also drop, they say. Many in the hunting community advocate that wolves and other predators be managed in the context of maximizing a single resource: ungulate populations. In other words, wolves must be managed in such a way that they do not pose a serious threat to game populations. Of course, many scientists, environmentalists, and wolf advocates see wolves in an entirely different light. Instead of managing wolves and other wildlife to "maximize the resource," they emphasize ecosystem interconnectivity and place wolves in a larger ecological context.

Many living within the greater Yellowstone ecosystem see this paradigm shift as a real threat. One survey shows that nearly two-thirds of rural community residents in the area fear that ecosystem management will result in greater government control, and some 70 percent believe that it represents an attempt by government to control development of lower elevation lands.[23] Wolves thus remain inextricably tied to the debate over ecosystem management. It is a step in the right direction, say environmentalists, indicative of what needs to be done in other ecosystems with others species, from Canadian lynx to grizzly bears. For others, however, it is symbolic of a radical biocentric environmentalism becoming formally institutionalized in land management and wildlife agencies, and done so at the peril of traditional customs, cultures, and rural lifeways. This interpretation is embraced by people like Idaho Senator Larry Craig, who sits on the powerful Senate Appropriations Committee and the Committee on Energy and Natural Resources, among others. "Efforts to bring back the nearly obsolete gray wolf population in the region are wreaking havoc on our Western way of life," says Craig.[24] In discussing bears, wolves, and now lynx, Craig also sees a hidden environmental agenda. "It appears the lynx is being used as a tool to achieve a broader goal of locking up land. One of the components of the protection plan is to prevent new roads from being built, making it a perfect companion to the current roadless moratorium."[25] And, finally, Craig reminds us that humans are part of the ecosystem and must be included in the decision-making process. After all, says Craig, "'ecosystem management' is about more than the reintroduction of species, it is about balancing and finding a way for all species, including humans, to co-exist."[26]

The Government's Role in Wolf Recovery

One of the most important questions in the debate about wolf recovery throughout the country is what should be the proper role of government in restoring and protecting wolf populations. Whether wolves should be translocated from one place to another, as was done in Yellowstone and central Idaho, for example, or whether wolves should (or can) be allowed to return on their own was an important theme in almost all of my interviews and selected cases. Some interests believe that the key to successful wolf recovery is public support and acceptance, and that the best way of winning this support is to adopt a more hands-off and natural approach to wolf restoration. Wolf opposition, they say, is often directed more toward the federal government and perceptions of federal micromanagement and excessive animal manipulation than toward the wolf itself. How can we seriously reintroduce wolves as a symbol of the wild, they ask, when the FWS is so eager to collar, monitor, and record their every move?

Many wildlife managers believe that natural wolf recovery and recolonization are a key factor in lowering levels of wolf opposition. In Wisconsin, for example, a state with perhaps the most quiet wolf recovery program in the country (although certainly not free of controversy), natural recolonization from wolves in Minnesota is often pointed to as the major reason for such low levels of public opposition. The recovery, some say, is seen as a rather natural process, and provides proud proof that the state's northern stretches are still wild enough for wolves.

Montana is another interesting example. Personnel within Montana's Department of Fish, Wildlife and Parks (FWP) are quick to point out that the state of Montana's consistent opposition to wolf reintroduction was not toward wolves but to the reintroduction effort by the federal government. One manager in the department says,

> I think the major obstacle/threat to wolf recovery are public perceptions and values pertaining to wolves. The best case scenario would be a societal view of the wolf as desirable, appropriate, or at the very least, interesting, [a] "neighbor" that people want to coexist with. The worst case scenario is public perception of wolves as competitors (as a predator of ungulates or as a force that will close wild lands to resource development) and/or threats (potential attacker/killer of humans—especially children, livestock and household pets)... natural recolonization of wolves is more conducive to the former scenario. The fact that wolves were reintroduced to YNP [Yellowstone National Park] and central Idaho by the USFWS was viewed as big government "foisting" wolves upon the populace, and was conducive to the latter scenario.

One hunting advocate in northwest Montana uses the case of mountain lion recovery in his part of the state as an example of how important this distinction is between natural recovery and reintroduction by the federal government. Mountain lions have made a fantastic recovery, he says, with little public opposition (until a severe winter stressed the area's ungulate population), despite the fact that mountain lions cause more trouble and depredation problems than does the area's wolf population. There was no widespread opposition to mountain lion recovery, he says, because they were perceived as being natural and were managed as a game species.

Perhaps the most illuminating illustration of this distinction between natural recovery and reintroduction is provided by Michigan's wolf history. In 1974, four wolves were captured in Minnesota and translocated to Michigan's Upper Peninsula.[27] All four translocated wolves were killed by humans: one was hit by a vehicle, and the other three were shot and killed. Some residents strongly opposed the experiment, largely out of concern for deer populations, which were precariously low at the time. Some joined the Baraga County Wolf Hunters Association, an organization formed with the express purpose of killing reintroduced wolves, with the slogan "Preserve Our Deer, Shoot a Wolf." Looking back on this "bittersweet" experiment in 1975, then FWS Director Lynn Greenwalt gave a glimpse into the possible fate of future reintroduction efforts: "The experiment was a complete success in providing the information sought: What might happen when a pack of wolves is transplanted to a new area where the native population has been all but exterminated by Man? It was the *answer* to this question that was disappointing."[28]

The context of the 1974 translocation is important, says one veteran wildlife manager in the state. There were record low numbers of white-tailed deer at this time, due to weather and antlerless deer hunting, and many deer hunters in the state blamed Michigan's Department of Natural Resources (MDNR) for the population decline. Nonetheless, this manager believes that differing public perceptions of natural recovery versus government reintroduction are not to be dismissed and are a major factor in explaining different levels of support from 1974 to the present. From analyzing the public comments made about the proposed Michigan wolf recovery and management plan in the early 1990s, he concludes that the major theme was one of people wanting natural recovery, not reintroduction. This was due, he says, to the costs associated with translocation and perceptions of the more "natural" process of recolonization.

While many people believe that natural recovery bodes best for successful and long-term wolf recovery, or at least that this belief explains lower levels of public opposition in some parts of the country, many observers I spoke with also believe that the choice between the two methods of recovery is irrelevant with regards to future strategy. One prominent wolf advocate in Colorado simply concludes that we do not have time to wait for natural recolonization in the Southern Rockies and questions whether a natural recovery could even take place given the natural barriers to wolves moving from the Northern to the Southern Rockies. He believes that there is an urgency in restoring wolves to the Southern Rockies, partly as a way to check the nation's largest elk population, and partly because the Colorado public favors federal reintroduction. In other words, why wait for something that may never happen. While these differences in public support between natural recovery and reintroduction cannot be easily translated into political strategy, they do clearly illustrate that public opposition to wolf reintroduction is often not as simple as it first appears.

Popular conceptions of "natural" are also perplexing to many of those involved in wolf restoration. While the romantic idea of wolves returning naturally and on their own terms would certainly alter perceptions and alleviate some concerns, many wolf advocates also remind us that wildlife recovery in general usually requires that human choices be made—to act or not to act in certain ways. New England's remarkable wildlife recovery is due in part, they say, to choices that have been made to help it along at critical junctures. From beaver in the Adirondacks to deer, wild turkey, and moose recovery, humans have taken an active role by reintroducing some species, and, for others, protecting their habitat and regulating hunting seasons.

Some wolf advocates and conservationists in New England are suspicious of calls for natural wolf recovery. After all, a number of "unnatural" barriers—superhighways, sprawl and development, icebreakers on the St. Lawrence Seaway—will likely preclude natural wolf recovery from southeastern Canada. Still, others think that even natural wolf migration is not a passive process. If wolves are to migrate from Canada into New England, for example, human action in the form of protecting habitat and establishing connectivity between core wolf habitats will also be necessary.

Wolves as a Biological Problem

Wolf recovery and management have often been framed as a biological issue. For many in the debate, the field of conservation biology offers a relatively holistic framework in which to view the complex interrelationship among humans, habitat, and biodiversity. Edward Grumbine, who has thoroughly examined the ecological and political threats to the grizzly bear in the greater North Cascades ecosystem, describes the field this way: "Conservation biology is an applied science. It differs from other natural-resource fields such as wildlife management, fisheries, and forestry by accenting ecology over economics. Most traditional resource management is reductionist, mainly concerned with species of direct utilitarian interest: How can humans have bucks to bag, trees to harvest, salmon to catch?"[29] The conservation biologist, as one leading textbook in the field points out, "recognizes that diverse and functioning ecosystems are critical not only to maintenance of the few species we harvest, but also to perpetuation of the nearly limitless variety of life forms of which we know little or nothing [and] that intact and functioning ecosystems are also important as life-support systems for the planet, and are critical to our own continued survival and well-being as a species." Given the scope of conservation biology, the authors of this text state that the field "fully recognizes and embraces the contributions that need to be made by non-biologists to conservation of biodiversity. In particular, the social sciences, economics, and political science may ultimately have more influence on real advances or losses in conservation than the biological sciences."[30]

Various pillars of conservation biology appear in the debate over wolf recovery and other large carnivore conservation efforts.[31] These include the following:

1. Large areas of interconnected wildlands are often needed for both large predators like wolves as well as other biodiversity.

2. Continued human population growth threatens the protection of interconnected wildlands and thus biological diversity. Many threats to wolves and other carnivores—the increasing number of roads and highways, for instance—are not a root problem but are instead symptomatic of human population growth.

3. Viable populations of a species often depend on the size of an area. The study of viable populations and island biogeography demonstrates that, put simply, large islands usually possess a greater diversity of habitats and ecosystems than do smaller islands, which usually have less diversity, fewer species, and smaller populations.[32] These findings are significant not only for wolves on Isle Royale—a true island population—but for species that inhabit a park, wilderness, or preserve, yet are cut off and isolated from other populations, as if on an island in the sea.

4. Habitat loss and fragmentation are a major threat to large carnivores and biodiversity in general. Conservation biologists have learned that fragmented landscapes pose serious threats to many species. A habitat patch must be as large as that required by the species that live within it; thus, many species are currently isolated (on islands) and do not have enough habitat to become viable. This situation becomes even more troublesome given the fact that many of our reserves and designated wilderness areas are comprised of "rocks and ice" (mountains, not rich valley bottoms, for example) and are not heterogeneous enough to support many species' needs.

5. The importance of greater ecosystems and biological corridors. Studying the habitat needs of the grizzly bear, conservation biologists point to the amount of land these animals need to survive. In studying grizzlies in Yellowstone, for example, some biologists quickly saw that the park's boundaries were simply not large enough for the needs of this animal. Instead, these bears require a much larger area, or greater ecosystem. Because setting aside such greater ecosystems is not currently politically feasible in many situations, biological

corridors, connecting strips or swaths of habitat, have been proposed by conservation biologists as a way for animals to move between isolated patches of landscape. These corridors, moreover, allow for greater genetic exchange and thus decrease the threats to small isolated populations.

Conservation biology's focus on habitat, core reserve areas, and corridors will be critical to wolves and how they are managed in the future. If we fail to address habitat, say many in the debate, wolves will increasingly be managed in unnatural zoolike settings. Thus, interrelated with questions pertaining to "natural" recovery are those regarding what steps society is willing to take to ensure the survival of wildlife in wild landscapes. Conservation biology forces us to ask some difficult political and cultural questions about what we are willing to do to safeguard natural processes. If we are not willing to reconsider some collective practices, then the model of red wolf recovery in North Carolina will likely become the norm: captive-bred wolves intensely managed in a harsh isolated landscape. Jan DeBlieu says that when working with predators, managers face many political constraints: "Their cautious attitude was typical of endangered species recovery programs, which are almost always designed to be convenient for people. The predominant goal of such programs is not to restore animal populations to their original conditions but to reshape them so they can exist in a thickly populated, heavily developed, economically expanding nation." The repercussions of this policy are vast, says DeBlieu: "The animals will be given the territory they need to prosper only if they do not come into direct conflict with development or special interests."[33]

Within these broad principles of conservation biology are a number of other issues specifically related to wolves and other large carnivores. Reed Noss and others remind us that Aldo Leopold considered carnivores a critical test of how committed a society is to the principles of conservation. "Saving a small woodlot for a rare lily is one thing," they say, "protecting millions of hectares for grizzly bears (Ursus arctos) is quite another."[34] Although much depends on the species and the spatial and temporal scale that is employed, carnivores do play important ecological roles in an ecosystem. They can, for instance, affect prey numbers and play the role of an umbrella species (a species whose habitat requirements encompass the habitats of many other species). In other words, conservation areas that are able to support viable populations of large carnivores are likely to be able to support a variety of other species as well. Large carnivores are also susceptible to threats such as road building and habitat loss due to development. Roads, for example, most often built for logging operations, pose a formidable threat by providing easier access for hunters and poachers, and contributing to a general loss of isolation. One study of grizzly bears, for instance, found hunting and poaching that resulted from road access caused the most deaths in the bears they were studying.[35] Another example is the number of wolves that have been illegally killed along roads in Arizona's Apache National Forest. Nevertheless, our efforts to protect large carnivores from roads and highways, says Paul Paquet of the University of Calgary, is akin to putting a filter on the end of a cigarette—not really addressing the real problem.[36]

Relying on the assumptions and tools of conservation biology will likely affect future debates regarding additional wolf reintroductions. In Adirondack Park in New York State, for example, there are important questions pertaining to the biological and ecological feasibility of a persistent wolf population given habitat fragmentation and the general perils of living in a human-dominated landscape. As discussed in greater detail in chapter 4, the Adirondack Park Citizens Advisory Committee, organized by Defenders of Wildlife, was asked to examine the issue of gray wolf recovery in Adirondack Park. An important part of this examination was commissioning the Conservation Biology Institute of Corvallis, Oregon, to study the biological feasibility of wolf reintroduction. The study draws a number of important conclusions about wolves in the Adirondack ecosystem. First, the institute believes that the park has a number of characteristics that are good for wolves, such as enough prey and adequate secure core areas and other high-quality habitats to maintain a small population of wolves. On the other hand, the institute also found that the park is highly fragmented with high road densities, and that linkages between the park and other good wolf areas in New England are tenuous and unreliable. Given these and other important factors (many of which have to do with questions about the genetics of wolves in the Northeast), the institute concluded:

we do not believe gray wolves can be permanently reestablished in the AP [Adirondack Park]. Though our analyses suggest that the AP comprises sufficient habitat to support a small population of gray wolves, regional conditions are not conducive to sustaining wolves over the long term (e.g., 100 years) . . . a small population might exist for, say 50 years. However, we should not confuse existence with persistence. The latter implies perpetuity, which we believe is the unstated objective of most reintroductions.[37]

Given this regional isolation, the institute believes that reintroduced gray wolves would face the typical problems associated with island species and small populations.[38]

Any serious discussion of wolf reintroduction in the Adirondacks also includes a concomitant discussion of conservation biology—what it is and what role it should play in political decision making and wildlife management. While environmentalists have been receptive to a science regularly verifying the importance of their agenda, when that science cuts the other way, some of the assumptions and tools of that science suddenly come up for debate. Some environmentalists in the Northeast were not surprised by the institute's recommendations against reintroduction because they fully understand the basic pillars of conservation biology, but others are caught in an important strategic dilemma. On the one hand, they have often used conservation biology as a scientific foundation on which to bring back wolves and other carnivores while also defending their habitat needs. On the other hand, if they want to bring wolves back to the park, they are now forced to question the assumptions and tools of this type of biological assessment. Others ask if wolves can and should be reintroduced in the "non-wilderness" Adirondacks, then why tie the fate of wolves to wilderness in other parts of the country? For wolf advocates, this dilemma also illustrates the perils of defending wolves on purely biological and scientific grounds. If wolves are defended first on the basis of public values, however, then a scientific report like this loses some of its weight in the larger political debate.

Principles of conservation biology are also interwoven into the debate over land-use politics. Several groups and individuals fear that recovered wolves will mean increased land-use restrictions. Many environmentalists have tried to alleviate some of these concerns by emphasizing the flexibility afforded to managers under the ESA's experimental rules. At the same time, however, many of these same environmentalists are embracing the important work of conservation biology and its holistic approach to biodiversity. While this position is certainly not hypocritical, nor unexpected, it does illustrate why some of those groups opposing wolf recovery contend that they receive mixed messages from the environmental community. From one side they are told that they have nothing to fear, but from another, they see a slippery slope based on an increasingly popular applied science.

This discussion of wolves and conservation biology also helps us better understand the importance of problem definition. Whatever the field may offer wolves and other wildlife, it is important that the "wolf problem" is not defined simply as a "biological problem." While habitat fragmentation is critically important, framing the problem and the solution in terms of habitat fragmentation alone is inadequate. Tim Clark, Peyton Curlee, and Richard Reading of the Northern Rockies Conservation Cooperative emphasize this point: "Too many public programs, including conservation efforts, accomplish little because they fail to define problems adequately.... Problem definitions that fail to appreciate the history, science, trends, and socioeconomic, organizational, and political contexts will lead to faltering programs because they are not sufficient to clarify goals, generate practical alternatives, and justify the goals and the selected alternative to the public and to decision and policy makers."[39]

Wilderness Preservation and Large-Scale Land Conservation Strategies

Whether in Italy or central Wisconsin, the "plasticity" of wolves means they can survive outside of classically conceptualized wilderness areas.[40] Due to a range of factors, however, including the willingness of humans to live with the animal, the wolf's future has been inextricably tied to the fate of American wilderness. Long-term and large-scale carnivore conservation is thought by many to require the existence and enlargement of either officially classified wilderness areas or at least sparsely populated environments in which human-predator conflict can be minimized.

The wolf has long symbolized wilderness. In 1969, legendary conservationist and wolf researcher Sigurd Olson summarized the importance of the wolf in Minnesota's northland: "The howl of a wolf in the north means wilderness. It is the background music of a great symphony of sound coming from a multiplicity of living things upon which it depends. The wolf is a creature of beauty, significance, and power, occupying the very peak of an ecological structure built of infinite relationships."[41] Well before this, however, some thoughtful observers noticed the threats facing these last "webs of wilderness." Writing about her experience with wolves and caribou in Alaska's Brooks Range in the early 1950s, Lois Crisler saw the connection in no uncertain terms: "Wilderness without its animals is dead—dead scenery. Animals without wilderness are a closed book."[42]

The wolf still figures prominently in the fight over wilderness preservation and the enlargement of either federally classified wilderness or additional roadless areas. The wolf problem has thus often been defined as a wilderness problem. While sometimes the importance of wilderness is concealed in the debate, its presence in the advocacy community is unmistakable. For many wolf advocates, the wolf symbolizes the virtues and necessity of wilderness—how close we have come to losing it and the possibility of safeguarding its future.[43] Says writer and wilderness advocate Rick Bass, "My affinity, my allegiance, is with complete landscapes, with wild places. I'd rather try to protect an undesignated wilderness area—a landscape's wild qualities, which comprises millions of variables—than spend energy on lobbying for the return of some single species—a grizzly, a caribou, a wolf."[44]

The issue of wilderness is also important in the debate over how protection of the wolf and biodiversity should be framed and "sold" to the public. Issue framing is a critical part of the policy process because it helps determine what gets on the decision-making agenda and what alternatives are then considered. Consider, for example, how the northern spotted owl controversy was framed by the timber industry: jobs versus owls—not an issue of increasing automation, exports, and conspicuous consumption. For people such as passionate wolf and wilderness defender Dave Foreman, the answer is simple: wilderness sells, and if we protect and enlarge wilderness areas, we will also be protecting wolves and biodiversity.

Environmental organizations often use species recovery to advance other goals on their agenda. Wolves and grizzly bears, for example, are often seen as wilderness species and are therefore used to argue for protection or designation of more wilderness areas. James MacCracken and Jay O'Laughlin, for instance, believe that "The Wilderness Society has used grizzly bear recovery policy to further its objective of protecting undeveloped areas in the Northern Rocky Mountains because of the difficulties involved in passing legislation to create additional wilderness areas for the region."[45] In short, the wolf and the grizzly are two important symbols that have been used effectively in political strategizing.

The political relationship between wilderness and wolves has also been recently documented in the case of Mexican wolf reintroduction in the American Southwest. The Center for Biological Diversity (formerly the Southwest Center for Biological Diversity; labeled as "the most important radical environmental group in the country and a major force in the life of Arizona and New Mexico") believes that officially classified wilderness is absolutely essential for successful wolf recovery in the Southwest.[46] The Center contends that wolves were released in Arizona's nonwilderness Blue Range Wolf Recovery Area (BRWRA) instead of the official Gila Wilderness of New Mexico because of New Mexico's powerful livestock industry. The Center advocated that the Blue Range be designated as formal wilderness and that a second primary recovery zone be established farther east in the Gila–Aldo Leopold wilderness complex. The Center, along with dozens of other environmental organizations, believes that the Gila-Leopold offers a safer haven for wolves than does the Blue Range. The group also believes that the BRWRA and the Gila-Leopold wilderness complex should be connected by biological corridors allowing for easier wolf travel, that the U.S. Forest Service should begin closing unnecessary roads within the entire recovery area, and that all grazing permits within the primary recovery areas and travel corridors should be phased out.[47]

The political wolf-wilderness relationship is also evident in the Northeast and will likely become even more so in the future. RESTORE: The North Woods, an important and vision-based environmental organization in New England, made a conscious and deliberate attempt to tie the fate of wolves to that of wilderness as a way to get the public thinking of the two as synergistic, inseparable, and complementary. Instead of a perceived myopic concentration on a single species, they work in a more inclusive fashion to bring back biodiversity and the evolutionary process to New England. A psychological shift is needed, they say, to get the public thinking of the North Woods as an ecosystem—wilderness and wolves—and not just as a woodlot and "working forest." While some organizations work on the premise that you should ask for what you can get, not what you want, RESTORE works on the latter. They thus wage concurrent battles to bring back the wolf to the Northeast while also proposing the visionary but controversial Maine Woods National Park. According to RESTORE, their strategy is not to choose between fighting for wolves or fighting for wilderness, but instead to restore wolves

to these landscapes and then come up with plans to protect and connect them.

RESTORE's Kristen DeBoer leaves no doubt that wolf restoration in
New England goes well beyond wolves:

> It is this broader mission to craft a wilder future that has helped the
> specific goal of wolf recovery to flourish. Wolf recovery is not just about
> restoring the wolf. It is about beginning to reweave the whole fabric of
> life. It is about biodiversity and wilderness restoration. It is about how
> we define our role in nature. It is about our worldviews. It is about
> lifestyles. It is about values.[48]

RESTORE's executive director Michael Kellett is similarly quite straightforward in discussing the political importance of the wolf. Says Kellett,
"RESTORE chose wolf recovery as our first campaign because we realized that the idea of wolves in New England could help us ignite a wilderness restoration movement. The wolf's ecological role is essential. But
just as important is the wolf's symbolic connection to wilderness."[49]

The Wildlands Project (TWP) is also unmistakably interwoven into
the story of wolf management and restoration. The mission of TWP is
as simple as it is sweeping:

> to protect and restore the natural heritage of North America through
> the establishment of a connected system of wildlands.... To stem the
> disappearance of wildlife and wilderness we must allow the recovery of
> whole ecosystems and landscapes in every region in North America....
> we live for the day when grizzlies in Chihuahua have an unbroken
> connection to grizzlies in Alaska; when wolf populations are restored
> from Mexico to the Yukon; when vast forests and flowing prairies again
> thrive and support their full assemblage of native plants and animals;
> when humans dwell with respect, harmony, and affection for the land;
> when we come to live no longer as conquerors but as respectful citizens
> in the land community.[50]

Although considered radical by its opponents in its scope and mission,
including its connection with former Earth First! leader Dave Foreman,
TWP has been endorsed by several scientific luminaries including E. O.
Wilson of Harvard, who writes in the allied journal *Wild Earth*, "Great
dreams, as opposed to fantasies, are those that seem to lie at or just beyond the edge of possibility. When I first learned of The Wildlands Project, I thought it must be beyond that limit, an admirable whimsy of

noble souls. But as quickly as I gave the ideas serious thought, I was converted. With imagination and will, I firmly believe, it can be done."[51] Paul Ehrlich of Stanford is also an enthusiastic supporter, and Michael Soulé of the University of California, Santa Cruz, is one of the project's founders. Many of the project's core ideas, albeit watered down, have also found their way into formal planning measures such as Florida's plan to protect the panther. The now mainstream use of terms such as the *Greater Yellowstone Ecosystem* and the *North Woods* is also an example of how many basic tenets of the project have seeped into popular discourse.

The scientific basis of the TWP is grounded largely in the work of conservation biology. Both recognize the same basic features of "rewilding": large, strictly protected core reserves, connectivity, and keystone species. These are the three C's of rewilding: cores, corridors, and carnivores.[52] Proponents of TWP and many conservation biologists focus on large predators like the wolf for a number of reasons: the diversity and resilience of ecosystems are often maintained by top predators, they require habitat connectivity for their long-term viability, and they often require large core areas and thus justify bigness.[53] Wolves are an important focal species according to TWP because their requirements for survival also represent factors important to maintaining ecologically healthy conditions. According to the TWP, "If native large carnivores have been extirpated from a region, their reintroduction and recovery is central to a conservation strategy. Wolves, grizzlies, cougars, lynx, wolverines, black bears, jaguars, and other top carnivores need to be restored throughout North America in their natural ranges."[54]

Although advocates of wolf reintroduction are not necessarily proponents of TWP, wherever there have been ideas or plans for wolf reintroduction, there are also ideas or plans for rewilding: the Yellowstone to Yukon Conservation Initiative, The Southern Rockies Ecosystem Project, the Greater Laurentian Wildlands Project, the Appalachian Restoration Campaign, and others. In southern Colorado's San Juan Mountains, for instance, the struggle over wilderness and reintroducing large predators like the wolf seem at times indistinguishable. The Wild San Juans wildlands network advocates restoring natural carnivores to the area, protecting and expanding large, wild core habitats, securing critical landscape corridors, and "rewilding the San Juans in the process."[55]

The maintenance or addition of more roadless land within core areas is a major goal of TWP. As discussed earlier, roads are a major threat to endangered species and most predators because they act as funnels for exotic plants and mortality sinks by exposing animals to dangerous vehicle traffic and making poaching easier. According to one ecologist, roads cause edges, and "edges let Bubba in to shoot endangered species. [Thus] everything within one six-pack of the point he parks is in trouble."[56] One prominent environmentalist similarly informed me that it is not just an issue of roads per mile, but one of "rednecks per mile."

It is easy to see why TWP is so controversial. Many of those opposed to wolf recovery see wolves' return as one part of a much larger and more radical and restrictive environmental agenda. Many, for example, refuse to use the term *Greater Yellowstone Ecosystem* because they interpret the language as coming from "the other side." One western-state Farm Bureau Federation official believes that wolves are simply a ruse for a larger and more inclusive environmental vision. He believes that wolves and grizzlies are but one way environmentalists are pursuing more land set-asides and wilderness designations. The issue is not just about wolves, he says, but about land-use restrictions and a once radical environmental agenda that is now mainstream. Terms such as *wildlife highways* and *biological corridors* are not only understood by opponents of wolf recovery but are used as evidence "that these environmentalists want a lot more than just wolves."

The Future of the Endangered Species Act

Essential to understanding both wolf management and reintroduction programs under way throughout the United States is the Endangered Species Act of 1973. As the pace of extinction quickens, the potential and failures of the ESA become more evident as well as politically manipulated. Since 1973, only eleven species have been removed from the endangered species list because of successful recovery.[57] This number is bandied about by both supporters of the act, who see it as a type of emergency room treatment and want it either strengthened or better funded and implemented, as well as by opponents, who use it as evidence that the act is unworkable and should be repealed. The wolf has become once again an important political symbol. This time, it either represents political validation of the much beleaguered ESA or yet another example of the act's social and economic costs.

Measuring the success or failure of the ESA is a difficult and value-laden process.[58] A conservative cost-benefit analysis, for example, would show more public expenditures than successfully delisted species. Contrasting the meager number of species that have been removed from the list against the comprehensive and far-reaching nature of the act leaves as much doubt as it does hope. As with other public policies, however, such simple accounting measures tell only part of the story. From an evolutionary standpoint, 1973 is not that long ago. It may be more advantageous to judge the merits of the act as providing a foundation on which future recoveries can be built. It is perhaps better to ask whether the act has secured a better future for many species, and whether it has forced us to better understand what they require for their survival. And we must of course ask how many species would have been lost without the act. However this piece of legislation is politically interpreted, it is clear that wolves are now an important part of this larger debate.

Apart from the number of species taken off the endangered species list, the act has been criticized for other reasons and from a variety of viewpoints.[59] For example, there is no statutory and absolute standard for determining when a species is in danger of extinction, and when a species has successfully recovered; instead, these decisions are made case by case. Some also think that the ESA has not been implemented as it was intended under Section 2(b) of the act (1973): "to provide a means whereby the ecosystems upon which endangered species and threatened species depend may be conserved." Others argue that undue and unbalanced attention is given to certain high-profile species and megafauna such as the wolf. The ESA has also been routinely criticized for the costs of reintroduction and habitat protection, and on other economic grounds.[60]

Although the act allows for economic considerations at various stages of implementation, it does not allow for such consideration during the listing process. It has consequently been attacked by opponents for its economic costs. Those who want the act strengthened, however, argue that such economic factors are deeply embedded, sometimes surreptitiously so, throughout the entire ESA policy process. The relationship between wolf recovery and various economic factors is a central theme found throughout all U.S. wolf programs. Use of the act's experimental 10(j) clause can be seen as one example of appeasing economic (ranching) interests in the intermountain West. One critic argues that "the wolf represents a threat—both philosophically and economically—to the industry's entrenched subsidies. In attempting to placate this polit-ically powerful industry, the agency charged with protecting the wolf has itself violated the Endangered Species Act."[61]

Running throughout many of these critiques is the argument that the ESA has been poorly funded and implemented. One comprehensive assessment concludes that "poor implementation of the ESA is itself a major cause of the continuing decline of species, and professionals and organizations are significantly responsible for the quality of implemen-tation."[62] For many, the failures or shortcomings of the act are not bio-logically based, nor are they due to the language and nature of the legis-lation, but are instead due to the act's poor implementation.[63] From a funding standpoint, even the heralded Northern Rockies and Yellow-stone wolf reintroduction programs have experienced several serious budgetary challenges.[64]

While the implementation critique is an important one, the ESA should be examined from a more political and strategic perspective as well. Groups such as the Center for Biological Diversity have been in-credibly successful in using the act as a battering ram, legal monkey wrench, and tool for institutional disruption.[65] They have seriously chal-lenged the status quo by using the ESA to protect species such as the Mexican spotted owl and pygmy owl in the Southwest. Successfully work-ing from within the system, they have challenged the old order, from urban development to public lands ranching. They have also been suc-cessful in getting the courts to make federal agencies implement and enforce existing laws. Given the language of the act, and those willing to force it, some fear that wolves are part of a larger environmental strategy.

Successful wolf recovery is also beginning to be used strategically as an example of the act's potential. Delisting the gray wolf in the upper Midwest, for instance, will certainly be one of the act's crowning achieve-ments. "This is truly an endangered species success story," says FWS re-gional director Bill Hartwig.[66] As of 2002, gray wolves in Minnesota, Wisconsin, and the Upper Peninsula of Michigan had been successfully restored, having reached approximately 2,500 wolves in Minnesota (es-timated at 750 in 1970), over 250 wolves in the Upper Peninsula (esti-mated at 6 in 1973), and over 300 in Wisconsin (0 in 1973). Perhaps more important, their recovery, while certainly not free of controversy, has taken place without many political fears and apprehensions being legitimized.

Once again, wolves and the ESA are often seen as a threat to land use and private property. Wolves, and most endangered species in the country, in many places depend on privately owned lands for their survival.[67] This threat is what often scares so many people and groups that are interpreted as being "anti-wolf." Wolf reintroduction is a slippery slope, they say, and sooner or later wolves will leave designated areas and find their way onto private lands. When they do, not only will they pose a threat to livestock, but they will also bring a heavy-handed federal government with them that will challenge these people's right to own and enjoy their private property. What will happen, they ask, when a key private holding separating two good publicly owned wolf habitats (a biological corridor) is identified as being essential to wolf recovery? Will they be precluded from using this land, and if so, will they be justly compensated for this taking?

The ESA is often viewed as being a prohibitive, negative, and threatening type of public policy, which precludes certain types of land use, diminishes property values, and embodies the legal justification for unconstitutional takings.[68] Critics contend that while the public-at-large and the environment may benefit from species protection, this public essentially pays nothing while a few landowners pay the concentrated costs and incur all of the risks. Wolves are on the periphery of this takings debate and are used in various "what if" and "would could happen" scenarios.

Many outspoken political representatives have also challenged the assumptions of the act, its environmental supporters, and those responsible for its implementation. Former Idaho Representative Helen Chenoweth-Hage, never short on condemnation of wolves or the ESA, simply asserts that the ESA does not work: "It has failed to save species, it has caused acrimony and gridlock, generated endless litigation, it has created brigades of possum cops, it has cost the American taxpayer and private property owner hundreds of billions of dollars in wasted effort, it has misappropriated property and lost production." She is especially critical of the FWS, who "insist on introducing wolves and grizzly bears into populated areas, devouring domestic animals and threatening the users of the forest, when these species exist in plentiful numbers in Canada and Alaska."[69]

Wolves have also provided an opportunity to reexamine the potential role of private property in endangered species protection. Wolves need and will inevitably use private property in some regions, especially east of the Rockies, if they are to recover successfully. One study by the General Accounting Office, for example, found that more than 90 percent of all listed species have some or all of their habitat on nonfederal lands.[70] Private property is a central issue concerning wolf recovery in the Northeast and Southeast in particular. In North Carolina, for example, two private landowners and two counties filed a lawsuit in 1997 to overturn the FWS regulation governing the killing or trapping of endangered red wolves on private property. The appellants asked the court (unsuccessfully) to invalidate a federal wildlife conservation measure found in the ESA because it exceeded Congress's constitutional powers. While the appellant's legal theory—that Congress's Commerce Clause power does not include federal measures to protect endangered species off federal lands—has been rejected by the courts on numerous occasions,[71] the lawsuit does illustrate the contested nature and overall importance of private property in long-term wolf recovery and conservation.[72] Even in the West, private property will play a critical role in wolf recovery. As elk and deer move out of the high country and mountains for their winter range, wolves will follow, and these lower elevation lands, valley bottoms, and river areas are often privately owned and are quickly becoming developed.

Many people believe that more positive, innovative, and incentive-based approaches are needed if wolves and other species are to be protected on private lands. Habitat conservation plans and safe harbor agreements have been put forward as a way to approach endangered species protection on private property. Although controversial, habitat conservation plans provide a permit that allows for the taking of endangered species incidental to otherwise lawful activities. To obtain this permit, a landowner has to develop a habitat conservation plan that mitigates the impact of this authorized taking. A "no surprises" policy is often worked into these plans, assuring landowners who prepare satisfactory plans that the government will not impose new requirements due to unforeseen future circumstances. Safe harbor programs work on the assumption that many landowners may eliminate an endangered species or the habitat they need to survive on private lands because of the perceived risk associated with having such species on one's private property. "Shoot, shovel and shut-up" before the FWS is the wiser. With a safe harbor agreement, however, a landowner can protect, restore, or enhance habitat or cooperate in a species conservation effort without incurring added liabilities as a result of such practices. These agreements, according to Michael Bean of the Environmental Defense Fund, "represent a small but significant breakthrough in designing an endangered species program that makes landowners allies, not adversaries."[73] These are but two approaches that could be used to reform or reinvigorate the ESA on private lands. Experiments with tax code reform, the creation of ESA special trust funds, government land exchanges, and the early use of stakeholders in decision making could also be implemented.[74] Estate tax reform, for example, would allow heirs to defer or avoid estate taxes on inherited land if they managed the land in a manner beneficial to endangered species.

Unwilling to wait for legislative change, one environmental organization has proceeded on its own. Understanding that hostility toward the wolf often stems from economic self-interest, Defenders of Wildlife uses private funds to compensate livestock owners who have lost cattle and sheep to depredating wolves.[75] Defenders has also helped pay for precautionary measures, such as the purchase of electric fencing to keep wolves away from livestock. "Putting its money where its mouth is," the Defenders' Wolf Compensation Trust paid one hundred ranchers over $96,000 in compensation from 1987 to October 1999.

The use of economic incentives in wildlife management was standard practice throughout much of America's history in the form of wolf bounties. First practiced by colonial Massachusetts in 1630, bounties for dead wolves were paid by several levels of government and private interests including states, counties, and townships. While the wolf bounty is no longer officially paid to the public, the economic principles on which it is founded are still being utilized. Defenders of Wildlife went beyond the compensatory and created a Wolf Reward Program, which pays landowners $5,000 whenever a pair of wolves breeds on their property, while at the same time offering a $5,000 reward to anyone providing information leading to the arrest and conviction of illegal hunters. The wolf compensation and reward program has been used as a defense against charges of absentee environmentalism: supporting carnivore conservation in someone else's backyard while assuming none of the responsibility or costs. This program is also often pointed to by wolf advocates as a way to illustrate the often "irrational" nature of the debate. Some believe that ranchers and other wolf opponents simply have nothing to fear, because of privately funded economic safeguards. Some ranchers, on the other hand, have little faith in such "safeguards" given the nature of western public lands ranching and the amount of evidence that is required to be compensated. Proving wolf depredation can be difficult, they insist. Thus, some see the program as a clever public relations ploy.

To summarize, it is not surprising to find that the debate over wolf recovery is entangled with a more far-ranging policy-related debate over the ESA. After all, wolves have returned as a result of this historic piece of legislation. For many policy participants, the wolf symbolizes either the promise of the ESA or its threatening and heavy-handed federal implementation. "Policy entrepreneurs," moreover, see the wolf as presenting a grand opportunity to refine and rework the act, to make it less threatening, more cooperative, incentive-based, and successful.

Implementing the ESA and Debate over Environmental Compromise and Capitulation

One of the most controversial aspects of wolf recovery in the Northern Rockies has proven to be the designation of reintroduced wolves in central Idaho and Yellowstone National Park as experimental populations. Section 10(j) of the ESA authorizes the secretary of the interior to identify and release an experimental population that is "wholly separate geographically" from nonexperimental populations of the same species. This designation was proposed as a way to give the FWS greater flexibility in the management of wolves in these areas. It can also be seen as a clear example of an implementing agency (under congressional direction) not only recognizing local customs and political culture but also incorporating these customs and local concerns into the policy and management process. Put simply, the debate over reintroducing wolves as experimental under 10(j) was as much about political compromise and capitulation as it was about agency effectiveness. Many people in the wolf advocacy coalition believe that successful recovery programs for the wolf and other endangered species require a certain degree of cultural recognition and resulting compromise. Some wolf advocates believe that if wolves and other endangered species are to be successfully restored, their most ardent defenders must recognize the difference between the paper protections provided by the ESA and the real on-the-ground protections provided, or not provided, by rural citizens.

The experimental designation has been used with different species and in different areas as a way to facilitate management and lessen state, local, and industry concerns about various land-use restrictions, unchecked depredation of livestock, and the depletion of big-game populations. Concerned about the lack of species successfully removed from the endangered species list, and the belief that people were often more afraid of the law and its restrictions than the animals themselves, Congress amended the ESA in 1982. Several political representatives believed that by providing wildlife managers more flexibility, species recovery could be facilitated in a less controversial and more conducive political climate. This amendment was added during the time of red wolf reintroduction in North Carolina and Tennessee. Farmers and hunters there, like ranchers in the Northern Rockies, were pledging to foil the program whether wolves were protected by the ESA or not. Some members of Congress and environmental interests feared the fate of the ESA without some type of reform and therefore proposed the 10(j) amendment as a way to achieve local cooperation, or at least local acquiescence or inaction.

In the ranching country of the Northern Rockies, this designation was chosen as the "preferred alternative" in order to appease local landowners and livestock operators and to assure them that wolf reintroduction would not unduly jeopardize regular ways of doing things. The FWS chose this experimental designation in part because it appeared to work well with red wolves in the Southeast. Unlike the naturally recolonizing wolves that are protected as "endangered" in northwest Montana, wolves in central Idaho and Yellowstone can be killed or removed from an area in certain circumstances.

Understanding that human-induced mortality is one of the greatest barriers to successful wolf recovery in the region, the FWS attempted to demonstrate, with the experimental designation as its primary tool, that federal agencies would act quickly to alleviate depredation problems. The debate over this designation is similar to a host of other policy implementation questions and concerns. Broadly stated, it pits the legislative *intent* of the original ESA against the ability of a bureaucracy to effectively *implement* this legislation. It is a conflict that is hardly unique in politics and public administration. With this statutory clause, Congress has given the FWS an ability to maneuver in a complicated and divisive political and cultural environment. From the perspective of the FWS, like that of many other agencies and implementers, this type of managerial flexibility is essential if wolves are to have more than just paper support and protection. They believe that protecting wolves on paper is different than protecting wolves on the ground. To do the latter, many implementing the ESA believe that state, local, and community concerns must be seriously and honestly addressed, and if they are not, successful wolf recovery over the long-term is improbable.

Many wildlife managers believe that achieving an acceptable level of human tolerance is the key to creating an environment that is most conducive to successful wolf management. Human conflict with deer (agricultural damage, auto collisions, deer attacks) is much greater than it is with wolves, but people nonetheless have a higher tolerance for deer. Wolves, given their strong symbolic quality and the negative feelings many people have toward them, are very susceptible to human persecution, especially by poison. Consequently, negative human attitudes, either toward the wolf itself or a related symbol or surrogate issue, can result in a failed recovery effort. As Ed Bangs, FWS wolf recovery coordinator for the Northern Rockies puts it, "Wolves have to be fit into the political landscape. If the local public isn't involved formally (as part of the solution), they will be involved informally (killing wolves)." He believes that the trick then is to have a level of conflict low enough so that eradication is not the only option available. For him, local attitudes are paramount, and if conflicts become too socially unacceptable, wolves will simply disappear. The key, he says, is reading what level of conflict is tolerable to local people, and what agency actions can be taken to keep conflicts at that level. The experimental designation is therefore seen as a way in which the FWS can best accomplish this important goal.

Before the reintroduction of wolves to Yellowstone, various constituencies in the area expressed a number of concerns, many that were especially Western in orientation. Issues and concerns included fears that wolves would kill a significant amount of livestock surrounding the park, that wolf management and control around Yellowstone would be prohibited by an overly restrictive ESA, that wolf regulations and management inside the park would restrict visitor uses, that once restored, wolves could not be controlled and managed and would therefore spread throughout the region, and finally, that the federal government would place additional restrictions on public land use, such as closing forest roads.[76] These concerns were addressed by scientists, managers, and some environmental organizations, such as Defenders of Wildlife, by supporting the latitude provided by the ESA's experimental designation. Responding to various objections to Yellowstone reintroduction, wolf biologist David Mech, for example, emphasized the importance of this managerial flexibility: "In fact, if necessary to restore wolves to Yellowstone, I favor a program allowing wolves to be killed everywhere outside of the designated reestablishment area. Everyone must understand that when wolves are restored to Yellowstone, wolf management outside the park will become a fact of life."[77]

The debate over how the ESA should be implemented, and whether it should be implemented at all, culminated in litigation over wolf reintroduction in Yellowstone and central Idaho. The litigation began with a lawsuit filed by the American Farm Bureau Federation (AFBF), who were represented by the Mountain States Legal Foundation (a wise-use oriented organization opposing wolf restoration). This lawsuit strategically charged that the nonessential designation of reintroduced wolves threatened the health and status of wolves that were possibly already in the area, as well as those that would disperse there, thus jeopardizing naturally recolonized wolves that were claimed to already be in Yellowstone. The AFBF used the 10(j) clause as a tool to halt reintroduction and force newly reintroduced wolves to be removed (or killed, said environmentalists, since government officials in Alberta, Canada, did not want these wolves returned).

A few environmental organizations also found themselves uncomfortably siding with their traditional adversaries in this lengthy legal battle. Unlike the AFBF, however, these organizations opposed the use of the experimental designation because they believed not only that it endangered naturally recolonized wolves, but that reintroduced wolves should be afforded the maximum protection allowed under the ESA. These pro-wolf groups argued that because wolves from Canada were naturally recolonizing parts of the Northern Rockies, the reintroduced Yellowstone and central Idaho populations were not "wholly separate geographically" from nonexperimental populations, as required by the ESA.

These cases were later combined into *Wyoming Farm Bureau Federation v. Babbitt* (1997) and heard by Judge William F. Downes of the U.S.

District Court for the District of Wyoming. Based on his reading of the legislative history of the 1982 amendment, Downes ruled that reintroduced experimental populations overlapped geographically with naturally recolonizing wolf populations, thus violating section 10(j) of the ESA. In other words, these experimental populations illegally reduced the level of protection granted to naturally expanding wolf populations, protected as endangered, not threatened. The ruling meant that Yellowstone and Idaho wolves would have to be removed from the experimental areas.

In January 2000, this ruling was overturned by the Tenth Circuit Court of Appeals in Denver. In reversing the district court, the Tenth Circuit interpreted the "wholly separate geographically" clause much differently while also deferring to the FWS. The district court in Wyoming interpreted the phrase to mean that any interaction among experimental and nonexperimental wolves, even between lone dispersing wolves, was a violation of the clause. The Tenth Circuit, on the other hand, emphasized the context in which it reviews matters of law, giving strict effect to the unambiguous intent of Congress. If there is congressional ambiguity, the court defers to the agency's construction (as long as it is deemed reasonable and permissible). Because the ESA does not define the relevant terms or address the precise issue at hand—whether "wholly separate geographically from non-experimental populations" means that a reintroduced population must be separate from every naturally occurring individual animal—the court ruled that Congress deliberately left this interpretation to the FWS. The court also reminded plaintiffs that Congress purposely designed section 10(j) to provide the secretary of the interior flexibility and discretion in managing reintroduction efforts. And finally, the court ruled that by definition, lone dispersers do not constitute a wolf population. Therefore, there is no violation of the "wholly separate geographically" requirement, and the wolves can stay in both Yellowstone and central Idaho.[78]

In enacting the ESA, Congress adopted a biological perspective on species conservation. Congress emphasized the importance of biological factors in deciding to list a species and proclaimed that economic considerations were to play no role in the listing process. Despite these intentions, for some critics, the role of economics—and in the case of the wolf, the ranching industry—has superseded that of biology and the intent of the ESA as it pertains to wolf recovery in the Northern

Rockies. According to University of Idaho law professor Dale Goble, "The *Plan*'s management strategies focus less on the biological needs of the wolf than on the pecuniary desires of the livestock industry. Placating the industry has produced a 'recovery plan' in which endangered species will be killed to protect the economic interests of ranchers. Maintenance of the subsidies enjoyed by beef and wool producers is the central political reality of the *Wolf Recovery Plan*."[79]

Critiques of this sort contend that the plan amounts to yet another indirect subsidy to the western ranching industry, and that ranching interests, not the interest of an endangered species, have been given the dominant position. For example, the plan does not set aside any critical habitat for the wolf, and its system of managing wolves clearly places ranching interests on equal footing with biological ones. A number of critics argue that the public should not be forced to bear the costs inherent in having a predator-free environment. They say that the beef and wool industry is trying to force the public to bear some of the costs of protecting livestock, costs that should instead be borne by producers, who are already enjoying considerable subsidies on the public domain. This livestock, they remind people, is grazing on public lands, and in a western environment that is replete with other risks beside that of predators—natural risks, such as floods and drought, and costs that are borne by both the citizen and other producers. This industry and its political representation have largely structured the basic parameters of wolf management and restoration. For longtime critics of the industry, wolves provide the latest opportunity to once again advertise the economic and ecological costs of the Western ranching culture, as well as what is perceived as the captured nature of the FWS.

These critics also see the flexibility the FWS believes it has in managing wolves as being unfounded and contrary to the intent of the original ESA, a law that they believe clearly places biological concerns above economic ones. Those implementing the ESA and other wolf recovery plans find themselves caught between two very different ways of interpreting the act and how it can be best implemented. On the one hand, there are those believing that the act and court interpretations of it are quite clear: recovery and biological considerations first, economics a distant second. Others see flexibility in the act, and believe that using this flexibility is the only way to rally public support—a support that is essential for successful wolf recovery.

Critics also point out that this is not the first time the FWS has struggled with its dual mission and conflicting roles of service and regulation. The agency's complex heritage dates to an 1871 act of Congress,
who feared the possible deterioration of national fisheries, especially in
Alaska. According to political scientists Jeanne Nienaber Clarke and Daniel
McCool, who have traced the agency's confusing parentage, "Given a
dual mandate from Congress—to conserve and protect while at the
same time promoting the fishery resource, the Bureau [the FWS was
formerly the Bureau of Fisheries] understandably was beset with difficulties in distinguishing between its two primary, and often conflicting,
functions."[80] The FWS, according to these authors, is perhaps best characterized as a "secondary service organization"; that is, "It has not been
able to break out of this conservative orientation. The attitude of agency
personnel is basically that of being enthusiastic, behind-the-scenes
helpers. Rather than becoming a leader in the environmental movement
that developed during the 1960s, the Service maintained its traditional
low profile and was frequently criticized for its timidity."[81]

It is quite common for a government agency to make the case for
flexibility in implementation and for an increase in its managerial discretion. But support for the experimental designation among several
environmental groups was surprising to many. That some groups supported the designation clearly illustrates the important philosophical
and tactical differences among environmentalists and their representative organizations. For some in the environmental community, reintroducing wolves as experimental populations is not only an example of an
agency kowtowing to entrenched economic interests (unsurprising and
expected), but also an alarming example of environmentalists bending
over backwards to accommodate these interests.

Strategic conflict over wolf reintroduction in Yellowstone and central
Idaho presents an interesting case in this larger political debate. Influential groups like the Wolf Fund (formed for the sole purpose of reintroducing wolves to Yellowstone) supported reintroduction under 10(j).
Defenders of Wildlife was one of the most important players supporting the experimental designation. Learning from the Minnesota wolf
program, Defenders' Northern Rockies field representative Hank Fischer
saw the amount of leeway that "threatened" wolves in Minnesota allowed
wildlife managers, and believed that this type of flexibility was essential if
wolves were to be successfully restored in the West. According to Fischer,

"Experimental reintroduction would restore wolves more quickly, with much greater assurance, and at less cost than would a highly uncertain natural recovery.... the goodwill generated by addressing the concerns of local people would save far more wolves than any number of carefully worded laws."[82]

Others involved in the Yellowstone reintroduction saw the compromise as something new in the environmental movement. Thomas McNamee, former president of the Greater Yellowstone Coalition, remembers that he (not the Coalition) saw a beautiful synthesis of pessimism and optimism in Section 10(j): "The pessimistic assumption was that some people were going to kill wolves no matter what. The optimistic assumption was that this was okay, because the wolf population was going to prosper anyway. Conservation was almost always saying no: stop this timber sale, end that abuse, promulgate new rules against such and such. Wolf reintroduction was saying yes."[83]

Many environmental groups did not see it this way. The Sierra Club Legal Defense Fund (now Earthjustice Legal Defense Fund) filed suit against the experimental designation and argued that the endangered wolves that might already be in Yellowstone and central Idaho would be mistakenly managed as threatened wolves under the provisions of 10(j). They argued that it would be impossible to distinguish between reintroduced wolves protected as threatened under the ESA and naturally recolonized wolves that would be protected under the more stringent endangered status. Many groups that Earthjustice represents, such as the Montana-based Predator Conservation Alliance (formerly the Predator Project), are concerned about this "new era of compromising legal protections to gain public acceptance of species recovery efforts."[84] According to the Alliance, despite its declared "victories" in the reintroduction of wolves, the FWS is treading a slippery slope in its attempts to implement and enforce the ESA: "On the ground—where it really counts—political deals and pro-development bargains between agencies, big corporations and land developers provide loopholes and exceptions to ESA compliance [and] these special interest deals continue to allow destruction of plants, animals and habitat, pushing imperiled species closer to the brink of extinction."[85] The Alliance is worried not only about wolf recovery in the Northern Rockies but about what 10(j) portends for grizzly bears in central Idaho, wolves in Maine, and lynx in Colorado. It now appears, says the Alliance, that the FWS has the discretion to designate those populations as experimental and relax full ESA protections.

Michael Robinson of the Center for Biological Diversity is equally critical, arguing that such flexibility and compromise have failed to help Mexican wolf recovery. He says,

> Throughout the United States, the Fish and Wildlife Service acts on the notion that endangered wildlife, and particularly predators, can be recovered only with local support, which the agency garners by suspending almost all protective regulations. . . . The Southwest experience with Mexican wolves and the early indications with jaguars illustrate the failure of this policy. As polls have long demonstrated, the majority of local residents in the Mexican wolf recovery area already support the animals' return. Only one identifiable social group—ranchers—stands almost monolithically in opposition, and that groups represents less than one percent of the rural region's population and economic base. The fact that the designation of Mexican wolves as "experimental, nonessential"—the legal mechanism under the ESA that allows for highly intrusive management—*manifestly failed* to prevent wolves from being shot should cause a reevaluation of the premises of our predator policies.[86]

This debate will likely continue in the future. In proposing their sweeping recommendations to downlist or delist wolves throughout much of the country, the FWS is accentuating the importance of managerial flexibility more than ever. Among other reasons, the agency believes that moving wolves from endangered status to threatened throughout much of the country will help alleviate local concerns while giving the agency as much flexibility and discretion as it needs to handle problem wolves. This action has proven to be very controversial. Some environmentalists believe that the agency should be emphasizing the habitat needs of large carnivores and not just the management needs of the FWS. They insist that if wolves were given adequate habitat in the first place, they would not need as much management. They question the agency's unyielding focus on special management rules when the real issue is habitat degradation. Learning from the Mexican wolf program in the Southwest, moreover, some wolf advocates also question the effectiveness of the experimental designation. They argue that Mexican wolves continue to be illegally killed despite this designation and should therefore be fully protected as endangered.

The Future of Rural Places

As the Idaho Department of Fish and Game was preparing its state wolf management plan in 2001, the Idaho legislature was writing a "joint memorial" regarding wolf recovery efforts in the state. The memorial emphasizes an important sociopolitical dimension:

> WHEREAS, Idaho's rural areas are suffering near depression-like economic disasters and America is becoming a nation of battered rural communities; and
> WHEREAS, natural resources are the lifeblood of Idaho, the genesis of wealth and the hub of America's economic wheel, and that eliminating resource production is a poor trade-off for wolf and grizzly recovery which has no basis in common sense, legitimate science or free-enterprise economics; and
> WHEREAS, our natural resource industries are declining in large part because of the federal government's policies and management; [THEREFORE, BE IT RESOLVED] that this legislature not only calls for, but demands, that wolf recovery efforts in Idaho be discontinued immediately, and wolves be removed by whatever means necessary.[87]

Wolves have provided another opportunity for those in the debate to discuss the role and future of rural communities. Some see the wolf and the danger it poses to livestock as yet another assault on rural communities, which are often bound to the fate of unpredictable commodity markets and extractive economies. Some rural citizens also view wolf support as being largely an urban phenomenon. For instance, while public attitudes toward wolves are generally favorable in both urban and rural areas, urban residents are generally more supportive of wolves and their reintroduction than are residents of rural areas.[88]

Rural places throughout the nation are facing a number of daunting challenges. They have often been used (by those inside and outside the region, and often voluntarily so) in a colonial-type fashion and simply as a source of cheap natural resources. The lack of economic vertical integration—providing only one part of the entire economic production process—leaves many rural areas increasingly susceptible to international economic cycles of boom and bust and external decision making. It is imperative, say some environmentalists, that those involved in the debate recognize the challenges facing rural communities—communities that will inevitably play the largest role in successful wolf restoration. As

Renee Askins, executive director of the Wolf Fund, a Wyoming-based organization that worked for the return of the wolf to Yellowstone, emphasizes:

> If I were a rancher I probably would not want wolves returned to the West. If I faced the conditions that ranchers face in the West—falling stock prices, rising taxes, prolonged drought, and a nation that is eating less beef and wearing more synthetics—I would not want to add wolves to my woes. If I were a rancher in Montana, Idaho or Wyoming in 1995, watching my neighbors give up and my way of life fade away, I would be afraid and I would be angry. I would want to blame something, to fight something, even kill something.[89]

Now that wolves are in Yellowstone, they are still an important symbol and surrogate. Hank Fischer of Defenders of Wildlife, a veteran of predator politics, contends that "the problem with wolves is they are reflective of people's attitudes and often a substitute for other issues. Wolves can become a target for anger that people feel for the federal government, or they can be a substitute for anger that livestock producers may feel toward an economic system that doesn't always treat them very fairly."[90] If these issues do not have a hearing, and public outreach does not take place, say some environmentalists, wolf restoration will be seen as yet one more example—from the move toward corporate agriculture to falling beef prices—of what little regard the government and the environmental community has for quickly disintegrating rural communities.

Also evident is what little trust many rural farmers and ranchers have in the "outsider," whether it be stereotypical perceptions of the elite urban environmentalist or of the aloof and out-of-touch federal bureaucrat. This lack of trust is often manifest in several areas of wolf politics. Take, for instance, statistics pertaining to the amount of wolf depredation on livestock in Minnesota provided by U.S. Department of Agriculture's (USDA) Wildlife Services.[91] Many farmers simply do not believe in the accuracy of these numbers, arguing that there is much more depredation than is verified by the federal government. This skepticism also illustrates the problems inherent in a purely scientific or nonpolitical definition of the wolf problem. The debate does not proceed from these scientifically objective "facts." Instead, a key constituency often questions their legitimacy and the government that is doing the counting.

Tribal Participation and Management Authority

Wolf recovery has provided an opportunity for many in the debate to reexamine the role of tribes in wildlife management. First Nations play an important but varied role in the story of wolf recovery. First, of course, there is no one uniform tribal role. Often, different rules and regulations pertain to fish and wildlife management that are specific to a particular band, not to the tribe as a whole. For example, in northern Minnesota, northern Wisconsin, and the Upper Peninsula of Michigan, the eleven bands of the Chippewa (often referred to as Ojibwe or Anishinabe) could in theory have eleven different sets of wolf management rules and regulations. While the Great Lakes Indian Fish and Wildlife Commission (GLIFWC), an intertribal organization, helps ensure that off-reservation hunting and fishing rights guaranteed by various treaties are protected, it does little pertaining to fish and wildlife policy on the various reservations. These reservations are not as large as those found farther west. Nevertheless, this example does illustrate the managerial complexity involved and the need for meaningful intergovernmental (international) communication and cooperation. Wolves will increasingly find themselves in a complicated federal, state, and tribal legal landscape consisting of different management guidelines, cultures, and values.

Take, for example, the San Carlos Apache and White Mountain Apache (or Fort Apache), both located immediately to the west of the Blue Range Wolf Recovery Area (BRWRA) in Arizona. Both initially adopted resolutions opposing Mexican wolf recovery in the BRWRA.[92] (Recently the White Mountain Apache tribe has taken a leadership role and has written a wolf management plan, hired a wolf biologist, and secured federal funding to help support tribal wolf management.) For both tribal governments, livestock depredation and budgetary constraints were important concerns. Also, both reservations generate significant revenue from game hunting by people outside the tribe. For the San Carlos Apache, for instance, trophy elk hunting by nonmembers provides approximately $500,000 in hunting revenues annually. Significant revenue is also generated by small-game hunting, trapping, and fees from guiding. Similarly, the White Mountain Apache generated approximately $1 million in nonmember hunting revenues in 1995 and sell trophy elk permits at $11,000 each.[93] The impact of wolves on game species migrating onto the reservation is therefore a major concern. The San Carlos Apache, as do Anglo populations near the BRWRA, often see wolves as another threat to an insecure rural economy. Multiple-family and tribal cattle operations exist on the San Carlos reservation, and these families, as well as other tribal members, face numerous economic hardships.

The tribal role in wolf management must also be placed in its larger cultural context. Some native communities in Alaska, for example, have called for increased wolf control (killing more wolves). Many natives in Alaska depend on moose and caribou meat for their basic dietary and existence needs. Many are unable to substitute other food for this game; thus, wolves are seen as a threat not only to this game but to a subsistence culture as well. The issue of wolf control is therefore seen in cultural-laden ways by these natives. Many are resentful or suspicious of outsiders, whether it be the urban hunter who kills too much game, the animal rights group that opposes their traditional trapping activities, or the wolf advocate who seems to care more about wolves than about natives.

The tribal role in wolf recovery is much different in Idaho. In 1995, the Idaho legislature barred the Idaho Fish and Game Department from cooperating with the federal wolf recovery program. Idaho's staunch political resistance to the FWS's reintroduction of wolves into central Idaho opened the door to tribal participation in wolf management. The Nez Perce tribe acquired the role, as outlined in the Final Environmental Impact Statement (FEIS), that the state of Idaho did not want. After the Idaho House of Representatives voted down the revised state wolf management plan, with one member contending that the issue had "little to do with wolves and lots to do with state sovereignty," the Nez Perce and the FWS worked out a cooperative management and recovery plan.[94] This five-year agreement gave the tribe responsibility, with FWS funding and oversight, for tracking and monitoring, disseminating information, and public education. Unlike the state of Idaho, the Nez Perce (a member of the EIS advisory team and wolf recovery planning participant) actively sought out an important role for the tribe in wolf recovery. In the Draft EIS, for example, the tribe stressed that it wanted to be a participant in program management and that whatever alternative was chosen, the tribe "should be 'a' or 'the' major player in Wolf Recovery."[95] In contrast, for some opponents of wolf recovery in Idaho, the prospect of devising a state wolf management plan that was acceptable to the FWS, while also paying for this new state management responsibility, was a hard pill to swallow. As one state legislator put it, "If they think we're going to raise taxes to pay for wolves we didn't want in the first place, well maybe that's what it will take to get the public to tell the Fish and Wildlife Service to take a flying leap."[96]

The symbolic importance of Nez Perce wolf management is hard to miss. According to Jaime Pinkham of the Nez Perce Tribal Executive Committee, their wolf recovery effort put a spotlight on the tribe for a couple of reasons. First, this was the first time that an Indian tribe had taken the lead role in the reintroduction of an endangered species under the ESA. And second, "It highlighted the fact that a tribe has the scientific capability as well as the political savvy to take on a project such as this."[97] Pinkham, who now heads the tribal fisheries department, sees a historic connection between what happened to wolves and Indian people during frontier settlement. The wolf and the Nez Perce are still following parallel paths, but the journey is a more optimistic one now, says Pinkham. "You see the tribal status elevated as a natural resource manager, and you see the return of the wolves to Idaho. Both of us are regaining our rightful place on the landscape."[98]

Despite the historic and successful role the Nez Perce have played in wolf recovery in Idaho, an important question lingers: What role does the tribe, in relation to the state of Idaho, play in the future delisting and state wolf management? "If the tribe is removed from wolf management, what is going to be the fate of the tribe, and what is going to be the fate of the wolf?" asks Pinkham.[99] While the tribe would like to continue playing an important role, especially given their hunting and fishing treaty rights on millions of acres, it also understands the state's traditional wildlife management responsibilities. One thing is certain, the tribe has accumulated a great deal of knowledge about wolves in Idaho before and after reintroduction. How that knowledge and other tribal resources are used, or not used, will once again send an important and symbolic message.

Implications for Conflict Management

Wolf recovery and management transcend issues strictly pertaining to wolf behavior and possible livestock depredation. As noted by Tim Clark, Richard Reading, and Alice Clarke, "Many obstacles to species restoration are rooted in the valuational, economic, or political dimensions of the situation." Sociopolitical and holistic approaches, moreover, are important for those responsible for wolf management and reintroduction programs. As these authors conclude, "Attempting to restore species by ignoring everything but the species' biology invites failure."[100] Understanding the human dimensions of wolf recovery, Northern Rockies gray wolf recovery coordinator Ed Bangs and other team members note the importance of the wolf as symbol and its management implications: "the remarkable attention that people give to wolves is particularly striking given the minor impact that wolves have on the physical lives of modern people. Humans have long viewed the wolf as a symbol of their values and beliefs, and we do not see that changing in the near future. Consequently, wolf restoration and management will continue to be far more complicated, expensive, political, and controversial than seems rational."[101] As the debate over wolves and state wolf management proceeds, it is important to recognize these larger issues and concerns. From the possible wolf reintroduction in the Northeast to the more established programs of the upper Midwest, Northern Rockies, and Southwest, the wolf debate will continue to be about more than just wolves. These issues and sociopolitical dimensions certainly make wolf conservation and restoration complicated and rancorous. There is little doubt why the wolf remains such an important symbol and surrogate, for in facing the future of the wolf, we are unmistakably facing our own.

These symbol and surrogate issues also illustrate why a strict techno-rational approach to wolf policy is so difficult, and why it will inevitably miss as much as it captures in explaining the true essence of this political value-laden debate. In discussing the social construction of Yellowstone wolf reintroduction, for example, Matthew Wilson says that "by remaining narrowly focused on the minutia of the rational planning process, planners in the past have often missed these underlying sources of land use conflict in the American West. If future policymakers are unwilling or unable to grapple with the more fundamental social issues driving land use debates in the future, their plans likely will fail."[102] From today's perspective, with more cases and contexts to examine, Wilson's assessment is even more relevant. Wolves are still linked to deeper social forces, but these forces have multiplied in number and are often more nuanced and complex than the relatively clear environmentalist wise-use categories. A more sophisticated understanding of these issues could also help us attain the type of "civic professionalism" necessary for successful endangered species management. A policy orientation will help civic-minded professionals better understand problems in their political context.[103]

As discussed in chapter 4, stakeholder-based collaborative conservation is being increasingly used by wolf, wildlife, and natural resource managers. These stakeholders often include representatives from environmental organizations, animal welfare groups, livestock producers, extractive industries, rural and urban citizens-at-large, and others. While the management design in which these participants work and on which they base their decisions often differs, participants are usually asked to reach a group compromise or consensus on wolf management or policy. One might surmise asking these participants to broaden their discussion to include the symbol and surrogate issues discussed here would be akin to adding fuel to a fire, making collaboration, compromise, and consensus even more difficult to achieve. But this is already the case. Although these groups are asked to deal specifically with the wolf issue, these symbol and surrogate issues inevitably find their way into the mix. Moreover, the way in which they work themselves into the debate is often not conducive to informed dialogue, mutual comprehension, collaboration, consensus-building, or conflict resolution.

Controversial and volatile policy problems that are interrelated with others are susceptible to a "spiral of unmanaged conflict": problems emerge, sides form, positions harden, communication stops, resources are committed, conflict extends beyond the original community of interest groups, perceptions become distorted, and, finally, a sense of crisis emerges.[104] If symbol and surrogate issues were worked into these decision-making processes from the outset in a comprehensive and educative manner, they would facilitate, not hinder, a more meaningful debate and dialogue. If these issues, which are sometimes central and sometimes only tangentially related to wolves, were acknowledged early in the process, the multiple dimensions of wolf management and restoration could be more constructively examined. While acrimony cannot be entirely removed from the process (nor should it), the debate can be made "smarter." By providing participants in these decision-making processes with valuable and well-balanced information, decision making can become more enlightened and empathetic.

If wolf policy and management are to be debated in a more inclusive and democratic arena, then participants in this debate should strive for more understanding and "mutual comprehension." Michael Briand of the Community Self-Leadership Project says, "Reciprocal understanding and appreciation, or 'mutual comprehension,' makes it possible to recast a political issue as a question of how jointly to prioritize goods that everyone can acknowledge as legitimate sources of political motivation. It allows us to reformulate a political disagreement as a political choice—a shared, collective choice—that both enables and encourages us to deliberate together to reach a sound judgment about how to resolve the underlying conflict."[105] This type of mutual comprehension, says Briand, can be aided greatly by analyzing and presenting issues of public concern in a way that facilitates understanding and appreciation of different perspectives. These issues can also sometimes be reframed in a way that will help achieve a more constructive and productive discussion.

How much common ground can be shared by those involved in the wolf debate remains uncertain. Perhaps many issues will present too great a challenge for this type of dialogue and comprehension. It is hard to see, for example, how any common ground could be found among those advocating a public harvest of wolves and those vehemently in opposition due to their moral and ethical beliefs about animals. On the other hand, common ground may be found among wolf advocates and those ranchers who fear the federal government more than they do wolves. What remains perfectly clear is that we will never know what common ground exists until we make explicit the underlying issues of this debate.

CHAPTER THREE

Wolves and the Politics of Place

This chapter examines the context of wolf policymaking and management by placing the value-based conflict discussed in chapter 1 and the symbol and surrogate issues discussed in chapter 2 in their larger political setting. I begin with background information on wolf politics and management in Minnesota, the Northern Rockies, and the Southwest and refer to these cases throughout the chapter. After a short discussion about wolves and federalism, I briefly discuss the importance of place in wolf politics. It is then analyzed in four ways. First, the historical context of the Western frontier helps us understand not only what was done to wolves but the essence of much of our natural resource policy as well. Second, urban-rural value conflict and the story of "new wolves in a new West" illustrate the importance of cultural context. Third, the political-economic context is examined by focusing on the debate over ranching and rural economies. Finally, I consider the overall management context as it is shaped by backlash from a pervasive federal presence, public opinion about wolf recovery and management, and political-institutional structure and support (or the lack thereof).

Case Background

Minnesota

In the United States, nowhere but in the great wilderness of Alaska have wolves recently done so well as in Minnesota. While the return of the wolf to Yellowstone and the West has prompted headlines and controversy throughout the nation, wolves in Minnesota have quietly, in comparison, flourished and are perhaps the most remarkable story of all. Gray wolves (popularly known as timber wolves) in Minnesota have reached a population of approximately 2,500 animals, a number unparalleled in the lower forty-eight states, and have recolonized other parts of the Lake Superior region. While the Southwest, with more public land and officially designated wilderness, agonizes over the (seemingly remote) possibility of 100 free-roaming wolves, Minnesotans somehow manage to live with twenty-five times as many.

Not everyone, of course, sees the Minnesota wolf situation as successful. Minnesota is often used as an example by both proponents and opponents of wolf recovery throughout the country. Champions of the ESA use the story of wolf recovery in Minnesota as an example of the statute's promise and fulfilled expectations. Opponents, on the other hand, see the Minnesota wolf population as one that is "out-of-control." For example, one western state Farm Bureau Federation official uses the "runaway" wolf population of Minnesota as an example of how wolves can quickly get out of control, and how difficult, if not impossible, management can become once they repopulate an area.

The habitat of Minnesota's northern reaches is an important component of the wolves' success. A landscape of thick woods and glacial lakes, this forest stretches from central Minnesota well into the Canadian provinces of Ontario and Manitoba, where roads and development become increasingly scarce to nonexistent. This ecosystem provides gray wolves important connectivity and room to roam. Taken together, various state forest and park lands, two million acres of the Superior National Forest (roughly half of which is the million-acre Boundary Waters Canoe Area Wilderness, one of the largest federally designated wilderness areas east of the Rockies), and Ontario's Quetico region to the north provide essential habitat for Minnesota's wolf population.

Minnesota's gray wolf did not escape the now familiar story of human vilification and persecution. Unlike the Ojibwe, Dakota, and other native cultures that lived with the wolf, northern settlers embarked on yet another eradication program—this time to eliminate a threat to their livestock and a competitor for wild game. The state eradication effort became official in 1849 with Minnesota's wolf bounty system and lasted through 1965. Wolves were not completely protected in the state before 1973 and were regularly taken by public hunting, trapping, and various government programs, including an aerial shooting campaign. While the federal Endangered Species Preservation Act of 1966 provided wolves protection on federal lands (Superior National Forest), not until the 1973 ESA did wolves have full legal federal and state protection. Beginning with the 1978 *Eastern Timber Wolf Recovery Plan,* wolves in Minnesota were reclassified as a threatened species and managed as such.

Gray wolves in Minnesota, Wisconsin, and Michigan have increased their numbers and expanded their range to a considerable extent since federal and state protection was first granted. Consequently, these populations would meet the recovery criteria stated in the recovery plan with a target recovery date of 2005.[1] As a result, these three states have developed state wolf management plans. In Minnesota, the plan had to be presented to the state legislature for approval, whereas in Wisconsin it did not. When these plans meet federal guarantees of continued wolf survival and success, the FWS proposes delisting the wolf from the endangered species list.

As in a number of environmental issues, the federal government (in this case the FWS) has provided these states flexibility in how they devise their management plans, insofar as they ensure the survival of the wolf at or above recovery levels. Minnesota's first Wolf Management Plan (not approved by the state legislature and discussed in greater detail in chapter 4) was drafted based on a series of public meetings followed by an eight-day stakeholders' discussion (Minnesota wolf management roundtable) that led to a "consensus" plan. The roundtable was made up of representatives from environmental, agricultural, hunting, trapping, and wolf advocacy organizations; government agencies; and other affected citizens and stakeholders. The purpose of the roundtable was not perfunctory nor merely advisory: the commissioner of Minnesota's Department of Natural Resources (MDNR) pledged to support the roundtable consensus, whatever that might be, as long as it assured the survival of the wolf, and the recommendations were biologically sound. Along with a number of other important recommendations, the roundtable agreed that wolves in Minnesota would continue to be allowed to naturally expand their range in the state, and that to assure their continued survival, the minimum statewide winter population goal would be 1,600 wolves, with no maximum goal or ceiling.[2]

The roundtable's plan was later defeated in the Minnesota legislature. After this setback, the MDNR prepared a new wolf management bill in

2000. This revised bill incorporated many roundtable recommendations but was also modified to reflect issues raised by legislators the previous year. The basis of this bill, passed by the Minnesota legislature and signed by the governor in 2000, was used by the MDNR to devise a state wolf management plan.[3] In brief, this controversial bill and the following plan created different wolf zones in the state that determine how wolves will be managed. Under the new plan, wolves will have far greater protection in the wilderness "gray wolf zone" (northeastern Minnesota) than they will in the state's "agricultural zone." Put simply, the new plan implements the roundtable agreement and its restrictions on more than 90 percent of the current gray wolf range in Minnesota but also provides far more protection and flexibility to farmers and landowners in the agricultural zone, who worry about potential wolf-caused losses.[4] As summarized by Ron Refsnider of the FWS, this bill gives wolves the benefit of the doubt in the designated wilderness zone, while in the agricultural zone it gives this benefit to landowners.

Wolf management in Minnesota has been both controversial and closely watched. As in other areas of public policy, the federal government remains the proverbial "gorilla in the closet." When delisting occurs, FWS management policies will be replaced by state ones. To ensure a successful changeover, however, the FWS will continue to monitor the status of wolves in Minnesota for five years following delisting. And most importantly, the FWS reserves the right and has the authority to immediately relist the species if Minnesota or any other state manages wolves in a manner that results in population declines below the 1992 recovery plan goals. Nearly all of the procedural requirements necessary for listing, usually a lengthy and highly uncertain process, can be temporarily bypassed in the case of an emergency (relisting) posing a significant risk to the well-being of any species.

Northern Rockies

Gray wolves were eliminated from Idaho, Montana, and Wyoming by the 1930s as official government policy. Following regulation in southwestern Canada in the 1960s, wolf populations began to expand southward. It was not until 1974, however, after the passage of the ESA, that wolves in the Northern Rockies received full legal protection in the United States. Following the finding of a small litter of wolf pups in Glacier National Park in Montana in 1986, the *Northern Rocky Mountain Wolf Re-*

covery Plan was written by the FWS. The plan was written as "a 'road map' to the recovery of the wolf in the Rocky Mountains. The primary goal is to remove the Northern Rocky Mountain wolf from the endangered and threatened species list."[5] The recovery plan identified northwestern Montana, central Idaho, and the Greater Yellowstone Area (GYA) as recovery areas and established a biological goal of more than ten breeding pairs of wolves in each of these areas for three successive years. To avoid potential human-wolf conflict, these three areas were chosen because they contained large amounts of public land, abundant wild ungulates, and less livestock than in other areas in the region (although cattle and sheep numbers are still typically twice that of wild ungulates in these areas).

In 1995 and 1996, wolves from Alberta, Canada, were caught and soft-released (held in pens before being released) in central Idaho and Yellowstone National Park. These wolves were designated under section 10(j) of the ESA as nonessential, experimental populations in order to give the FWS greater management and flexibility and a way to address state and local concerns. Wolves in northwestern Montana remained listed as endangered and thus receive a greater degree of protection than do experimental wolves in Idaho and Yellowstone. After these releases, the plan called for natural recolonization of central Idaho and Montana via wolf dispersal from Alberta and British Columbia. Since reintroduction, and despite the perpetual legal challenges that have cloaked Yellowstone wolf recovery in a blanket of uncertainty, wolves have successfully established themselves in the Northern Rockies region faster than predicted. While the idea of removing the gray wolf in the Northern Rockies from the endangered species list was thought by many to be far-fetched at best, and for good reason given the legal and cultural challenges that faced the program from the outset, the process of reclassifying wolves as threatened was quickly under way.[6] Because of the rapid success of the program, Idaho, Montana, and Wyoming are writing and debating state wolf management plans. Once wolves are removed from the endangered species list, states become responsible for their management. The political culture of the Northern Rockies region will thus become even more important in the future.

It is also important to keep in mind the symbolic importance of Yellowstone National Park in this debate. Since the park's designation in 1872, it has been a lightning rod for environmental controversy.

High-stakes issues pertaining to wilderness, fire, wildlife, land use, and ecosystem management have played out in this highly symbolic environment. It is not only the world's first national park and one of the nation's largest intact ecosystems but also an important scientific, philosophical, legal, and economic battleground.[7] Restoring the highly symbolic wolf in a such a symbolic park only raised the rhetoric and importance of the debate. From a wolf advocacy standpoint, moreover, the question of whether wolves could be successfully restored in Yellowstone was in essence asking whether wolves could be restored anywhere in the lower forty-eight states. If it cannot work here, they asked, where could it work.

Southwest

The Mexican wolf is the southernmost occurring and most endangered subspecies of gray wolf. Unlike wolves in Minnesota, the Mexican wolf was extirpated from the wild in the United States by the mid-1900s by hunting, trapping, poisoning, and digging pups from dens.[8] The Mexican wolf was listed as endangered under the ESA in 1976. The Mexican Wolf Recovery Team was formed by the FWS three years later and was responsible for preparing the *Mexican Wolf Recovery Plan*. This plan called for a captive breeding program as a way to ensure the survival of the Mexican wolf and reestablish a viable, self-sustaining population of at least 100 wolves within the Mexican wolf's historic range.[9] Consequently, 4 males and 1 pregnant female were live-captured in Durango and Chihuahua, Mexico, from 1977 to 1980. Reproduction from this "certified lineage" began shortly thereafter. With successful breeding and additional lineages added to the breeding program, by 1999 the captive population consisted of 178 individuals held in forty zoos and wildlife sanctuaries in the United States and Mexico.[10] The secretary of the interior approved the reintroduction of Mexican wolves to establish a wild population of more than 100 wolves in 1997. Under this approved plan, captive-raised Mexican wolves were released into the Apache National Forest in eastern Arizona and were allowed to recolonize the Blue Range Wolf Recovery Area (BRWRA) in east-central Arizona and west-central New Mexico. The White Sands Wolf Recovery Area in south-central New Mexico will be used as an additional recovery area if the goal of 100 wild wolves cannot be achieved on the Blue Range. Annual releases of 10 to 15 wolves, or about three family groups, will occur for three to five years in order to achieve natural reproduction and a self-sustaining population of 100 or more wild Mexican wolves.[11]

State and local concerns over wolf reintroduction culminated in the experimental designation these wolves received as found in section 10(j) of the ESA. This designation, causing so much controversy and litigation in the Yellowstone and Idaho programs, provides the FWS more flexibility, latitude, and administrative discretion in managing wolves. Wolves caught depredating livestock, for instance, can be legally removed or killed. Despite this managerial flexibility, the Mexican wolf program has experienced extensive problems with human-caused mortality.

Federalism and Wolves

Humans and wolves share a remarkable number of social similarities. Both can be quite territorial, for example. A dispersing wolf traversing through another pack's territory risks serious injury or death. While conflict between the federal bureaucracy and the states has sometimes reached an uncomfortable level, it has not yet reached this level of seriousness. Nevertheless, conflict pertaining to political and managerial territory is an important part of the wolf debate. Questions concerning the proper role of the federal government and state wildlife agencies run throughout this story. Just as wolves do not often accept interlopers into their territory, will states such as Idaho, Wyoming, Arizona, and New Mexico, all vocal critics of wolf reintroduction, successfully manage and pay for an animal they never wanted in the first place?

These cases also provide an excellent opportunity to explore environmental decentralization and wolf policy: the politics, potential, and risks of ESA delisting and resulting state wolf management. States in the Lake Superior region and Northern Rockies will help answer questions regarding environmental decentralization that have, until now, been posed largely in the abstract and hypothetical sense. These states will soon find themselves in the policy spotlight regarding the management of America's most well-known and controversial carnivore. In the context of environmental federalism—who should do what—the stakes have rarely been so high. The case is of historic importance. Whereas the return of the wolf to the American West was the wildlife story of the 1990s, state management of the wolf may prove to be the wildlife story of the future. While delisting the recently reintroduced Mexican wolf from the endangered species list is still years or decades away (if restoration is successful), state wolf management in Arizona and New Mexico is what the program is ultimately seeking. As legally codified, successful wolf restoration will inevitably result in state wolf management. The ESA is not a permanent wolf protection bill. It attempts to save a species from extinction and does so with federal involvement. Generally speaking, once a species is recovered, management returns to the states.

Federalism and intergovernmental relations are an important part of wolf politics for a number of reasons, including the following: (1) the transnational nature of wolf management, for example, wolf dispersal from Canada into the Northern Rockies and Minnesota; (2) the interstate nature of wolf management and reintroduction, for example, wolves from Canada dispersing into northern Minnesota and then recolonizing parts of northern Wisconsin and the Upper Peninsula of Michigan; and (3) the role of native tribes in managing wolf reintroduction efforts, for example, the Nez Perce Tribe cooperating with the FWS in the reintroduction program in Idaho.

A number of useful frameworks can help describe or explain state environmental policy variation. Political scientist James Lester, for example, provides four popular explanations for state responses to environmental protection based on the severity of environmental problems, state wealth, partisanship, and organizational capacity.[12] According to this framework, Minnesota, for example, is labeled as a "struggler," a state with a "strong commitment to environmental protection but with limited institutional capacities . . . willing, but often structurally unable, to implement federal environmental programs effectively" (54). Arizona and New Mexico, on the other hand, are labeled regressives: "states with weak institutional capacities as well as a limited commitment to environmental protection" (55). For these states, according to Lester, "decentralization of environmental programs will likely be a disaster. They may fail to adequately implement federal laws in this area, and they are unlikely to take independent actions" (55).

The wolf is also once again an important political symbol. If successfully and popularly managed by the states after ESA delisting, the wolf may well be used as an example by states' rights advocates and others of how competent and "green" the states have become. If, on the other hand, states make politically unacceptable decisions regarding wolf management, proponents of environmental centralization and federal authority will certainly argue that the states are still too beholden to some interests and too scientifically inept for such an important responsibility. While there are numerous examples of both devolutional success and failure, state wolf management promises to be one of the most carefully watched and scrutinized by political decision makers, the conservation community, and the general public.[13] Unlike policy regarding environmental problems that are measured in parts per billion, the wolf resonates strongly with the American populace—both friend and foe. Wolf reintroduction under the ESA in the Northern Rockies, for example, has been bitterly opposed by political representatives in Idaho, Montana, and Wyoming.[14] Many state and local officials in these western states see the recovery effort as an affront to their traditional responsibility over wildlife management and yet another symbol of federal intrusiveness. The Idaho legislature, for instance, had precluded its Department of Fish and Game from cooperating with federal officials in any manner on wolf reintroduction. The state of Wyoming also formally opposed the Yellowstone reintroduction program. Wyoming officials argued that the initial recovery plan failed to adequately address questions regarding the impact of wolves on big game and how wolves could be controlled upon leaving the designated recovery zones. Furthermore, all of these states are concerned about the economic costs associated with wolf management upon delisting, as well as the question of who will and should be responsible for livestock compensation programs. Many state wildlife officials believe that the federal government, not Defenders of Wildlife, should be responsible for compensation programs. If reintroducing wolves is in the national interest, with the national public in favor of reintroduction, they ask, then why shouldn't the national government pay for these programs?

Ironically, intergovernmental cooperation has a relevant precedent. Not so long ago both levels of government, through bounties and government initiative, effectively organized a massive wolf eradication campaign.[15] From the vantage point of the wolf, it did not matter where it found itself—it was hunted, trapped, and poisoned on private, federal, and state lands. Many western states, moreover, actively sought federal assistance in eliminating wolves because of their transboundary nature. Robert Keiter and Patrick Holscher note, "In short, the wolf eradication campaign stands as an unusual early example of harmonious federal-state cooperation in the realm of wildlife management on the public domain."[16]

U.S. wildlife policy is subject to federal, state, and local government involvement and jurisdictional complexity. States have come to play an ever increasing role in most areas of environmental and natural resource policy. The sometimes striking disparity between state environmental programs and the political context in which they operate is usually at the heart of the debate over federalism and policy decentralization.[17] Decentralists see devolution and its various incarnations as the logical next step in the contentious history of American federalism, with some states becoming more sophisticated than the federal government in various environmental policy areas (e.g., California's air quality standards). Detractors, however, point to state and regional inequities in fiscal resources, state organizational capacity and legislative design, technical expertise, partisan makeup, political pressure and interest group environment, and the outright environmental antagonism in some states as reasons why such enthusiasm for environmental devolution should be tempered or held in check by federal authority—the much maligned "gorilla in the closet."

American wildlife policy has largely followed the same path as other environmental policies regarding federal versus state and local control and prerogative—a dynamic and often adversarial relationship.[18] This relationship has often been more complicated than in other areas, in part because of the transboundary nature of wildlife, the amount of federal lands in many states, federal legislation such as the ESA, and the jurisdictional complexities originating from international treaties such as the Convention on International Trade in Endangered Species (CITES) and the Migratory Bird Treaty Act.[19] Nevertheless, given the states' reserved powers in the U.S. Constitution, common and statutory law, the amount of state-owned land, and the influence states have in decisions and policies related to economic development and habitat protection, they will continue to play an important role in managing wildlife and biodiversity in the twenty-first century.[20] American wildlife policy has been described as one of dual federalism, with the federal government and state governments dominant within their own jurisdiction.[21] Simplified, state wildlife agencies have managerial responsibility for all species within their boundaries, on state and federal lands (except national parks). Federal agencies, on the other hand, have primary responsibility for many migratory species and federally classified endangered or threatened fish and wildlife.[22]

Throughout most of American history, the states have managed wildlife in line with consumptive and utilitarian principles.[23] The federal government increased its share of responsibility for wildlife throughout the 1970s with national legislation such as the National Environmental Protection Act of 1970, the Marine Mammal Protection Act of 1972, and the Endangered Species Act of 1973. Many nonconsumptive wildlife organizations supported increased centralization of wildlife policy. Certainly, one of the primary reasons for support of federal responsibility among wildlife nongovernmental organizations (NGOs) is the way that wildlife management is funded at the state level. As discussed later, most state wildlife management agencies derive their funding from the sale of hunting and fishing licenses, thus directly or indirectly supporting a consumptive-use philosophy.

The Context of Wolf Recovery and Management

The Importance of Place in Wolf Politics

The story of wolf recovery and management will not unfold with a unified and coherent national narrative, but instead as a series of disconnected stories taking place in different regions throughout the country. The context of these states and regions will play an important role in future wolf restoration and management programs. The reintroduction of wolves in the intermountain West provides one example. Those with the most wolf experience in the Northern Rockies emphasize the importance of the cultural history and politics in the region. Bob Ream, wolf researcher and professor emeritus of wildlife biology at the University of Montana, who among other things pioneered the Wolf Ecology Project, believes that the political history of the region is critical, for "those that ignore their history are doomed to repeat it." The "War on the West" theme, says Ream, continues to be an important part of the wolf debate in the Northern Rockies.[24] In Alaska the political context is essential in understanding wolf politics in the state (see chapter 4). Special issues pertaining to federal control and land use (and the Alaska National Interest Lands Conservation Act of 1980), subsistence rights, urban-bush conflict, and the history of state wildlife management are just a few items that distinguish the politics of this place from others.

Minnesota also has a particularly interesting and well-recognized political context. The state has a reputation, one that has been noted by various observers, for clean, open, and issue-oriented politics, political independence, and policy innovation.[25] People in the state tend to have more trust in their state government and are more likely to get involved in politics than people elsewhere. While it is a relatively high-taxing state, it is also a high-spending state. These characteristics affect the content of the state's public policies as well. From passing the nation's first anti-smoking bill, to promoting the first statewide educational choice plan and charter schools, to electing a professional wrestler-turned-governor, Minnesota is either bucking or starting national trends. The state has often been the first, or among the first, to experiment in other policy areas, including pay equity and comparable worth, innovations in bureaucracy, and health care reform.

Belying its big-government liberal image, pragmatic public-private partnerships often characterize the state's problem-solving policy approach. According to one comprehensive assessment of the state's culture and politics, "Minnesota is the archetypal example of a state informed and permeated by the moralistic political subculture: both the general public and the politicians conceive of politics as a public activity centered on some notion of the public good and properly devoted to the advancement of the public interest." In this moralistic and communitarian-style culture, "there is a commitment to using community power to intervene in private activities for the good or well-being of the polity. Government is considered a positive instrument with a responsibility to promote the general welfare." They go on to suggest that from a policy standpoint, "Minnesota's bureaucracy is very professional, and its lawmakers are often interested in taking bold steps to solve public problems, both characteristics typical of a moralistic political culture."[26] The important differences between Minnesota and states in the intermountain West require little elaboration. On a number of policy fronts, Minnesotans and their political representatives are willing to use government to solve collective problems. This is not often the case in the American West, where a rhetorical "Marlboro Man" rugged individualism is still found. Solving collective policy problems in the exaggerated individualistic American West is often a challenge.

This subcultural distinction must also be qualified. The environmental policy context of northern Minnesota is quite similar to that found in the intermountain West. Minnesota is one of the few non-western states to have a large amount of federal land (5,377,366 acres) and federally designated wilderness areas (815,154 acres).[27] Together, federal lands, wilderness, a rural populace, and the importance of the timber and mining industry have given northern Minnesota a particular Western flare at times. In the struggle over the Boundary Waters Canoe Area Wilderness (BWCAW), for example, national patterns of environmental conflict emerged: urban versus rural constituencies, wise use, and the usual issues over private property, logging, mining, roads, and motors consistently reappeared.[28] However great the differences between various states and regions may be, context will continue to affect wolf policy and management throughout the country in important ways. This will become more evident when these states become responsible for wolf management. The following examines these contexts and their political implications.

Historical Context

The political subculture of the intermountain West, most often pronounced in rural areas, has affected everything from wilderness designation, to mining reform, to water law, to endangered species management. This subculture often sets the parameters of the environmental debate in the region. Western history is also reflected in the natural resource law governing the West. The 1872 Hardrock Mining Act, the 1934 Taylor Grazing Act, and the prior appropriation doctrine of water management are but a few examples of how Western political history is embodied and codified in statutory, common, and administrative natural resource law. As described by law professor Charles Wilkinson, natural resource policy is dominated by the "lords of yesterday, a battery of nineteenth-century laws, policies, and ideas that arose under wholly different social and economic conditions but that remain in effect due to inertia, powerful lobbying forces, and lack of public awareness." These lords of yesterday, says Wilkinson, "trace to one of the extraordinary eras in all of history, the American westward movement of the nineteenth century."[29] The story of wolves, and western natural resource law in general, is better understood in this larger historical context.

The historic importance of manifest destiny and a frontier ethos are commonly believed to have encouraged Western environmental values that were domineering and utilitarian. Given the immensity and sometimes hostile nature of the western terrain, settlers often interpreted the landscape as one to dominate. According to environmental historian Roderick Nash,

> Wilderness not only frustrated the pioneers physically but also acquired a significance as a dark and sinister symbol. They shared the long Western tradition of imagining wild country as a moral vacuum, a cursed and chaotic wasteland. As a consequence, frontiersmen acutely sensed that they battled wild country not only for personal survival but in the name of nation, race, and God. Civilizing the New World meant enlightening darkness, ordering chaos, and changing evil into good. In the morality play of Westward expansion, wilderness was the villain, and the pioneer, as hero, relished its destruction. The transformation of a wilderness into civilization was the reward for his sacrifices, the definition of his achievement, and the source of his pride.[30]

The relationship between this frontier movement, the wolf, and other wildlife is well known. Wolves, grizzlies, mountain lions, and other predators were systematically eliminated from the western landscape in the most brutal fashion. As bison and native ungulates were slaughtered by the millions to make room for domestic cattle, wolves were forced to change their diet and did so quite successfully. And as cattle losses mounted, so did the highly symbolic opposition to the wolf. This war on the wolf took a toll on all wildlife, due in part to the common use of poison as a control method. As Stanley Paul Young, FWS biologist and predator-control expert, noted in 1946, "A sort of unwritten range law was adopted and adhered to, whereby no range man, when riding, would knowingly pass by a carcass of any kind without inserting in it a goodly dose of strychnine sulphate, in the hope of eventually killing one more wolf." Young estimated that as a result of action by the government and "wolfers" throughout the country, over 24,000 gray and red wolves were taken between 1915 and 1941.[31]

The history of this slaughter still affects the debate over wolf recovery and the methods by which wolves are managed. According to one leader of a prominent hunting-based conservation organization in the Northern Rockies, there is a "societal guilt factor" related to wolves, grizzlies, and bison: people understand what was done to these animals in the past and want to make sure that such harm does not happen again. He believes that this factor will become even more evident once the debate shifts from reintroduction issues to the public hunting and trapping of wolves.

It is worthwhile to keep in mind the historical and cultural context in which the slaughter of wildlife took place not only to better understand and explain the dark side of manifest destiny but also to provide a historical grounding for political change. If we are to reevaluate our natural resource and wildlife policies, we must also understand why they were written as they were in the first place. Given the cultural values and national objectives of frontier America—settle and develop the arid West—the war on the wolf, along with other management practices and resource subsidies, can be more easily understood.

Placing wolves within their frontier context is relatively easy. Harder, however, is discerning what has changed since historian Frederick Jackson Turner's famous pronouncement declaring the end of America's frontier. University of Utah natural resource law professor Robert Keiter observes that the controversies engulfing the greater Yellowstone region are now taking place in a new context:

> Modern ecological knowledge has changed the terms of the debate, auguring a fundamental reorientation in public land management policy. Indeed, a revised preservationist ethic is displacing the ethic of consumption that has historically determined public lands management policy, and it is now rising to a dominant position on the Greater Yellowstone public domain. This revised preservationist ethic is based on the principle of preserving ecological components and processes on a system-wide or ecosystem scale.[32]

Just as historical context helps answer the question of why the war on the wolf was waged in the first place, context also sheds valuable light on why wolves are now being restored in the region. Certainly a lot has changed since the last wolf was trapped in Yellowstone in 1926. There is a new scientific understanding of the important role that wolves and other predators play in ecosystems. There is a new environmental paradigm that while perhaps not dominant, does at least challenge old ways of thinking and doing things. And finally, the challenge of manifest destiny and how to develop the arid West has been replaced with an even more daunting challenge of how to accommodate more people wanting more things.

Cultural Context

URBAN-RURAL VALUE CONFLICT

An important theme running throughout wolf politics is the difference between urban and rural perspectives toward wolves, wildlife, and the natural world. Of course, it is important not to generalize and stereotype. Urban people are not all "pro-wolf," and rural people are not necessarily "anti-predator." Nevertheless, my interviews often found serious differences in how urban and rural residents think about wolves and the human-nature relationship. Many rural residents talked of out-of-touch urban residents who for some reason separate themselves from the natural world. Certainly many of these rural people had an intimate connection with the land and its wildlife and wanted decision makers to use this local knowledge base. Many also voiced resentment toward urban residents for thrusting wolves on them and their communities. One native elder in Alaska, for example, told me of his wish to drop darted wolves from Alaska into New York City. It is only then, he says, that they will truly know what it is like to live with this animal.

Someone living in a small bush community in interior Alaska or a small ranching community in western Montana is likely to see wolves and other predators in a different light compared to someone living in Anchorage or the Twin Cities. In short, urban-rural value conflict is an important part of this story. Stakeholders are often speaking a different language and doing so in very different worlds. Furthermore, the process by which this conflict has been dealt with in the past, from the courtroom to the ballot box, simply encourages communication breakdown.

NEW WOLVES IN THE NEW WEST

The intermountain West is changing. Like an untamed river meeting the concrete of a dam for the first time, the West is filling up. And while dams are emblematic to environmentalists of everything that is wrong with the Old West, the wolf is often seen by ranchers and other Old Westerners as a symbol of everything that has gone awry in the New West. This "New West" poses a challenge to old ways of doing business, and some ranchers interpret the wolf as being its most loathsome mascot. According to the perceptive Renee Askins, who worked for Yellowstone reintroduction,

The wolf is an ideal target: It is tangible, it is blamable, and it is real. Or is it? When ranchers talk about wolves they say, "you know, it's not the wolves we're worried about, it's what the wolves represent; it's not what they'll do, it's what they mean." Wolves mean changes. Wolves mean challenges to the old ways of doing things. Wolves mean loss of control. Wolves aren't the cause of the changes occurring in the West any more than the rooster's crow is the cause of the sun's rising, but they have become the means by which ranchers can voice their concern about what's happening around them.[33]

Although compromises and accommodations were made, wolf reintroduction in the Northern Rockies can be seen as a historic blow to the entrenched ranching establishment. The days of closed networks, iron triangles, and captured agencies, while certainly not dead, are being challenged by powerful forces operating in a quickly changing political context.

The New West and its regional population change have several implications for wolves and wildlife management in general. A number of new values, interests, and constituencies are challenging the traditional consumptive-oriented wildlife management paradigm. Despite the popular image of the rural American West held among many non-westerners, most of the region's residents live in an urban setting. In Colorado, for example, over 80 percent of the state's population resides in urban locations.[34] Urbanization is important to wildlife management because urban residents often possess different values and attitudes toward wildlife than those citizens residing in more rural areas. One study of Colorado found that urban (Front Range) residents were more likely to possess strong value orientations toward wildlife rights and were least likely to have strong positive value orientations toward wildlife use and hunting.[35] The authors conclude that as long as these differences hold, "continuing urbanization in the New West is likely to be linked with increased pressure for managers to attend to these values."[36]

There is little doubt about how much Western culture and economy have been transformed in the past few decades, and the greater Yellowstone and Northern Rockies region has witnessed some of the most sweeping changes. Resource industries like timber, mining, agriculture, and ranching are now joined by new sources of growth spurred by recreation, telecommuters, retirees, and new technology and information-based industries.[37] Of course, not everything in this New West bodes well for wolves and wildlife. Population growth will ultimately determine the fate of wolves and humans, and nowhere in the United States is the pressure of population growth being felt more than in the intermountain West. Poorly planned growth and decentralized development pose one of the greatest threats to wolves, carnivores, and biodiversity in general. While ranchers have received their share of blame for the demise of the nation's predators, a more insidious threat comes from the cumulative impact of one more golf course, ski resort, Wal-Mart, and developed parcel replete with a new "starter castle." Such threats to wolves and all wildlife prompt the question: Will history repeat itself? Will wolves be returned to the Southern Rockies, for instance, only to be forced out in the future—this time not due to poisons or snares but instead by strip malls and second-home development?

Some environmentalists and wolf advocates are thus caught in an important dilemma: although they have challenged ranchers and their perceived stranglehold on government for decades, while at the same time rolling their collective eyes whenever the "custom and culture" retort is made, many now believe that preserving ranch land and ranching communities is essential if wolves and other wildlife are to make it in the long run. In other words, ranching means open space, and open space means habitat for wolves and wildlife.

Sprawl, or low-density development, affects wolves in a number of ways. It leads to degraded and fragmented habitat or the outright loss of habitat, blocks traditional wildlife migration routes, increases pollution, facilitates the spread of noxious weeds, alters important ecological processes such as fire and hydrologic cycles, and increases the chances of human-wildlife conflict and thus human-caused mortality. From a legal standpoint, moreover, the ESA requires that the listing and delisting process determine future threats to species and their habitat; thus, all future discussion regarding delisting should seriously consider these habitat threats and development trends.

The Greater Yellowstone Ecosystem (GYE) provides a classic example of the threats posed to wolves and other wildlife by increased residential growth and development. Although the GYE is one of the largest and most intact ecosystems left in the United States, the twenty counties within the GYE are among the fastest growing in the nation.[38] The Sierra Club Grizzly Bear Ecosystems Project (working to protect and restore wild grizzly populations and their habitat in the lower forty-eight states and Canada), for instance, has found that there has been unprecedented growth within this ecosystem, and that more future development has already been approved. The project has also found that this development is occurring most in rural county areas rather than clustering near existing cities, and that much of it appears to be concentrating in areas of critical wildlife habitat, like river corridors. The project suggests that due to these trends, the goal of bear recovery may be difficult to attain.[39]

Development occurring on private lands presents one of the greatest challenges to wolf habitat protection. While private lands make up just 18 percent of the 18 million core acres of the GYE, they are vitally important to wildlife and the health of the larger ecosystem. Wolves and humans are often attracted to the same type of habitat, like valley bottoms, big basins, and river areas. Both wintering elk and humans are attracted to low-lying south-facing slopes, for example. These areas, however, are often already developed or will soon be so in the near future. Therefore, focusing solely on national forests, wilderness areas, and parks for wildlife survival misses an important part of the picture. Wildlife ecologist Richard Knight summarizes the ramifications of this public lands focus: "While we have been preoccupied with struggles to protect public lands from never-ending assaults, an alarming trend has occurred, largely unnoticed, on the 'back forty': we are losing private lands to commercial and residential development at rates seldom equaled in history."[40] Organizations such as the Greater Yellowstone Coalition similarly believe that residential growth and development are one of the most serious problems facing the GYE. Many believe that the Coalition and other environmental groups will thus have to carefully weigh what they perceive to be the greater threat to wolves and wildlife—ranching or development—or at least find a tenable third way.

It is also possible to reject having to make such a choice. Many people believe that framing the problem this way is dubious and not supported by the facts.[41] It is a case, they say, of environmentalists buying into the ranching industry's problem definition of "cows or condos"; that is, if you want to protect open space and wildlife habitat, you must also protect ranching. But many disagree with this assessment, arguing among other things that only small parcels of private land are at risk, not the massive amount of publicly owned acreage that is currently being degraded and managed for maximum beef production, not wildlife habitat.

A sense of an environmental hypocrisy is also evident in this New West. What, for example, are we to predict about future wolf recovery in Washington State given the area's tremendous growth and development? Another projected twenty-nine Tacoma-sized cities in fifty years does not bode well. What about the staggering development along Colorado's Front Range and the more threatening forms of subdividing and ranchette development in its more rural areas? This New West may be less extractive, but the pressures placed on wildlife will still be as severe, if not more so. Furthermore, the new players in the New West— industrial recreation, for instance—are just as potentially harmful to wildlife and its habitat as are other users of the land. Finally, what are we to make of those New Westerners who have long chided rural "anti-environmental" residents for being backward-looking and reactionary but are the first to bitterly complain of Canada geese ruining their manicured golf courses and deer and elk eating their perennials?

Political-Economic Context

As discussed in chapter 2, the debate over wolf recovery in the intermountain West is inextricably tied to political interpretations of the past, present, and future of rural economies. For wolf proponents examining various regional economic reports and indicators, wolves represent a change but not a challenge to the way most people in the region make their living. For opponents, however, wolves represent yet one more nail in the coffin, symbolizing what little regard urban residents have for the people and communities that provide them their lumber, beef, and fleece jackets. Put simply, while many urban citizens in the region see the return of wolves as an asset, many rural citizens and ranchers see them as a real and symbolic threat to rural communities and their economic viability.

The ranching culture of the rural intermountain West still provides the most straightforward and useful explanation of why settlers showed such an outright antipathy to predators. While other cultural factors are not to be dismissed, the Western war on the wolf sometimes boils down to a rather simple explanation: wild ungulates were killed to make room for cattle, wolves ended up killing this livestock, ranchers killed wolves. As the livestock industry grew, so did the scale and ferocity of the war on wolves. Self-interest, and some cases of pure economic self-preservation, still serves as a useful explanation of why this war was waged, and on whose behalf.[42] The cattle culture of the West continues to be the most powerful obstacle to wolf recovery.

Economic analyses are often used as political currency in this debate. For environmental interests, it is important to distinguish between how the Western economy is often popularly portrayed and politically framed, and what some believe is the current economic reality. Although some advocates of Western custom and culture view the "environmental juggernaut" in the region as the cause of needless unemployment and economic instability, evidence pointing to the contrary is also often used in the political debate. Studies done at the national level, for instance, show environmental regulations have not resulted in any significant overall job losses.[43] In fact, the amount of effort taken by a state to protect the environment through government regulations is positively correlated with a state's gross product, total employment, and labor productivity.[44]

Despite the emergence of a new, more diversified regional economy, coupled with the decline of the natural resource industry, the belief that extractive industry is the economic essence of the West is still pervasive. According to University of Montana economist Thomas Michael Power, often cited by the environmental community, this "view through the rearview mirror" poses a dangerous threat to the economic health of local communities.[45] Power maintains that "folk economics"—the belief that the extraction and processing of natural resources are the heart of the economic system—is a powerful but misleading myth that should not dictate current or future economic policy in the region. This economic "view through the rearview mirror" is an important factor in the greater Yellowstone area as well. According to Power, a community's perception of its local economy tends to be tied to past patterns of economic activity rather than current economic reality. In many ways, says Power, individuals, businesses, and organizations in the area collectively create a shared community vision of what the population "does for a living."[46] This view is important because the perceived importance of resource-based industry in the area often leads these communities to assume that ecological protection and economic well-being are incompatible goals. Analyzing federal data on income and employment at the county-level, Power shows that the primary economic activity tied to greater Yellowstone is recreation-based, not resource-based industries, and that the natural amenities of the area attract both permanent residents and temporary visitors. Furthermore, he concludes that "protecting the integrity of the Greater Yellowstone Ecosystem is not only not in conflict with local economic well-being but is a crucial element in any economic development strategy for the region."[47]

The debate over the ESA is also affected by these perceptions of the economy, held by those inside and outside of the region. Critics often argue that the ESA—and the wolf as its most prominent symbol—is impeding state economic growth and prosperity. Certainly, anecdotal evidence abounds, from the northern spotted owl imbroglio to the more recent pygmy owl case in the Southwest. But focused studies on the ESA and the economy show something else. Stephen Meyer of MIT, for example, examined the impact of endangered species listings on state economic development for the period 1975–90.[48] Data show not only that such listings have not depressed state economic development activity, as measured by growth in construction employment and gross state product, but that in fact the converse is true.

Whatever the merits of each case, it is important is to see wolves as once again part of a larger and more inclusive political debate. Those opposing wolf recovery often do so on economic grounds: wolves are a threat to livestock and resource-based industry and are therefore a threat to rural communities—the essence of the West. Many wolf advocates, on the other hand, understand that it is not enough to publicize research showing what little livestock depredation is likely to occur from recovered wolf populations. They believe that it is also necessary to challenge what they see as an antiquated conception of the Western economy. Appropriating various economic analyses, they hope to convince decision makers and the public that not only will wolves present minimal risk to the rural Western economy, but that this economy is no longer the real economic engine of the region.

This economic context is different in other places, however. Unlike mining in the intermountain West, the iron ore industry is an important part of the northern Minnesota economy and wolf range. In northeastern Minnesota, for instance, recent economic analysis shows that despite efforts to diversify, the region's economy continues to be deeply affected by the taconite mining industry.[49] While the livestock industry in Minnesota is not as large or politically powerful as that found in the West, one does exist and is inevitably affected by wolf depredation. Livestock depredation in western states has attracted national attention and become an important part of the crusade against wolf reintroduction in parts of the region. What is interesting, however, is that livestock depredation in Minnesota occurs, due to the number of wolves in the state, more frequently.[50] What is perhaps most surprising about such contrasts are not the numbers themselves but the attention relatively smaller conflicts have received in the western states. Support for wolves in Minnesota is not due to the absence of livestock, farms, and personal losses. Human-wolf conflict happens in this state on a larger scale than in the West. But the importance of this larger regional political economy cannot be emphasized enough: wolves do not eat iron ore, and their habitat needs do not pose a threat to the industry. Moreover, some observers believe that the area's significant timber industry has little reason to be overly concerned given the fact that logging can create favorable deer habitat, which is also good for wolves.

It is also important to note that many ranches in the West operate differently than do ranches and farms in Minnesota and the upper Midwest. Because of rainfall, vegetation, and other factors, ranching on public lands in the West often means "turning them loose in the spring and rounding them up in the fall." Farmers in northern Minnesota, on the other hand, can more easily monitor their animals and are grazing them almost exclusively on private land. This important difference is cited by some western ranchers as a reason why a Minnesota comparison is not always useful or fair. As noted earlier, the Minnesota case is often used by wolf advocates as a touchstone for other wolf recovery and management programs—"they can do it there, so we can do it here." But western ranchers continue to point out this important difference of scale and management style in citing reasons why it is not so simple.

More similar to that of the Northern Rockies region, the rural economy of the Blue Range Wolf Recovery Area (BRWRA) in the Southwest is much more dependent on the livestock industry. The BRWRA supports an estimated 57,000 deer, 16,000 elk, and 82,600 head of cattle.[51] There is perhaps no other statistic that is more important than this one to the future of the Mexican wolf. Although many historical accounts of livestock depredation in the Southwest are now suspect, potential livestock depredation by wolves remains the most serious political impediment to successful reintroduction and management. Once again illustrating the symbolic importance of wolves, Mexican wolf reintroduction has often been as much about the perceived power, privilege, and future of the livestock industry as it has been about documented wolf behavior.

The Southwest wolf debate is best seen in this larger political-economic context. Wolves are but the latest endangered or threatened species forcing southwesterners to address the public lands ranching issue. An ad placed by the Center for Biological Diversity in the *New York Times* condemning the livestock industry's war on wolves is illustrative: "The livestock industry has waged a war against wildlife for over a century. It slaughtered thousands of wolves, bears, mountain lions, jaguars, deer, antelope, and beaver. . . . unwilling to share even a tiny portion of America's vast public lands, it sued to put the wolves back in cages."[52]

Few environmentalists hesitate when asked to describe the greatest challenge posed to Mexican wolf recovery. The Center for Biological Diversity sees it in simple terms: the ranching industry dominates the environmental politics of the Southwest. According to the Center, "When compared with other occupations, the number of ranchers in Arizona is miniscule: less than .1% of Arizona's 4.7 million residents are ranchers. Yet they are disproportionately represented in politics."[53] They go on to list the impressive number of legislators who are ranchers in the region, while also discussing their past environmental voting records. The Southwest's ranching industry, they say, is a very powerful local elite who dictate the states' politics and have a chain of political control extending all the way to Washington. This elite's power is manifest in state-based institutions like predator control districts, water districts, and, most of all, in politically manipulated game and fish commissions. Privilege is also evident, they say, in the lush subsidies and "elaborate support system our states and nation provide to the ranching industry." According to the Center, while more than 60 million acres of federal and state lands are currently grazed by cattle in Arizona and New Mexico, there are surprisingly few ranchers in the region, and even fewer who depend on cattle-ranching income. Nevertheless, says the Center, this industry enjoys numerous tax breaks and subsidies, from below-market public lands ranching fees (AUMs) to federally administered predator control programs. The Center, as do other environmental organizations in the region, believes that this political power is so entrenched that litigation based on sound science is the only way to counter it, and is also the most effective way of getting cows off public lands.

It is not only the political power of ranchers that unsettles some environmentalists, it is also their behavior and animal husbandry practices. According to outspoken critic George Wuerthner, there are no problem wolves, just problem ranchers. Ranchers, he says, have externalized what should be the cost of doing business on the public domain—protecting one's livestock by reducing opportunities for predation. Wuerthner believes that it is no longer acceptable to leave livestock unattended for weeks at a time without direct supervision. Campers are not allowed to leave out picnic baskets to tempt bears, he says, so why should ranchers be able to leave their four-legged picnic baskets out to tempt wolves. According to Wuerthner, "Trying to restore wolves to the West without changing the basic way ranchers operate or even removing cows from more of the public lands is analogous to trying to restore salmon without talking about protecting riparian areas, leaving tree buffers along streams, or removing dams. We are treating the symptoms rather than the causes of the problem."[54]

Some in the Southwest's ranching industry, on the other hand, see the return of wolves as yet another potentially devastating threat to their livelihoods, customs, and culture. An erratic beef market was a difficulty, but at least ranchers' cattle were relatively safe from depredation. The return of the wolf signifies to many rural ranchers yet another affront by an all-too-removed and unsympathetic federal government. Many ranchers also argue that the paper protections they are granted under the ESA's experimental designation are administratively cumbersome and unrealistic. Given the vast amount of private and public land that is grazed in the arid Southwest, many ranchers harbor little hope that they will catch wolves in the act of depredating their livelihoods and thus be able to harass or kill the predator. And because wolves leave little evidence behind when they do kill livestock, many ranchers dislike the sort of proof that is required to be compensated.

Most disconcerting to some, in both its symbolism and substance, is the absence of a government-controlled method for compensating ranchers who lose livestock. Some argue that without a government-run compensation program in place (as there is in Minnesota), the reintroduction effort does not pass constitutional muster under the Fifth Amendment's just compensation principle.[55] The lack of a federally implemented compensation program is due to the legal complexity of operating on the public domain. In other words, the FWS believes that not providing compensation is within its constitutional boundaries. Defenders of Wildlife also continues to administer its privately run compensation program. Either way, many ranchers are distrustful of a federal

agency proclaiming that livestock depredation will be minimal but re-
fusing to provide compensation for supposed minimal losses.

Management Context

PUBLIC OPINION AND POLITICAL SUPPORT

Over the course of a century, wolves have swung like a pendulum from
their place as sinister symbols of evil incarnate to that, for some, of being a spiritual and ecological necessity. This swing is part of a larger
shift in American environmental values and opinions.[56] As Aldo Leopold's
poignant description of his transformation in *A Sand County Almanac*
shows, personal values toward wilderness and wildlife—of thinking like
a mountain—can change. Not surprisingly, so too can new generations
reassess their environmental values and attitudes. Public opinion played
a role in the violent history of the wolf, and it is now playing a role in its
return. Issue intensity is also a critical factor when assessing public opinion toward wolf recovery. According to one veteran wolf manager in
the Northern Rockies, wolf support is a mile wide and an inch deep,
while opposition is one hundred yards wide but a mile deep.

While the founders of the republic were skeptical of the "ticklish nature" of the public's opinion, there remains an often positive relationship between public opinion and public policy at different levels and
branches of government. In other words, there is often "belief congru-
ence" between public opinion and public policy.[57] (Cases of important
incongruence also exist, of course.) When American policy preferences
shift, it is more likely than not that changes in policy will follow. Wolf
restoration should therefore be seen, at least to some degree, as the broad
enactment of America's changing values toward wolves and wildlife.
Furthermore, as more Americans find themselves in urban settings,
more crowded and with less open space, wilderness and its most prominent symbol gain additional significance and symbolic value.

Public opinion surveys about various wolf management and reintroduction programs illustrate these changing and often complex environmental values, beliefs, and attitudes. In Minnesota, for example, numerous studies by Stephen Kellert show that state residents (as do human
cultures in general) possess a wide range of values toward wolves, and
these values are shaped by an equally complex set of variables ranging
from demographics, urban-rural residency, age, income, education, and

others.[58] Drawing on twenty years of survey research, Kellert maintains that contemporary attitudes "remain at the cusp of a transition in the perception of wolves, wildlife, and wilderness. Many now view wolves as innocent victims of a society that lost its bearings and place in nature; [while] others continue to hold antagonistic values toward this animal and other large predators."[59]

Effective management becomes difficult with a lack of public support, especially in a case that is this symbolic and volatile. Differences of opinion often place wildlife managers in a difficult position. Kellert's work, for example, shows that Minnesotans possess a wide range of values, beliefs, and attitudes toward wolves and wolf management.[60] Within Minnesota, these differences are usually analyzed by dividing the state into its major metropolitan area (Twin Cities and surrounding suburbs), the northern public, and the state's farmers. When examined as a whole, however, Minnesota residents are quite supportive of wolves. After extensive longitudinal surveying, Kellert finds that "the Minnesota public clearly values wolves, viewing this animal as ecologically important, scientifically fascinating, aesthetically attractive, recreationally appealing, and significant for future generations. Only a small minority fear and dislike wolves, or believe Minnesota would be a more desirable state without this predator, or object to living within relative proximity to this animal."[61]

Kellert's work also shows that Minnesotans are ready for state wolf management. Most respondents (over 70 percent of northern residents, non-northern residents, and the farming public) favor the state rather than the federal government assuming primary responsibility for managing the wolf in Minnesota.[62] A substantial majority, moreover, expressed confidence in the ability of the Minnesota Department of Natural Resources (MDNR) to manage the wolf effectively.[63]

Public opinion regarding Mexican wolf reintroduction follows similar patterns. Despite state political rhetoric to the contrary, the majority of Arizona and New Mexico residents generally support wolf reintroduction in the Southwest. There is widespread support as well as a very vocal minority opposing reintroduction. Pockets of anti-wolf attitudes are often very localized. While a large number of rural residents living in proximity to the wolf recovery zone are supportive of restoration efforts, stronger support is often found among urban residents. There is a NIMBY (not in my backyard) dimension to wolf reintroduction efforts (*no wolves in my backyard).* One survey of Greenlee County, Arizona (within the wolf reintroduction area), for instance, found that 58 percent of respondents oppose while 22 percent support wolf reintroduction.[64] Most respondents in this area cited ranching and concern for livestock safety as a reason for their opposition. A survey commissioned by the League of Women Voters of New Mexico shows similar urban-rural variation.[65] This survey found that residents of New Mexico statewide were more supportive (62 percent) and less opposed than regional residents (50 percent supporting) toward reintroducing wolves into the Blue Range recovery area. Twenty-two percent of statewide residents and 30 percent of regional residents opposed reintroduction into Arizona. Regarding White Sands reintroduction, 70 percent of statewide residents and 60 percent of regional residents were supportive. Before the release of wolves, a cross section of Arizona residents were in favor of reintroduction.[66] This survey of 3,221 Arizonans revealed that licensed hunters (71.5 percent), Defenders of Wildlife members (92.7 percent), rural residents (63.3 percent), metropolitan residents (75.7 percent), and employees of the Arizona Game and Fish Department (80.6 percent) either "strongly like" or "like" the idea of having Mexican wolves in the wild in Arizona. More recent polling in New Mexico shows that close to three-quarters of New Mexico residents agreed with the following statement: "Although I may never see a Mexican wolf in the wild, it is important to know they exist in New Mexico."[67] Of little surprise, the major concern about wolf reintroduction was the potential danger to livestock.

The divide between supportive public opinion regarding wolf reintroduction, on the one hand, and formal political opposition, on the other, presents a troublesome dilemma for some wildlife managers. When asked what he sees as the major obstacles and threats regarding successful wolf recovery in the Southwest, wildlife biologist David Parsons, former leader of the Mexican wolf program, responded by pointing to this democratic divide. He believes that there is a disproportionate influence exerted by livestock interests and private-rights and anti-government organizations in the political process, despite polls showing them to be in the minority regarding wolf recovery. He believes that the political environment of the Southwest is very negative to the idea of wolf recovery. As a result, Parsons believes "that the most important factor influencing the success of wolf recovery programs is strongly demonstrated grass-roots citizen and NGO support with poll results that verify the level of support." Under these conditions, says Parsons, "few politicians (if any) will openly support or facilitate wolf recovery, but neither will they seriously attempt to undermine recovery efforts."

Parsons is correct in emphasizing the importance of political and institutional support for successful wolf management. Despite widespread public support, key Arizona and New Mexico state and national political representatives and other decision makers opposed Mexican wolf recovery, including the New Mexico Game and Fish Commission, the Director of the New Mexico Department of Game and Fish, and others.[68] Arizona's Game and Fish Commission (ADFG) has threatened to pull the state's wildlife agency out of Mexican wolf recovery unless a number of specific requests are met by the FWS. These include meetings being held in small communities in the recovery area, including hotbeds of anti-wolf sentiment, and the FWS becoming fully responsible for all reintroduction costs related to litigation and other claims against ADFG, the commission, and the state of Arizona.[69] Because wolf restoration programs are ultimately working toward ESA delisting and state wolf management, this state political and administrative opposition raises serious questions regarding possible state responsibilities for future wolf management.

While the wolf debate in Minnesota has been in part over how many wolves should exist in the state before an active wolf control program is instituted, and in what areas wolves are best maintained (wilderness versus agricultural zones), many political and administrative decision makers in the Southwest see no reason for any wolves, however small that population may be. This divide—state public opinion toward wolf recovery versus state political and administrative opposition—is quite apparent in the Southwest. While there are voices for increased wolf control in Minnesota, especially in the more rural and northern parts of the state, there is generally no widespread or mainstream support for eliminating the state's wolf population. Minnesota's DNR appears to recognize such general support, as well as the legitimate concerns over safety and livestock depredation in rural Minnesota, and proclaims itself eager to manage this state's resilient wolf population.

While it may seem premature, given the struggle to have any wolves in the Southwest, it is important to ask what happens if this viable population objective is achieved and these two states are asked to take control of wolf management. The contrast between Minnesota and Arizona and New Mexico is again instructive. Minnesota's DNR declares itself "committed to ensuring the long-term survival of the wolf in Minnesota, and also to resolving conflicts between wolves and humans."[70] In contrast, the New Mexico Department of Game and Fish (NMDGF) opposed Mexican wolf restoration on both biological and political grounds, declaring the lack of any suitable wolf release sites and the scarcity of support by local residents in potential release sites.[71]

The importance of state wildlife commissions, from who sits on them to what authority they have, will also become more evident with state wolf management. While the Game and Fish Departments of Arizona and New Mexico administer the wildlife laws of their states, control of these departments is vested in game and fish commissions. Commission members are appointed by the governor, with various criteria having to be met. In New Mexico, for example, the commission is comprised of seven members appointed by the governor with senate approval to serve four-year terms. No more than four of these members are to be from the same political party, five specified state districts must be represented, and two members are to be appointed at-large. The commission is empowered to do such things as establishing open and closed seasons for the taking of game, setting bag limits, and prescribing the manner, methods, and devices that can be used in killing game.[72]

Wildlife commissions in both Arizona and New Mexico are often pointed to as a major obstacle to successful wolf recovery. David Parsons, for instance, candidly asserts that "my biggest fear is that wolf management by the states will be dictated by political decisions imposed by the governor through the power of the game commissions, [and] science-based management recommendations and citizen interests will have little bearing on ultimate management programs and decisions." He believes that the Southwest's wildlife agencies are subject to intense political oversight and political influence and that "state agency directors are largely powerless pawns, and few decisions are based on sound science." Other wolf advocates I spoke with concur with Parson's assessment and believe that these commissions must become more balanced in the future, representing a broader spectrum of values, interests, and perspectives.

State wildlife commissions date to the 1930s, when the nation's sport hunters fought and won protection for wildlife from widespread market hunting. As a way to institutionalize this protection, sport hunters were placed on commissions that were to adopt and enforce state wildlife laws. Years later, state wildlife commissions continue to be dominated by hunters, trappers, and other consumptive users of wildlife. As I will discuss in greater detail in chapter 4, many interests now believe that state wildlife commissions are antiquated, represent minority interests, and undermine the principle of the public interest in wildlife.

Among the most vocal critics of this type of decision making is the Humane Society of the United States (HSUS), an important player in the national wolf policy debate. According to the HSUS, although more than 90 percent of the public does not hunt, governors continue to appoint hunters, trappers, and other consumptive users of wildlife to fill commission openings. Many of these commissioners, they say, also have potential conflicts of interest, representing the public's interest in wildlife as well as their own, as hunting guides, commercial fishers, taxidermists, resort owners, and so on. The system for state wildlife funding and determining what interests are represented on state wildlife commissions is unsurprising and self-perpetuating, says the HSUS: "So while the financial contribution of hunters is hardly voluntary, it is the public relations engine behind a circular system designed to ensure its perpetuation. The more licenses hunters buy, the more influence they have over wildlife agencies and wildlife management." The HSUS demands that the system be changed so that more wildlife and the greater public can benefit. Non-hunters, says the HSUS, "must demand places at the table which reflect their representation in society."[73]

The structure and funding of state wildlife management are one reason why the HSUS is opposed to state wolf management in Minnesota. In fighting against the delisting of Minnesota's wolves, the HSUS contends that "unfortunately for the wolf, state departments of natural resources and state legislatures have not changed their attitudes toward wolves since 1973 [and] this makes the prospect of returning management of wolves to the states chilling."[74] Many wolf and wildlife advocates throughout the country are fearful of the same thing: what they see as unbalanced hunting-oriented state wildlife commissions requiring that wolves, like other predators, be managed and controlled for special hunting and trapping interests.

INSTITUTIONAL CAPACITY

An important question is whether a state has the institutional and bureaucratic capacity to effectively manage a resource or policy area. The issue is not only maintaining appropriate funding levels but also where these funds come from and where they are directed. A large percentage of funding for state wildlife management comes directly from the sale of hunting and fishing licenses, or indirectly from federal assistance funds generated from excise taxes on fishing and hunting equipment. Consequently, state wildlife agencies most often direct their resources and energies toward the management of game species. One study, for example, shows that state expenditures for nongame species amount to roughly 3 percent of the amount spent on game species.[75] The source of funding creates a "tremendous barrier to a redirection of state programs toward a more comprehensive management approach."[76] The move toward environmental decentralization in general, and in state wolf and nongame management in particular, raises important questions regarding the way in which these agencies are funded: Given their sources of funding, can states that want the responsibility of managing wolves, and biodiversity in general, do so effectively? And what should be expected in those states that initially opposed wolf restoration but will soon be asked to manage these wolves?

Some critics of the dominant wildlife management paradigm believe that fish and wildlife programs funded more via general tax revenues (as in Missouri, for instance) than through the more common game and fish funds tend to have different and more progressive attitudes about wildlife management. In a system with a broader base of funding, the general public not only might have more of a voice in wildlife decision making but would also pay for the costs associated with game and nongame management. The consumptive-oriented management paradigm will certainly affect future wolf political conflict as well. Aggressive wolf management in Alaska, for example, is advocated in the context of maintaining large moose and caribou numbers. But critics believe that these game populations need enhancing, in part, because of over-hunting allowed by the state's wildlife agency. Environmental writer Ted Williams summarizes: "Wolves do not purchase hunting licenses, and most state wildlife managers draw their pay from revenue derived from sale of hunting, fishing, and trapping licenses. That, in brief, is what is wrong with wildlife management in America, why in most cases it really is sportsman management."[77]

In answering these questions, important differences between Minnesota and Arizona and New Mexico should be noted. In Minnesota, 22.8

percent of the DNR's operating budget comes from its game and fish fund (anglers and hunters, for example).[78] Minnesota relies more heavily on state taxes (49 percent) and other types of natural resource funds, user fees, lottery proceeds, and nongame licenses and permits than Arizona and New Mexico do. The department does, however, face a number of fiscal constraints and challenges. Although the number of outdoor recreationists in the state has grown, the department has struggled to sufficiently fund the bare minimum number of officials and field stations required to effectively manage the state's natural resources and wildlife. Several of the state's conservation officer field stations have been vacant due to a lack of funding. Thus, while the agency awaits its new wolf responsibilities, it has also made these financial constraints a political issue and has asked the state to modestly increase its hunting and fishing license fees. The lack of enforcement personnel in the field is especially alarming. Says Captain Craig Backer, who manages the northern third of the state, "We have more people than ever out there using the resource, doing more things. But there are fewer of us trying to see that the laws are upheld and the resource is protected."[79] Before recent staff reductions, Minnesota ranked forty-fifth among the states in the ratio of conservation officers to the number of hunters and anglers.[80] The majority (67 percent) of the department's law enforcement revenue originates from its game and fish fund. Furthermore, wolf management will be one of several relatively new responsibilities for the agency. Not only does the agency oversee hunting, fishing, and poaching, but it now manages and enforces regulations pertaining to snowmobiles, all-terrain vehicles, boats, and water bikes, as well as water and wetland pollution and violations. The cost of wolf management in the state—funding new positions, doing population studies, and running the wolf control and trapping program—will certainly be an important issue by itself. While the state may want to regain management control over its wolf population, skeptics want to know how they are going to pay for this important responsibility.

The ADFG receives an even larger amount of its revenue from its game and fish fund.[81] In fiscal year 2000–01, the department received $20,084,400 out of its total revenue of $54,716,100 from its game and fish fund (over 36 percent of its revenue). New Mexico's Game and Fish Department is even more dependent on its sale of hunting and fishing licenses, receiving 59.5 percent of its budget from this fund.[82] These differences in funding sources are important, according to many involved in the debate over wolf recovery. It is a question not only of whether a state wildlife agency is willing to manage a recovered wolf population but also of whether it has the institutional and resource capacity and incentive to do so.

Given that consumptive users pour millions of dollars into wildlife management, it is not surprising that most of this money is allocated to the management of game species. What is absolutely necessary for successful state wolf management then, according to almost all of the wildlife managers I spoke with, is a consistent and reliable source of nongame wildlife funding. The Conservation and Reinvestment Act (CARA) was repeatedly emphasized as a way to achieve this goal and manage the majority of species that are not hunted, fished, or listed as threatened or endangered, and are therefore not adequately funded. CARA, widely considered the most significant conservation funding legislation ever considered by Congress, would have provided nearly $3 billion a year to states and local communities for wildlife management, land restoration, coastal protection, conservation easements, outdoor recreation, and other conservation efforts. CARA funding would have come from revenues tied to oil and gas leases on the Outer Continental Shelf.

State wildlife managers are not the only ones to accentuate the importance of a permanent stream of nongame wildlife funding. Environmental organizations like the National Wildlife Federation believe that a permanent conservation funding bill would be comparable to the passage of landmark laws like the Clean Air and Clean Water Acts. Moreover, Many Native American tribes that lobbied for CARA, including the White Mountain Apache and Nez Perce, believe that they have the capacity but not always the resources to successfully manage wildlife and environmental protection on tribal lands.

Those opposing CARA did so on a constitutional, ideological, or cultural basis. Former Idaho Republican Representative Helen Chenoweth-Hage, one of the more vocal opponents of wolf recovery and environmentalism in general, opposed the bill using the policy story of the slippery slope.[83] "When did we conclude that the government can manage the land more responsibly and efficiently than the private property owner?" she asks. She also believes that CARA "will dramatically expand the scope and power of the federal government, and it will dramatically reduce the constitutional role of Congress to control the purse strings."

And central to her opposition to CARA, wolves, and other natural resource policies is her deep-seated mistrust of the federal government:
"The truth is that a private property owner categorically does a better
job of utilizing and conserving private property. Government, by its
very nature, is inefficient and unhealthy when it comes to managing
land and water."[84] The bill would have provided states large sums of
money for conservation purposes without first having to go through
the potentially dangerous annual appropriations process. Therefore, some
representatives simply opposed CARA because they saw it as a threat to
the congressional power of the purse.

CARA's slow death in Congress presents a case study in Washington
politics. A strong Republican and Democratic coalition supported CARA.
So how can a bill supported by 315 House members, 66 senators, and
the president not get passed? Whatever their reasons, a few influential
senators did not allow the bill to get on the floor for debate and consideration.[85] It was replaced with a milder and less threatening piece of
legislation: the Land Conservation Preservation and Infrastructure Im-
provement Act of 2000 (LCPII). Although this replacement legislation
was still significant, the story of CARA is a vivid reminder of how power
and influence—not debate and deliberation—often characterize our
democratic process.

Implications for State Wolf Management

What does the politics of place mean for future state wolf management?
First, it is important to keep in mind that there is a cushion underlying
the hand off of management responsibilities from the FWS to the states.
This federal oversight—the ability to step back in and use the ESA's
emergency clause to relist the wolf—is often cited by federal managers
and some wolf advocates as a reason why they are not overly concerned
about state wolf management. One prominent wolf manager in the
Northern Rockies believes that western states will do an acceptable job
of managing wolves because the threat of federal relisting will be hang-
ing over their heads. He thinks that they would rather have wolves back
than have federal bureaucrats involved in their affairs. This "gorilla in
the closet," he says, will also give state wildlife agencies enough cover to
conduct a scientifically sound wolf management program. There is a
sense here that while many western wildlife agencies are up to the task,
some state legislatures are not, and that without the threat of federal

reintervention, wolves would once again be eliminated outside of the most remote and protected areas. Feelings of assurance have also been conveyed by several environmentalists in the region. Some point to the fact that many states have a constitutional duty to protect and enhance wildlife within their borders. In Montana, for instance, the legislature finds and declares that "it is the policy of this state to manage certain non-game wildlife for human enjoyment, for scientific purposes, and to insure their perpetuation as members of ecosystems [and that] species or subspecies of wildlife indigenous to this state which may be found to be endangered should be protected in order to maintain and enhance their numbers."[86]

Lack of trust, on all sides, was regularly expressed during interviews. Many ranching interests have very little trust in the FWS and the environmental community and see delisting as a vague and hollow promise. Some believe that the FWS will raise the bar just before delisting by raising the population threshold or by requiring additional habitat connectivity. One Stockgrowers Association representative complains that ranchers do what they are told only to find out later that the rules and criteria have been changed. One Farm Bureau official also believes that environmental lawsuits will never let state wolf management happen. He also sees the current wolf management framework as an effective way for the FWS to get the states to pay for a program they never wanted, while at the same time giving them little flexibility in how they manage it.

In the most important sense, successful wolf recovery and management are directly related to two of the greatest challenges for carnivore conservation. I think most wolf and wildlife advocates would agree with wildlife biologist David Mech that these are, first, curbing human population growth, and second, preserving as much as we still can of the natural world.[87] On another level, however, various elements need to be aligned if wolves are to recover successfully with as little conflict and human manipulation as possible. They can be seen as tributaries emptying into a larger river. While one or two of them may be dammed with little overall effect on the larger course of water, if too many of them are held back and altered, the entire process and natural flow may be jeopardized. It is also difficult to generalize and make predictions across varying places and contexts. What may pose a threat to one river may not pose a threat to another. Likewise, it is difficult to state in any rigid fashion what political factors are always necessary for successful wolf recovery and minimal human-wolf conflict.

Similar to the magic that takes place when divergent streams converge and become one in a larger system, many things critical to wolf recovery connect in important and unpredictable ways. Timing and context can be everything. Wolf recovery in Michigan's Upper Peninsula is instructive here. Michigan's 1974 wolf reintroduction program failed badly (four wolves dead in eight months, all by human causes) because of plummeting deer numbers and the resulting public mistrust of the Michigan Department of Natural Resources. These four wolves had nothing to do with the deer decline, nor the rough winters that caused it, but still paid a price for being in the wrong place at the wrong time. Roughly twenty-five years later, wolves have returned to an Upper Peninsula that is contextually different: deer overpopulation is now a problem, wolves were not reintroduced but naturally recolonized the area, and environmental education and awareness have changed some opinions.[88]

Michigan's wolf recovery story is but one case in a particular place. Elsewhere, the players, processes, and context may differ in important ways. As wolves become delisted, the politics of place will become even more consequential. There are, however, some general themes and issues that appear to be universal in the wolf debate such as a concern for human safety, potential livestock losses, and perceived threats to private property. State wolf management will have some serious limitations as well. Wolves are a transboundary policy issue, and they will continue to float across political and management boundaries. Throughout most of the country, and especially in the West, wolf recovery will also be affected by land-use decisions made by federal land management agencies. Wolves will also present an important test of state wildlife management capabilities as well as how committed these and other agencies are to the new paradigm of ecosystem management.

The politics of place also mandates a flexibility in approach to future wolf conflict. Wolves become symbols, and these symbols often differ to suit their contexts. Asked if he could share any policy-related advice with other wolf management programs throughout the country, one FWS wolf manager urges us to keep in mind the following: "wolves and wolf management has nothing to do with reality! The issues are mainly symbolic and about human values and perceptions rather than an animal.

[Therefore] encourage diversity in approaches, and recognize what does well in one situation would fail miserably in another."

The politics of place helps us understand the history and possibly the future of the wolf. Wolf recovery and management do not take place in a vacuum. Important contextual factors have serious policy implications for future state wolf management. Four have been discussed in this chapter: historical, cultural, political-economic, and management. The intermountain West as place provides one example. It seriously affects everything from how the "wolf problem" gets defined (wolves versus ranchers, for example) to how wolf policy finally gets implemented (experimental, nonessential designation). This context helps us better understand the history of wolves in the West and the prospects for successful recovery. And like all political cultures, this one is not static. It is changing and being challenged in significant ways. Wolves are often but one part of a larger and more inclusive cultural debate that is taking place in the West, while once again becoming an important symbol or surrogate for these larger conflicts among the region's citizens and stakeholders.

CHAPTER FOUR

The Use of Stakeholders and Public Participation in Wolf Policymaking and Management

The "stakeholder" now occupies an important role in many environmental, natural resource, and wildlife policymaking and management decisions. Once charged with being dominated and "captured" by various consumptive-oriented constituencies, many public land and wildlife agencies have attempted to draw the public and various interest groups into the decision-making process. While public input has been solicited and used in a variety of ways, ranging from the pro forma public hearing to Minnesota's inclusive "wolf roundtable," those responsible for implementing our environmental laws now consider (in some cases because they have been forced to) other voices and public values in their decision-making methods. The case of wolf reintroduction in Yellowstone and the Northern Rockies is a textbook example of muddling-through and environmental politics at its most adversarial and contentious, with years of legal maneuvering and millions in court costs. In other places, however, wolves are among the latest and most controversial issue to test the promise and pitfalls of stakeholder-based collaborative conservation.

The return of wolves throughout the United States has taken place while a number of natural resource and wildlife agencies experiment with these relatively new and more inclusive management designs, from the use of vaguely defined "public input" to the more controversial collaborative and consensus-based models. We now have a situation in which one of the most important issues of American wildlife policy (the what of wolf politics) has been tied to the debate over the wildlife policymaking process (the how of wolf politics). Examining wolf politics without exploring the use of stakeholders would be similar to investigating forest policy in the twentieth-century without discussing the ideas of "progressive conservation" and Gifford Pinchot's conception of "the greatest good, to the largest number, for the longest time." In both cases, a large part of the story would be left out. And it is important to bear in mind that, as in most areas of public policy, process affects substance. Just as the Administrative Procedures Act (APA) and the Environmental Impact Statement (EIS) fundamentally changed the rules and therefore the content of many public policies, so too may these new and more participatory management designs affect the direction and content of our natural resource and wildlife policies.

This chapter begins with a broad discussion of stakeholder approaches to environmental, natural resource, and wildlife management, including a summary of arguments for and against these approaches. Following this discussion, I briefly examine four cases of wolf politics (Minnesota, Wisconsin, New York, and Alaska) and the use of stakeholders and public participation in the policymaking and management process, and discuss the policy lessons relevant to these and other cases. In brief, I make the case that the use of stakeholders and public participation offers a promising way to deal with future wolf policy and management issues.

Stakeholder Politics

The use of stakeholders is part of a larger movement in environmental and natural resource policy toward using methods of alternative dispute resolution and public participation in formal and informal decision making.[1] Collaboration, consensus building, and other approaches fall under the broad heading of a more inclusive, democratic, and participatory management. Philip Brick and Sarah Van de Wetering describe it as follows:

> Often called "collaborative conservation," this new movement represents
> the new face of American conservation as we enter the twenty-first century. Although no single strategy, process, or institutional arrangement
> characterizes this movement, collaborative conservation emphasizes
> the importance of local participation, sustainable natural and human
> communities, inclusion of disempowered voices, and voluntary consent
> and compliance rather than enforcement by legal and regulatory coercion.
> In short, collaborative conservation reaches across the great divide con-

necting preservation advocates and developers, commodity producers and conservation biologists, local residents, and natural interest groups to find working solutions to intractable problems that will surely languish unresolved for decades in the existing policy system.[2]

Methods of participation can be differentiated and evaluated using criteria such as feelings of efficacy among participants (whether groups and individuals felt that their needs, concerns, and values were considered in the process), the amount and type of representation and access that is provided, opportunities for information exchange and learning, the continuity of participation, and the amount of decision-making authority given to participants.[3] These approaches have been used with a number of natural resource, wildlife, and endangered species conflicts. The Quincy Library Group in northern California, the Applegate Partnership in Oregon, the Colorado Plateau Forum in the Southwest, and dozens of collaborative approaches to watershed management are examples of more inclusive approaches to conflict resolution.

Many of these alternative approaches are so experimental and are happening so quickly that there is often a general confusion over terminology. According to Barb Cestero of the Sonoran Institute, a leading organization in community-based conservation efforts, a collaborative conservation initiative is "a cooperative process in which interested parties work face-to-face to resolve a natural resource problem, create a new policy, or develop a management plan [and] brings together people from across the spectrum of diverse, typically adversarial, perspectives regarding conservation and natural resource issues."[4] Collaboratives include input from those who can influence the outcome, who are affected by the outcome, who implement the outcome, and who want to participate. Fundamental to such an approach is the inclusion of multiple, diverse, and opposing perspectives.

The Sonoran Institute describes two important categories of collaboration, both of which are important to wolf policy and management. *Place and community-based initiatives* focus on a specific geographic locale with which residents identify, including public land and encompassing nearby human communities. In contrast, *policy and interest-based initiatives* use a collaborative approach to tackle problems of a broader geographic scale or address policy and land management issues of regional and national significance. Watershed groups active throughout the country are excellent examples of place and community-based efforts.

They are often practiced on a smaller (bioregional) scale and can result in improved public participation and community stewardship. Policy and interest-based initiatives, on the other hand, involve issues of a larger and often transboundary scale, and as such usually include a number of organized interest groups. This kind of initiative can result in improved public participation as well as shared management authority between stakeholder organizations and a land/wildlife management agency. These two types of collaboration differ in both structure and success. Evaluating various cases, Cestero found that smaller-scale place-based efforts seem to be more successful than the inherently complex collaboration over large landscape management and broad policy issues. Policy-based initiatives often become mired in political questions and controversy pertaining to proper representation, outreach, and management authority.

The "collaborative relationship" can include a number of different arrangements. According to Julia Wondolleck and Steven Yaffee, who have studied hundreds of these relationships in detail, each involves an important linkage or bridge connecting agencies, organizations, and individuals. While acknowledging that they are not a magic bullet, these authors remain unabashedly optimistic about the potential good that can come from collaborative relationships. They contend that the bottom line is this:

> The dispersed and finite nature of existing human and financial resources, both public and private, the complexity of problems that we face, and the sheer diversity in our society mean that there really is no choice. Creative ways to bridge multiple capabilities and concerns will be a necessary part of American life in the twenty-first century. They offer an exciting way to foster the traditional values of shared responsibility and democratic involvement while dealing with complex issues in a highly diverse society.[5]

The Use of Stakeholders in Wildlife Policy and Management

Some agencies responsible for wolf recovery and management have made serious attempts at incorporating public participation into decision-making processes and have done so for a number of reasons. First, a certain amount of public input and participation is often required by law (the public comment period during an EIS, for example). Perhaps most important, however, wildlife managers are beginning to recognize the importance of the human dimensions of wildlife management. As noted by Aldo Leopold half a century ago, the problem of wildlife management is not how we manage animals but how we manage humans.[6] Stakeholders will have as much to do with wolf recovery as will a range of other ecological and biological factors.

Stakeholders are being given more decision-making authority, and their management plans are increasingly being adopted by managing wildlife agencies. Proposed grizzly bear recovery in the Bitterroot ecosystem of western Montana and central Idaho provides one example. Here, a policy and interest-based collaborative of environmentalists and timber industry representatives devised a "Citizen's Management Alternative" and proposed it to the FWS. This collaborative was comprised of interest-based groups such as Defenders of Wildlife, the National Wildlife Federation, and the Resource Organization on Timber Supply (ROOTS). Their management proposal was later adopted by the FWS as its "preferred alternative" in the Final Environmental Impact Statement (FEIS).[7] The collaborative group laid out a plan to achieve grizzly bear recovery while minimizing the social and economic impacts on the Selway-Bitterroot community. Grizzlies would be reintroduced as an experimental population and be managed by a Citizen's Management Committee (CMC), appointed by the secretary of the interior in consultation with the governors of Idaho and Montana. According to the FEIS, "The CMC would consist of a cross-section of interests reflecting a balance of viewpoints, be selected for their diversity of knowledge and experience in natural resource issues, and for their commitment to collaborative decision making."[8] In this important case, stakeholders not only devised a management plan that was chosen by the FWS but gave the CMC authority over questions pertaining to implementation and management. In short, this proposed plan provided stakeholders with an unprecedented amount of management authority over a federally threatened species.

The use of stakeholders in wildlife management is a relatively recent phenomenon. Fish and wildlife agencies have historically served what they perceived to be their "constituents" or "clients." As is the case with agency-client relationships in other policy areas, fish and wildlife agencies developed a special and cozy relationship with a narrow set of interests:

anglers, hunters, and trappers. Dissenting voices and nonconsumptive interests were treated as impediments and obstacles to be overcome, not as legitimate stakeholders having an interest in the *public's* wildlife. This client-manager paradigm was challenged in the early 1970s.[9] An increasing number of Americans were "nonconsumptive" users of wildlife, possessing an array of values toward wildlife and the natural world. Many were unhappy with the special privileges, influence, and access conferred on hunters, fishers, and trappers. There was more interest in environmental issues in general, and more groups emerged to represent them. And these groups and individuals were seeking a more meaningful part in governmental decision making. As a result of these and other important factors, since the 1980s, many wildlife managers have sought out and incorporated other interests and concerns held by a wider spectrum of stakeholders. These stakeholders generally have either legal standing, great political influence, the political power to block policy implementation, a sufficient moral claim, or some combination thereof.[10]

While the stakeholder approach to wildlife management is certainly more difficult to carry out than the old paradigm because it involves different players and values, many see it as an important step in the right direction, and critical for the long-term success of wildlife management and the wildlife profession. According to Daniel Decker and his colleagues at Cornell University, who have long studied the important human dimensions of wildlife management, the future outlook is not yet clear: "Adoption of this new, broadened perspective about whose interests and concerns should be considered and who should have input in fish and wildlife management decisions is a vital step in keeping the profession in a viable, central role in conservation. Failure to recognize and consider the breadth of public interests in fish and wildlife can diminish management credibility and effectiveness. Despite the importance of this broader perspective, the transition has been subtle, slow, and resisted by some fish and wildlife professionals."[11]

Decker and his colleagues are nevertheless adamant about the importance of this task: "In our opinion, the future of the profession will be inherited by those managers who adopt, refine and practice the evolving stakeholder approach for fish and wildlife management." They discuss a number of challenges still facing the stakeholder approach. What values ought to be included when making management decisions? How are managers to distinguish between what is scientifically defensible and what is morally or legally defensible? What ought to be the role of the legislature in providing wildlife mandates, goals, and management guidelines? How is the stakeholder to be shielded from special interest power and domination? How do we define who is a stakeholder in order to avoid it being too broadly construed to mean the public-at-large or too narrowly construed to simply be a pretext for special interest privilege? As these authors explain, "Like explorers of old, fish and wildlife managers will face both the dangers and the thrills of navigating uncharted waters."[12]

There are a number of different ways of making wolf and wildlife management decisions. One typology, used by Cornell's Human Dimensions Research Unit, is helpful in better understanding these different approaches and in analyzing stakeholder involvement in general.[13] It will also help distinguish the four wolf cases discussed later. This assessment places various management approaches on a continuum. At one end is the authoritative approach where agencies follow an "expert model," making all decisions and taking management action without stakeholder consultation. Next is the passive-receptive approach where agencies are open to input when stakeholders take the initiative to be heard, such as by writing letters, making telephone calls, or testifying at commission meetings. The inquisitive approach occurs when agencies invite input from stakeholders, such as at public meetings and listening sessions and from surveys. Here, human dimensions inquiry can augment an agency's information base, informing them of stakeholder values, beliefs, and opinions. The transactional approach is a significant change in the way agencies interact with stakeholders. It allows stakeholders to become directly involved in making decisions, not just in providing input. It also means that wildlife agencies must be willing to give up some managerial control. At the other end of the continuum is the next innovation in stakeholding, co-management. This model differs from the transactional approach in that stakeholders are involved in multiple stages of the management process, not just in decision making.

Stakeholder Debate

Before examining recent examples of wolves and stakeholders, I will quickly summarize the general case for and against various stakeholder approaches to environmental, wildlife, and wolf decision making. Wolves have been and will continue to be affected by this larger debate.

The Case for the Stakeholder Approach

A New Approach to Problem Solving. There have been generally two dominant methods of decision making and policy problem solving: resource allocations through a free market, and technical solutions through expert decision making. When conflict and problems not easily handled by market mechanisms arise, a technical-rational approach is often put forth as a way of problem solving. As discussed earlier, there are some policy issues that cannot be "solved" using the traditional tools of instrumental rationality. A technical-rational approach to many wolf-related issues will fail because it cannot adequately address their sociopolitical and value-based dimensions.

The complexity and value-based character of wolf politics and policy may therefore be best addressed in a community-based public sphere, with concerned citizens and identified stakeholders resolving problems and value-based conflicts in their own unique ways. Recognizing that often there is no one best way of solving a problem, the stakeholder approach is inherently more flexible and site-specific—two important components of resolving value-based sociopolitical conflict. Believing that human-caused grizzly bear mortality in the Rocky Mountains cannot be "solved" with technical-rational scientific tools, Steven Primm of the Northern Rockies Conservation Cooperative believes that a localized and site-specific stakeholder approach offers the greatest hope of dealing successfully with this important problem.[14] According to Primm, grizzly bear management and conservation in the Rocky Mountains are bound up with a number of other contentious policy issues and are very much a matter of individual and local behavior. Therefore, effectively listening to and communicating with these local citizens are essential for lowering levels of human-caused grizzly bear mortality. Listening to others is very beneficial, says Primm: "By recognizing that local residents matter and have legitimate concerns, these processes would reduce the resentment that is often acted out against grizzly bears as 'surrogates' for the distant, callous federal government and environmental elitists. Local acceptance, mutual understanding, and reason-based public opinion . . . would greatly improve the outlook for this species in the Rocky Mountains."[15]

Getting Results. Many analysts view the traditional approach to natural resource management in general, and endangered species management in particular, as largely ineffective. For example, of the approximately 1,700 species listed on the endangered species list, as of 1997, only 11 had been delisted due to successful recovery.[16] So for some proponents of new ways of managing conflict, "trying out alternatives may be worth it simply because this historical baseline is not very encouraging."[17] For them, old ways of doing business—litigation, special interest maneuvering, power politics, lack of communication, vilification, fear mongering, top-down centralized Washington management, and process/procedure/delay ad nauseam—are often ineffective at advancing conservation goals. They equally emphasize results: on-the-ground benefits that have resulted from policy and management decisions. Successful wolf recovery requires more than process, procedure, and paper protection. For proponents then, the best way to get results is often with collaborative conservation.

Shortcomings of Traditional Approaches. The move, in rhetoric and in practice, to a more ecosystem-based management paradigm also requires that new values such as biodiversity be represented by a new and more inclusive set of stakeholders. The standard ways of incorporating public input have also been challenged. Barb Cestero of the Sonoran Institute says,

> The now familiar process mandated by federal law—in which an agency crafts a proposal, drafts the analysis, and presents it to the public for comment—is, in effect, an after-the-fact public review of decisions already made by "neutral" agency officials rather than by substantive public involvement in the decision-making process. This process seldom fosters any sense of public ownership in management decisions. Instead, it frequently leads to conflict among various interest groups, as expressed in contentious public hearings and significant detours to the courts and Congress.[18]

The stakeholder approach can also be examined as a way to effectively manage common pool resource problems (CPRs) and the "tragedy of the commons."[19] Garret Hardin's thesis that the rational self-interested actions of individuals ("utility maximizers") often have devastating collective consequences has been applied to a number of natural resource policy problems, such as public lands management and water pollution. Policy and management challenges posed by public resources and goods, such as air, water, public lands, and wildlife, are usually approached in one of two ways: by advocating privatization of the resource, or by advocating more centralized management of the resource. Rejecting this "grim trap" between privatization and leviathan, Elinor Ostrom persuasively argues that common pool resource problems can and have been resolved from the bottom up through "self-organized collective action."[20] According to Ostrom, communities affected by CPR problems can effectively create their own policy solutions with localized innovative arrangements. In other words, these policy challenges can be managed from the bottom up and not imposed by either centralized government or by the auctioneer. Ostrom presents numerous detailed cases in which participants enter into binding contracts that they create themselves and help monitor and enforce. This type of self-organized collective action also incorporates local environmental knowledge and is often dynamic and tailored for a particular place, time, and local context.

Importance of Process. Public policy debates are often as much about how decisions are made as they are about what decisions are made. Stakeholder-based approaches to conflict resolution recognize the importance of process in environmental decision making. Top-down, centralized, and unilateral decisions are almost always met with dissatisfaction and hostility, sometimes from all interested parties. President Clinton's use of his executive order privilege and the Antiquities Act in designating national monuments throughout the country, and the controversy and acrimony that it generated, is but one recent example of how important process can be in environmental politics. Questions pertaining to process run throughout wolf policy as well. Who should be defined as a stakeholder? Who should set the parameters of stakeholder debate and dialogue? How should public administrators reconcile the sometimes conflicting viewpoints of scientists, the public, and stakeholders? Who, and by what means, should set wolf population targets, viability numbers, and wolf management zones? These issues and others like them are often as important as questions regarding the "what" of wolf policy.

Inclusion, Efficacy, and Issue Ownership. Federal and state natural resource agencies have historically been criticized as being captured by or beholden to narrow consumptive-use constituencies: the U.S. Forest Service to the timber industry, the Bureau of Land Management to livestock and grazing interests, and the FWS to commercial fishers, to name a few.[21]

Several state wildlife agencies continue to be criticized for being too dependent on hunters and anglers because of the important revenue their activities bring to severely strained budgets. With a more participatory approach, however, "iron triangles"—those cozy relationships often formed and defended by public agencies, legislative committees and subcommittees, and the industry being regulated—are opened up to more interest groups, the general public, and broader constituencies. These approaches to conflict resolution can also increase feelings of political efficacy and issue ownership. Successful implementation often requires "buy-in" from the communities, groups, and individuals most affected. Through a collaborative planning process that addresses the needs, concerns, and values of participants, stakeholders can feel as though they have helped create a plan and therefore have a greater stake in its outcome.

Facilitating Implementation. While more time-consuming in the short run, stakeholder approaches can save agencies time, energy, and resources in the long run. In other words, not only can participatory designs prevent costly lawsuits, but they can also facilitate policy implementation by resolving problems and conflict earlier in the policymaking process. Hank Fischer, the Northern Rockies representative for Defenders of Wildlife, for example, believes that cooperative efforts with the timber industry have benefited the proposed grizzly bear reintroduction in the Bitterroot, especially when compared to Yellowstone wolf reintroduction. Fischer says, "Remember that this isn't about bears—it's about process.... Wolf reintroduction in Yellowstone took 20 years, cost a lot of money, and a lot of people are still mad. The EIS itself took 10 years and $6 million. But it took us only two years and $250,000 to do this."[22] Participatory approaches to environmental conflict are often championed as a way to more effectively implement public policy by resolving important conflict at the planning stage. Implementing agencies and interest groups can save valuable time and resources if public input is honestly used early enough in the process.[23] Furthermore, for some, it is a way in which environmentalists can begin crafting effective and innovative solutions—getting their hands dirty, making choices, and solving problems—rather than informing others what is wrong and what *they* should do about it.

Building Community, Citizenship, and Sense of Place. At the very heart of these new approaches to conflict resolution is the belief held among proponents that local collaboration builds an important sense of community and place—a sense of rootedness that is a prerequisite for change and ecological restoration. Daniel Kemmis, former mayor of Missoula, Montana, and author of *Community and the Politics of Place,* asserts that "the emerging kind of citizenship, in which adversaries learn to solve problems through face-to-face collaboration," is really a rejection of the "procedural republic," "the politics of stalemate," efforts at keeping "citizens apart," and the notion of the "unencumbered self."[24] According to Kemmis,

> It would be an insult to these people to assume that they are incapable of reaching some accommodation among themselves about how to inhabit their own place. Such accommodation would never be easy, and it would probably always be open to some redefinition. But if they were allowed to solve their problems (and manage their resources) themselves, they would soon discover that no one wants local sawmills closed, and no one wants wildlife habitat annihilated. If encouraged to collaborate, they would learn to inhabit the place on the place's own terms better than any regulatory bureaucracy will ever accomplish.[25]

The stakeholder approach can also be a way to foster citizenship, social capital, and civic democracy, while also providing a user-friendly vehicle for community-based conservation.[26] The type of civic discourse and involvement, collective learning, citizen-friendly bureaucracy, and local empowerment found in the stakeholder approach is also seen as an important dimension of ecosystem management.[27] On an even larger scale, more democratic processes are seen as the only way of moving toward the goal of environmental sustainability.[28] Also embedded within these stakeholder designs is the belief that local citizens often know their place on a deeply personal and intimate basis and can therefore make an important contribution to saving it. Assumptions are sometimes made that "communities of place" will manage resources and wildlife differently than "communities of interest." The impressive number of place-based environmental organizations found throughout the country, from watershed councils to local forest watch groups, is evidence of how strongly many urban and rural residents feel about their place and the threats facing it.

The Case against the Stakeholder Approach

Compromise and Capitulation. Stakeholder methods of resolving disputes are criticized for many reasons.[29] As in the debate over reintroducing wolves into Yellowstone, Idaho, and the Southwest as experimental populations, some environmentalists see collaboration and consensus building as the institutionalization of a dangerous level of compromise and capitulation. Some see these efforts as feel-good hand-holding sessions, selling out, and an overall abdication of responsibility by those in the environmental community. More specifically, critics argue the following points: (1) environmentalists often have both science and the law on their side; thus, if they continue using these tools, sooner or later they will prevail on their own terms through traditional legal and political processes; (2) various industries and powerful interests are enthusiastic about collaboration and consensus building for a reason: they have the resources and expertise necessary to dominate the process; (3) consensus ideas are often lowest-common-denominator ideas; in other words, consensus solutions are not always the best solutions; and (4) conflict is not always a bad thing but is instead an essential part of the democratic process, raising public concern and demands that something be done. This critique is often used by politically important conservation organizations. One prominent environmentalist active in the conservation community for over fifty years echoes the late David Brower in summarizing his feelings toward this process: "It's not my job to compromise and seek consensus, that's what the politicians get paid to do."

But it is not only some environmentalists that are leery of this approach. Following my work in Alaska, two important members of a prominent consumptive-use interest group sent me the following quote on consensus: "Margaret Thatcher once said that 'consensus is the process of abandoning all beliefs, values and policies in the search of something in which no one believes, but to which no one objects, the process of avoiding the very issues that have to be solved, merely because you cannot get agreement on the way ahead. What great cause would have been fought and won under the banner "I stand for consensus"?'"

Strengths and Promise of the Legal Approach. While some believe that traditional approaches to natural resource and endangered species management leave much to be desired, others emphasize how successful some interests have been in using the courts. Various wolf advocacy organizations simply believe that science and legal mandates have a better chance of surviving in the courts than they do inside a collaborative framework. They are also suspicious of those interests advocating collaborative conservation. For example, Idaho Senator Larry Craig, widely considered by environmentalists to be no friend of endangered species, supports such an approach. About the controversy over wolves, bears, and now lynx in his state, Craig says, "The approach extreme preservationists used to get the lynx on the threatened list was litigation, which meant no collaboration and no compromise. The only venue that allows them to get away with this 'my way or the highway' attitude (because the public will not), is the courts. I recognize this brand of extremism represents a small portion of the environmental community, and the rest of us understand the better way to make decisions is to bring all interested parties together to facilitate the multiple-use of our public lands. This is a concept called collaborative conservation."[30] It is just this type of endorsement that keeps many environmental organizations focused on the courts and away from the stakeholder table.

Collaborative processes may not work simply because of the very nature of some groups' values and interests. The focus on rights by animal rights organizations, for instance, casts doubt on the possibility of meaningful compromise in the future. Many animal rights activists, in fact, are disillusioned with the normal give and take of most politics and policymaking, seeing it in part as "selling out" and not staying true to the cause.[31] Framing an issue in terms of "rights" will most likely lead to the courts, not the roundtable.

Outcomes or Process. While process should never be snubbed, some critics assert that there are too many unanswered questions concerning the final outcomes resulting from collaborative decision making. For some, these questions—about what constitutes the proper scope of participation, the balance of national versus local interests, transboundary confusion, legislative oversight, and others—need to be answered before we experiment with such an important and symbolic public policy issue as wolf recovery. Furthermore, some find the focus on process rather than outcomes maddening. Have watershed-based groups protected watersheds? Have forests and wilderness areas been saved from exploitation? Who cares, they ask, if a sense of place is developed among stakeholders if in the end that place turns into a dump.

Fundamental Value Differences. Not all disputes are amenable to stakeholder approaches to conflict resolution. Many natural resource and wildlife disputes involve issues that are based on fundamental and deep-seated value differences. For this approach to work, stakeholders must not violate the fundamental values and beliefs of their organization. This requirement poses a serious challenge to the ability of stakeholders to compromise and build consensus regarding wolves and their management because of the rare passion this animal often evokes in people. It is difficult to understand how consensus can be achieved regarding an animal that is spiritual shaman for some, and destructive varmint for others.

Accountability and Defining "Stakeholder." One of the most contested and problematic aspects of the stakeholder approach is the question of who defines who is and who is not a stakeholder. While this definition may be simple in a situation concerning a local garbage facility, with other issues it is loaded with politics, power, and values. Who, for instance, is a stakeholder regarding the future of wildlife and wolves on our *public* lands and *national* parks? Defining who is a stakeholder and who will sit at the decision-making table is perhaps the most controversial aspect of these alternative approaches to conflict resolution. And this question is embedded in complex and often competing conceptions of accountability.[32]

This challenge is also related to the earlier discussion of problem definition and issue framing. In other cases of collaboration, local coalitions have successfully redefined what was once considered a national issue (e.g., national forest management) as a local problem requiring a local solution.[33] Localization strategies can be successful in containing an issue. Opponents of this type of localization, on the other hand, contest this sort of framing by nationalizing, and therefore expanding, the scope of conflict. Put simply, strategies of problem definition—from the rhetoric of the local to the nationalization of an issue—are an important part of this story.

While environmental organizations such as Defenders of Wildlife and the National Wildlife Federation have supported local collaborative efforts, other national players, such as the Sierra Club, have waved signs of caution. For the Sierra Club and other Washington-based environmental organizations, local collaborative efforts challenge the legitimacy and power of their most important constituency: urban residents. Says Sierra Club Chairman Michael McCloskey, a skeptic of these collaborative efforts, "Local interests do not necessarily constitute the national interest."[34] Some critics, however, believe that the Sierra Club and other national environmental organizations are opposed to collaborative efforts for a reason: they have everything to lose and nothing to gain by having environmental problems solved at more localized levels.

Defining stakeholder is even more troublesome given the dimensions of public opinion toward the wolf and its management. While public opinion surveys document that wolves are often supported in both urban and rural areas of the country, most surveys do show that wolves have greater support in urban areas. Some see a risk of defining stakeholders as those living in relative *proximity* to wolves—northeastern Minnesota, communities near the Blue Range of Arizona and New Mexico, towns within the greater Yellowstone area—and not as those having an equally legitimate *interest* in wolves. Wolves are often managed or reintroduced on public lands and in national forests and parks. For some, then, it is not only an issue of defining urban residents as being stakeholders but also an issue of including those farther outside a wolf area, and the national public-at-large.

Because of complexity and issues of ownership, skeptics urge a return to the traditional arenas of conflict resolution: courtrooms and normal legislative processes. McCloskey says, "And, instead of hammering out national rules to reflect majority rule in the nation, transferring power to a local venue implies decision-making by a very different majority—in a much smaller population. . . . thus, the process has the effect of disempowering both national as well as local majorities. Those not represented by any organized interest in a community may be totally disempowered, and if the status quo is environmentally unacceptable, this process gives small minorities a death grip over reform."[35]

Power and Politics. Political power, one way or another, can be manifested in all decision-making processes, including stakeholder approaches. In environmental and natural resource policy, disparities in political and economic power—who has it and who doesn't—are an obvious fact of life. Environmental and other public interest groups cannot usually compete with private interest, commodity-oriented groups. In the legislative arena, environmentalists recognize these important dimensions of political and economic power. They are often at a disadvantage, and they know it. With the stakeholder approach, however, assumptions are often made that these more local, democratic, and participatory designs are somehow less susceptible to the type of political and economic domination found in other forms of political decision making. For some thoughtful observers of environmental mediation (a process that is more formal than many collaborative endeavors), the practice is a useful alternative form of conflict resolution, but one that needs to be demystified. According to Douglas Amy, who has studied the importance of political power in environmental mediation, "It is important that potential participants in environmental mediation keep in mind that mediation can be no more fair than the larger political context in which it takes place."[36]

Many proponents of the stakeholder approach subscribe to a pluralist model of political power. They see a variety of interests involved in the decision-making process, with power distributed relatively equally among all interested parties. For others, however, this rather cheery view of the stakeholder approach, and environmental mediation in particular, is both unfounded and dangerously naive. Political power, they say, is embedded in all decision-making processes, from litigation to interest-group lobbying. With the stakeholder approach, they say, inequalities of power are evident in many ways. First is the problem of access. Not all interests are invited to participate. Facilitators or sponsoring agencies often have an incentive to maintain limited participation. After all, the more interests that are invited to participate, the more difficult it is to find common ground and a recommendation that every interest can live with. Decisions about who should be invited to the stakeholding table are often based on perceptions of political power. If an interest has enough power or political clout to block or subvert a final agreement among stakeholders, then chances are that this interest will be invited to the table. If a group has a legitimate interest in the decision but not the requisite power or political clout to block it, there is little incentive to include yet another interest. According to this view, says Amy, "It is power that serves as the passport into these negotiation efforts."[37]

It is equally important to recognize that not all legitimate public interests are organized interests. There is also often a disparity in scientific and technical expertise among stakeholders in various environmental policy areas. Some stakeholders also enjoy what Amy refers to as the power of outside options. They have the clout and resources to wage a successful campaign in the courts or through lobbying and are thus able to abandon the negotiating table when they feel they can get more by taking a different route. They bargain from a position of strength. Weaker interests, on the other hand, lacking both clout and resources, often bargain from a position of weakness and are thus forced to make more concessions because they would likely fare even worse in another venue. Government also plays an important role here, setting the agenda and the parameters of stakeholder decision making. In other words, government decides what will and will not be decided upon. It also uses its power to determine how decisions are going to be made, in effect forcing some interests to the negotiating table. And finally, government agencies have often used stakeholders and public participation as a proforma way to manage conflict and defend decisions that have already been made. In sum, there are biases and inequities in many stakeholder designs. Compromise forged among unequals is bound to be unequal. These compromises, moreover, often become legitimated by the egalitarian myth of the stakeholder approach—that it is always participatory, fair, just, and inclusive. Often presented as an inherently more fair and democratic way of making decisions, especially compared to the traditional and often ugly legislative process, the stakeholder approach has its own share of problems.

Wolves and Stakeholders

The following sections describe how stakeholders have been used in four wolf policy cases: Minnesota, Wisconsin, New York, and Alaska. Together, these four examples help us better understand the case for and against the use of stakeholders and public participation in wildlife policy and management.

Minnesota's Wolf Roundtable

Minnesota's use of stakeholders and a consensus-based "transactional" approach to wolf management presents a complex and educational case study documenting the institutional and democratic challenges facing this type of conflict resolution. The FWS's 1992 *Recovery Plan for the Eastern Timber Wolf* provided Minnesota and other states flexibility in how they devised their state wolf management plans as long as these plans ensured the survival of the wolf at or above recovery levels. The Minnesota Department of Natural Resources (MDNR) created its first wolf management plan by using a consensus-based stakeholder approach: the "Minnesota wolf roundtable." The plan was developed by holding twelve public information meetings throughout the state in January 1998 and then convening a roundtable that held eight days of meetings to develop consensus recommendations regarding state wolf management. Understanding that this management is as much political and cultural as it is biological, the MDNR hoped that the roundtable could prepare a plan that was biologically acceptable to the FWS and socially acceptable to Minnesotans.

The roundtable was comprised of various stakeholders from around the state including representatives from environmental groups, such as the Sierra Club, Audubon, and the Izaak Walton League; agricultural interests, such as the Minnesota Cattleman's Association and Minnesota Farm Bureau; hunting interests, such as the Minnesota Deer Hunter's Association; wolf advocacy organizations, such as HOWL (Help Our Wolves Live) and the Animal Rights Coalition; and tribal representatives, such as the Indian Affairs Council and various tribal authorities. Six individuals were also appointed by the MDNR: three residents of northern Minnesota, and three representing urban Minnesotans. These thirty-four stakeholders played a historic role in the use of public participation in wildlife decision making. They were not assigned mere "advisory" responsibility for the nation's largest wolf population outside Alaska; the MDNR commissioner pledged to support the roundtable's consensus, whatever it was, as long as wolf recovery goals and objectives could be met. Furthermore, because the Minnesota wolf population is the keystone of timber wolf recovery throughout the Lake Superior region, the wolf roundtable, in effect, was also determining the fate of state wolf management in Wisconsin and Michigan. If the roundtable plan (or any other method of devising a state wolf management plan) was found unacceptable by the FWS, Wisconsin and Michigan would not be granted state management authority.

The roundtable consensus plan, later submitted by the MDNR to the state legislature for approval, included the following provisions: (1) wolf populations in Minnesota would be allowed to naturally expand, with a minimum population goal of 1,600. No maximum goal or ceiling on wolf numbers was set; (2) a general public taking or harvest of wolves was postponed for the first five years following delisting; (3) a state depredation control program, similar to the current federal program, which would trap or kill depredating wolves, would be created. The killing of depredating wolves would be limited to areas where conflicts with humans, livestock, or dogs occurred; (4) compensation for livestock losses would be increased, and compensation would also be provided for the loss or injury of pets and livestock guard animals; and (5) an integrated wildlife damage management program combining nonlethal deterrents, lethal wolf removal, and the use of best management practices (BMPs) by livestock owners would be implemented.[38]

In hindsight, the roundtable worked on a crucially flawed assumption: that the MDNR and the roundtable had the power of a legislative decision-making body. While the MDNR manages most wildlife in the state without legislative approval, it was not given a completely free hand in its policymaking authority with wolf management. While the MDNR pledged its early support for roundtable recommendations, no similar guarantee was made by political representatives elected to the state legislature. Reflecting on the use of the roundtable by the MDNR, Commissioner Allen Garber (hired after the roundtable plan) concludes that the fundamental mistake made was the failure to understand that the MDNR is not a legislature. This was an important political mistake, according to the commissioner, because the department cannot expect to write their own legislation and simply use a democratically elected legislature as a rubber stamp.[39]

Despite the roundtable plan being the preferred plan of the MDNR, the Minnesota House of Representatives controversially chose to ignore the consensus plan and instead wrote their own wolf management bill. While leadership in the MDNR now interprets this action as what one might expect from a democratically elected state legislature, some roundtable members believe that it was the result of agricultural-interested stakeholders sitting on the roundtable and negotiating in bad faith. These stakeholders assert that the livestock industry, while agreeing to the consensus wolf management plan, later lobbied key representatives in the Minnesota House to kill it. This is what Amy refers to as the power of outside options, or the ability of some interests to abandon stakeholding when they feel they can get more by shifting to a friendlier venue, in this case the state legislature.

Ultimately, the fate of state wolf management hung precariously on the politics of the state legislature. Ironically, two of the most controversial issues of the 1999–2000 legislative session—the wolf management plan and debate over the possibility of Minnesota adopting a unicameral legislature—were strangely connected. Governor Jesse Ventura had advocated a unicameral (single house) legislature as a way to curtail the influence of a few powerful legislators sitting on the relatively closed conference committees (used to resolve differences in the language of house and senate bills on the same topic). Ventura and other unicameral proponents argued, among other things, that a unicameral legislature would increase political accountability and make the policymaking process more open to the public. Due to differences between wolf management plans proposed by the house and senate, these bills finally found their way into a powerful and less-than-open conference committee. At one point, in fact, four different versions of a wolf management bill were being considered by the committee: a house bill, a senate bill, a MDNR bill, and a state-amended MDNR bill.

Of course, political gamesmanship played an important role in Minnesota's wolf policymaking process. Exhibiting typical legislative behavior, for example, one northern Minnesota state representative threatened to drop two bills related to increasing MDNR funding as a result of how the senate voted against his preferred wolf management plan. This same legislator also enlarged the debate by framing wolf management as one of an urban-rural divide: "If we want to start a battle between Greater Minnesota and the metro area today, we've done it. . . . It's beyond just the wolf bill. . . . Everything is dead."[40] In assessing how decisions regarding wolves should be made, it is important to consider this committee process. In other words, is stakeholder decision making less democratic than decision making by conference committee? And are the compromises made among stakeholders any different from those made among legislators?

The Minnesota legislature finally passed a more restrictive wolf management bill, which was later signed by the governor and sent to the MDNR to be turned into a more detailed wolf management plan. The new bill, a compromise between the 1998 roundtable agreement and a bill passed by the house that established an open hunting and trapping season in the state, creates a gray wolf zone in northeastern Minnesota and an agriculture zone in the rest of the state. Roundtable recommendations are to be implemented in the gray wolf zone, estimated to contain 98 percent of the state's wolf population and encompassing 90 percent of the current wolf range in Minnesota. More protection and flexibility are granted to farmers and landowners in the agriculture zone, approximately five-eighths of the state, with an estimated wolf population of one hundred. Citizens living in this southern zone are able to take wolves at any time or hire a state-certified trapper to protect livestock, domestic animals, pets, and private property.

Different wolf management zones were not created by the citizen's roundtable, and it is the flexibility provided to landowners in this new agriculture zone that caused so much controversy. As predicted, this new bill was seriously debated by those living in Minnesota and by various environmental groups. Defenders of Wildlife was adamant in their opposition to any proposed plan other than the citizen's roundtable agreement. In objecting to house and senate bills, they declared that "the introduction of these bills undermines the democratic process and shows a complete lack of respect for all those who reached a good faith compromise on the management of Minnesota's gray wolves during the five months of negotiations last year."[41] Defenders found the lenient standards for taking wolves in the non-wolf zone troublesome, akin to an open season on wolves. Because property owners would be allowed to kill wolves "to protect their property," Defenders wanted clearer language and guidelines as to what constitutes this sort of protection.

Holding views reminiscent of the debate over the experimental designation given to wolves elsewhere, some environmental organizations saw the roundtable-legislative compromise as acceptable and in the best interest of long-term wolf survival. The National Wildlife Federation and its Minnesota affiliate, the Minnesota Conservation Federation, both endorsed the plan and its basic principles. Both argued that with wolf recovery comes responsibility, and that the best way to secure the wolf's future is by minimizing human-wolf conflict. They made a clear distinction between the long-term health of the Minnesota wolf population and the protection of every individual animal. They made the case that long-term viability depends in part on public tolerance, and that anti-wolf attitudes can be inflamed by unnecessary human-wolf conflict. They also argued that the ESA was never intended to provide a permanent wildlife asylum managed by the federal government.

Wisconsin's Wolf Management Plan

The Wisconsin case represents a more incremental and "inquisitive" approach to stakeholding. The gray wolf returned to Wisconsin in the mid-1970s as wolves dispersed there from Minnesota. The 2002 population numbered over 300 animals residing primarily in the northern part of the state. Because of this successful recovery and the primacy states have managing recovered species, Wisconsin's Department of Natural Resources (WDNR) wrote a state wolf management plan.[42] Unlike in Minnesota, the WDNR was not required to obtain legislative approval for its management plan.[43]

The use of public participation and stakeholding in Wisconsin should be understood in its broader institutional setting. Reorganized in 1967, the WDNR represents the "umbrella concept" of resource management whereby responsibilities for forestry, fish, and wildlife are combined with environmental protection. The statute creating the WDNR put it under the control of a seven-member citizen board that has a high degree of statutory authority.[44] The board sets policy for the WDNR and "exercises authority and responsibility in accordance with governing statutory provisions."[45] Board members are appointed by the governor with the advice and consent of the state senate. An elected citizen-based "Conservation Congress" was also created as a statutory advisory body to the Natural Resources Board.

The process of developing Wisconsin's wolf management plan involved stakeholders in a way different from Minnesota's wolf roundtable, which made decisions about management guidelines. The WDNR has placed more authority with its science and biology-based Wolf Advisory Committee. It is at this level where decisions regarding wolf management are made. These plans are then subject to approval by the Natural Resources Board. Under this science-based wolf advisory committee is a stakeholder team that identifies issues for the science-based wolf advisory committee to consider and/or resolve. This stakeholder team is made up of various interests and individuals in the state such as environmentalists, trappers, hunters, Native American tribes, livestock and farming organizations, animal rights groups, and educators.[46]

Stakeholders in Wisconsin's wolf management plan play a purely advisory role, raising issues and concerns that may or may not be considered by the Wolf Advisory Committee (whose decisions are then subject to approval by the Natural Resources Board). The role of wildlife biologists and professionals in related fields is given priority in this plan. But unlike in Minnesota, the WDNR already has a citizen-based policymaking body and an advisory Conservation Congress. Perhaps because of this, the WDNR crafted a citizen involvement model that simply identifies issues through citizen input and use of the stakeholder team. At the first stakeholder meeting, for instance, various stakeholders were asked to comment on the Wisconsin wolf management plan and raise issues of concern. Stakeholders raised a number of issues that they wanted the WDNR to address more adequately in the future. Chippewa representatives voiced concerns over Wisconsin's "breach of protocol"—why a sovereign nation is being treated as yet another "stakeholder." Environmental representatives were fearful that the WDNR's management goal of 350 wolves would be politically misconstrued as a ceiling and limit on future wolf expansion. One "no compromise" environmental representative condemned participating in any process that could eventually lead to the public hunting and trapping of wolves. Some voiced skepticism about the accuracy of the wolf population count, whereas others defended its accuracy. An animal rights representative proclaimed that a hunting-dominated WDNR managing the state's wolves is akin to a fox guarding the henhouse. Livestock representatives wanted an expedited process for dealing with depredating wolves. And so on.

The discussion and debate over the fate of Wisconsin's wolves have been inextricably tied to a number of other policy issues. What is the "social carrying capacity" of wolves in the state is a central question. Stakeholders and scientists have emphasized a number of issues outside of wolf biology in trying to determine this capacity. Various land-use issues in northern Wisconsin, for instance, such as sprawl and cottage lakeside development, are seen by many as important wildcards in the wolf's future. Controversy over the state's growing game farm industry has also crossed over into the general wolf policy discussion. State regulations pertaining to deer farms in some places require only that deer are not able to leave these farms, not that wolves cannot enter. As a result, these deer farms are compensated by the state when wolves kill their deer. This is a major issue for some conservationists in the state who see this type of compensation as absolutely ridiculous. Wolves, they say, must not only leave livestock alone but must now distinguish between farm deer and wild deer.

Adirondack Citizen Advisory Committee

In 1992 the FWS identified Adirondack Park, along with an area in eastern Maine and one on the Maine–New Hampshire border, as potential wolf recovery areas deserving further study.[47] The 1992 *Recovery Plan for the Eastern Timber Wolf* stated that a complete recovery of the timber wolf would be achieved once two distinct populations were recovered: one in Minnesota and one elsewhere. Because of the rapid dispersal of wolves from Minnesota into Wisconsin and the Upper Peninsula of Michigan, a second wolf population in the Northeast was not given priority by the FWS. Because of the FWS's focus on wolf recovery in the upper Midwest, Defenders of Wildlife took up the requisite work and study necessary to restore wolves to the Northeast.

Beginning its wolf recovery project in 1994, Defenders' first step was to determine the biological and social feasibility of wolf restoration in this region. A number of important questions needed to be addressed before a government-initiated environmental impact statement (most likely by the New York Department of Environmental Conservation) would be prepared: Could wolves naturally migrate to the Northeast from central and eastern Canada? If not, could they be successfully translocated? Was there suitable habitat, or were there too many roads and too much habitat fragmentation in the region? Was there a suitable prey base? Were there corridors for wolf dispersal? And equally important, what were the greatest concerns of local residents, and would wolves be welcomed by the Adirondack community? While public opinion polls commissioned by Defenders illustrated widespread support among Adirondack, New York, and New England residents toward wolf restoration in the Adirondacks, some local opposition was particularly strong and often acted out violently in the form of death threats, slashed tires, and bomb scares.[48]

While public support is an essential component of all wolf management and recovery programs, it plays an even more important role in this case. Because the FWS chose to focus on the upper Midwest as a second wolf recovery area, wolf advocates had the responsibility of demonstrating to key decision makers in the state that local citizens were supportive of Adirondack wolf reintroduction. Therefore, NGOs such as Defenders and the Wildlife Conservation Society saw public participation as the key to successful reintroduction. If such support could not be proven, neither policymakers nor the FWS would have the political capital needed to successfully reintroduce wolves. According to Bill Weber, director of North American programs for the Wildlife Conservation Society, "Public opinion is perhaps the most critical issue. Failure to address concern of Western ranchers blocked the Yellowstone reintroduction for more than 20 years. Premature proposals to reintroduce wolves in the Northeast could cause similar problems." Weber also thinks that the biological feasibility of wolf recovery in the Northeast is no longer in question: "If we are willing to listen to others, acknowledge their concerns, and seek solutions that accommodate multiple interests—perhaps including a higher degree of local control than the Endangered Species Act might currently permit—we can break through remaining cultural and political barriers."[49]

The Adirondack case illustrates how a particular state and regional context can make the stakeholder approach even more appropriate. Because there is no federal land within the boundaries of the park, the state of New York and private landowners would play a bigger role in the wolf's possible return than they would farther west. In other words, land ownership patterns will make stakeholder participation in the Adirondacks and the rest of New England consequential to wolf recovery. Whereas in the West the FWS must consider national public sentiment and opinion regarding wolf reintroduction because wolves are being managed on federal lands, in the Northeast state and local opinion plays a more important role because of state and private lands.

Given this political context, Defenders of Wildlife raised funds to finance two feasibility studies: one focusing on biological questions (see chapter 2), and the other on social ones. Because the organization did not want to risk the credibility of this important research, they worked with Paul Smith's College of the Adirondacks, a natural resource and hotel management school located within the park. Working together, Defenders, Paul Smith's College, and the New York Department of Environmental Conservation (DEC) identified twenty representatives of various stakeholder groups within the Adirondacks representing such interests as hunting, trapping, farming, recreation, environmental, tourism, and property owners.

These stakeholders comprised the Adirondack Wolf Citizen's Advisory Committee (CAC), and they had a number of important responsibilities. First, they were to develop a list of issues important to their stakeholder groups that would be examined in either the biological or social feasibility studies, such as the effect of wolves on the white-tailed deer population, the taxonomic relationship between eastern coyotes and eastern timber wolves, the possible effect on livestock within the park, threats to human and pet safety, and potential limits on private or public land uses.[50] Once this issue identification was complete, the CAC was responsible for choosing prospective contractors to carry out the research. They chose the Conservation Biology Institute in Corvallis, Oregon, for the biological study, and Cornell University's Human Dimensions Research Unit for the social component.

While the CAC did not have the scope of authority that Minnesota's wolf roundtable did, some of those involved believe public participation at this stage had a number of beneficial effects, many of them typical of a successful stakeholder design. First, the involvement of the CAC is a clear indication that Defenders and others in the conservation community are beginning to understand the importance of local support in wildlife conservation. This is shown not only by the use of stakeholders but also by their having field offices and representatives do outreach and education in the rural communities of the north country. Second, the use of the CAC shows that if the stakeholder approach is to work, it must be viewed as credible from those within and outside of the decision-making process. For example, Defenders paid for a public opinion poll that ultimately showed that area residents were in favor of wolf reintroduction. The legitimacy of this poll was questioned by some in the community. As a result, Defenders quickly learned to take on a more politically acceptable role. Those questioning the legitimacy of the two feasibility studies had to attack not only a pro-wolf environmental organization but also a well-respected college and twenty diverse stakeholders and local citizens. Finally, the CAC's experiences illustrate the importance of the social and human dimensions of wildlife management and the stakeholder approach to conflict resolution. According to Nina Fascione, Defenders' director of carnivore conservation, and Stephen Kendrot, their Adirondack field representative, one of the keys to the committee's success was a discussion of issues that went beyond wolves. Before every CAC meeting, for example, participants had dinner together and were able to discuss a variety of issues and concerns. This component of the meetings, according to members, provided an important opportunity to build bridges and resolve disagreements.

Alaska Wolf Management

Like its physical environment, wolf conflict in Alaska is big and often extreme. The state has wrestled with issues pertaining to wolf management and control that people in the lower forty-eight will deal with in the future. State wolf management in Alaska thus offers important "policy lessons"—what to do and not do in the future when it comes to how wolf and wildlife policy decisions are made.

The context of wolf politics in Alaska is critical if one is to fully appreciate the claims made by the various stakeholders in the debate. In some respects the wolf debate in Alaska is simpler than it is elsewhere due to the vast tracts of wild public land in the state and the basic absence of livestock. Wolves are not managed in isolated islands of wilderness full of sheep and cattle. The debate is more serious, however, because it involves issues pertaining to subsistence. A large percentage of Alaskans, native and non-native, depend on wild fish and game for their basic dietary and existence needs. As a result, when wolves or other predators are seen as a threat to precarious moose and caribou populations, an important cultural lifeway is also perceived to be at risk. Complicating the debate are Alaska's land ownership patterns: about 60 percent is federal; 28 percent, state; 12 percent, native; and only 1 percent, private, non-native land. Because of the amount of federal lands and the environmental history of the state, non-Alaskans are much more likely to claim stakeholder status here than they are elsewhere.

Alaska is also a very symbolic place on which various stakeholders project their values and vision of the future. For some, it is still America's "last frontier," in which individual freedom and self-reliance are paramount. For others, the state represents the "last chance to get it right." Special places within the state also become key battlegrounds. For example, protecting the wolves of Denali National Park, the first professionally studied and most viewed wolves in the world, is a constant and bitter political struggle.[51] There are also a number of place-based symbol and surrogate issues stacked onto the wolf controversy. Stakeholders often talk of issues pertaining to the Alaska National Interest Lands Conservation Act, federal land regulations, and the role of "outsiders" meddling in "local problems."

The Alaska Department of Fish and Game's (ADFG) management context is also important. For example, the state's "intensive management" law mandates maximization of human harvests of moose and caribou as the primary objective of wildlife management. The state constitution reads that "fish, forests, wildlife, grasslands, and all other replenishable resources belonging to the state shall be utilized, developed, and maintained on the sustained yield principle, subject to preferences among beneficial uses." The state constitution also requires that these resources be made available for maximum use "consistent with the public interest" and that wildlife, among other resources, be "reserved to the people for common use." The ADFG thus finds itself between competing constituencies citing different statutes and constitutional articles. Pointing out that there are more nonconsumptive than consumptive users of wildlife in the state, many wolf advocates call for management in the public interest. Hunting interests, on the other hand, remind the agency of its sustained yield and intensive management obligations. And from a budgetary standpoint, approximately 90 percent of the ADFG's Division of Wildlife Conservation's funding is provided by hunters and trappers through license and tag fees and matching federal funds derived from hunting-related excise taxes.

Alaska's wolf history has gone through familiar phases, from indiscriminate wolf control to organized federal and state predator management.[52] Wolf conflict in the state has usually centered around questions pertaining to wolf control: if and when it is necessary, for whom it is being done, and how it should be implemented. The debate has often revolved around complex biological questions about predator-prey dynamics. Simplified, hunters and other consumptive users of wildlife argue that in conjunction with other factors (e.g., severe winters, bears, human harvest levels), wolves can keep moose and caribou populations at unacceptable low levels from a biological and social standpoint. They argue that wolves must therefore be managed and controlled, and control means killing wolves. Wolf advocates in the state reject the very premise on which these arguments are based. They contend that hunters and trappers, including the Board of Game (BOG), want the state's wildlife managed as a game farm. That is, they want the state's moose and caribou populations maintained at unnaturally high levels, and the only way to do this is by keeping wolves at unnaturally low levels.

Many wolf advocates, inside and outside Alaska, are also troubled by the methods in which wolves have been "managed" in the past by the public and the ADFG. The 1996, 1998, and 2000 initiatives provide examples. Voters in 1996 used the initiative process to ban the controversial practice of same-day airborne land-and-shoot wolf hunting (the practice of flying over wolf habitat, landing a plane near a wolf pack, and shooting wolves at least 100 yards from the plane). The initiative also prohibited the state from using aircraft in government wolf control programs except in the case of a biological emergency. In 1998 "Alaskans Against Snaring Wolves" were unsuccessful in passing a proposition that would, among other things, prohibit the use of snares in trapping wolves. And in 2000, Alaskans voted to reinstate the ban on public same-day airborne wolf hunting after the state legislature revived the issue.

Process is often at the center of these wolf conflicts. Wildlife management policies in the state are made by the BOG, a seven-member body whose members are appointed by the governor and confirmed by the state legislature. Wildlife management is carried out by the ADFG's Division of Wildlife Conservation. The ADFG is responsible for implementing policies approved by the BOG. The important role the BOG plays in setting wildlife policy in the state is criticized by environmentalists and wolf advocates. It is a clear example, they say, of single-use wildlife management made in an exclusive process by a select number of consumptive interests and values. They maintain that the BOG, dominated by hunters, fishers, and trappers, does not reflect the wildlife values of most Alaskans. As a consequence, they see any meaningful policy change regarding wolves and wildlife as an uphill battle unless the policy process is reconfigured in some way. Perceptions of the BOG as being exclusive and unreflective also help explain the 1996 and 2000 wolf initiatives. According to some wolf advocates, they were essentially forced to use the initiative process because of the way most wildlife policy decisions are made. If their values are not represented on the BOG, and these values are perceived as being in the majority, then the obvious route is to take their case to the public in the form of a ballot initiative.

SuzAnne Miller, former chief biometrician at the ADFG, focuses on the perceived representational problems evident in Alaska. Miller believes that sound public policy is based on a deliberative public process. Process is as important as the product, Miller says, and acceptance of government action and policies depends as much on how policies are developed as on their substance. Given these criteria, Miller is critical of Alaska's wildlife decision-making framework. She says,

> I believe that public demands on wildlife management now exceed the ability of the state's formal process set up to deal with them.... Right now you have the situation where the seven-member Board of Game has become by fiat the wildlife management policy making entity for the state ... yet their real job is to pass hunting and trapping regulations....

Since there is no other formal body, all wildlife issues come before them... hence the desire for the non-hunting (and anti-hunting) public to have representation on the board.

Ideally, says Miller, "the Board of Game would be passing hunting and trapping regulations that were consistent with broader wildlife management policies/goals/objectives established through some other public process.... Trying to develop wildlife management policies via an official group of hunters (the Board) established to regulate hunting is simply asking for problems."

Many consumptive users of wildlife, such as organized hunting and trapping interests, are of course suspicious of these complaints directed at the BOG and calls for new policy processes. They argue that there is a public and democratic process already in place. Not only is the BOG appointed by the governor and confirmed by the legislature, but there is also an elaborate advisory committee system that is open and grassroots (there are more than eighty advisory committees set up throughout the state, each with the ability to make proposals and recommendations to the BOG).

These interests support the BOG process because they are currently doing well in this venue. The ballot initiative process, on the other hand, is seen with some trepidation. Roughly 80 percent of the state's population resides in urban places such as Anchorage and Fairbanks. Comprehending the state's urban demography, they view "ballot box biology" as being antithetical to minority (rural) rights. They argue that the process is corrupt and too susceptible to imagery (especially suffering animals), scientific misrepresentation, outside influence, and big (often East Coast) money. Ironically, they and other outside interests put forth a proposed constitutional amendment in the 2000 election that would ban all future wildlife policymaking by the initiative process. Although unsuccessful, it is a clear indicator of the threats some see in an increasingly urban Alaska.

It was well before the term *stakeholder* became fashionable that the ADFG recognized the importance of process and including the public in wolf policy and management decisions. Mired in controversy over the agency's wolf control programs in the 1980s, the ADFG assembled a stakeholder and consensus-based "Alaska Wolf Management Planning Team" in 1990. According to planning personnel close to the team, the agency had an important realization:

Some staff, who had seen many apparently sound management programs stopped for nonbiological reasons, realized that department programs, and the system for involving the public in management decisions, had not kept pace with changes in societal values. It appeared that new approaches would be needed if the department were to retain the latitude to enhance some wildlife systems for benefits to people. An open planning process that fairly addressed the values and concerns of all Alaskans seemed to be the best means for meeting the legal mandate of providing a wide array of uses of wildlife.[53]

The diverse team was charged with making recommendations to the department and the BOG on how wolves should be managed in the future. The ADFG then drafted a Strategic Wolf Management Plan, based primarily on the team's final report, that in effect recognized that no single type of wildlife management can provide for a wide variety of uses. Hence, the plan recommended a zone system "where management strategies would range from complete protection of wolves to manipulation of wolf numbers to maintain or enhance human uses of ungulate species."[54] Shortly after this general recommendation was made, the process quickly fell apart. Area-specific management and implementation plans were prepared by the department with little opportunity for public input and participation. The breakdown of the process was compounded by actions taken by the BOG. The board made important changes to the plan in a closed process without any public involvement in their deliberations. According to those close to the process, the board failed to appreciate the magnitude of concessions made by environmentalists while also underestimating the strengths of concerns of those living outside Alaska. Following the board's actions, "the spirit of compromise among Alaskans diminished as rhetoric escalated and public opinion re-polarized."[55]

Release of the board's plans was followed by a call for a national boycott of tourism in Alaska organized by a coalition of animal rights and welfare groups. In an effort to salvage what planning progress had been made and to relieve some of the social and economic pressure on the state, a "Wolf Summit" was held in Fairbanks in 1993. About 1,500 people attended the summit, and 125 were invited to participate. While the structure of the summit invited failure, and a fair bit of grandstanding and public posturing took place, facilitators did identify areas of agreement. Among other items, participants agreed that the planning process used, especially that involving the Alaska Wolf Management Planning Team, was a good one; that the state needed to make the BOG and advisory committee process more representative of the public's diverse interests; and that more time was required for a fair and open public process to be successful.

Governor Tony Knowles inherited this explosive political situation. He approached the issue by suspending Alaska's wolf control program in 1994 while putting forth three criteria for the reinstatement of wolf control: (1) it must be based on solid science, (2) a full cost-benefit analysis must show that the program makes economic sense for Alaskans, and (3) it must have broad public support. The governor would not reinstitute predator control measures until these three criteria were met. To help clarify the scientific and economic components, the governor requested that the National Academy of Sciences (NAS) evaluate the biological underpinnings of predator control in Alaska and assess its economic impacts. The governor and the NAS recognized the difficulty of assessing the last criterion—determining what constitutes "broad public support"—while also acknowledging that disputed science and economic analyses do not help matters. The NAS began its evaluation with the following assumption:

> Scientific and economic approaches cannot resolve ethical and esthetic disagreements about predator control and management. However, management policies are more likely to be acceptable if the public has confidence in the scientific and socioeconomic analyses on which management is based than if the underlying science and economic analyses are in dispute. Once the distraction of disputed science is eliminated, conflicts in wildlife management that go beyond scientific issues can be better clarified, an essential step toward ensuring broad public support.[56]

While NAS was not asked to design a program that would have broad public support, they did emphasize the importance of process and perceptions of fairness:

> Consensus about goals and methods is unlikely to be reached soon, but decision-making can be carried out in a way that is perceived to be fair. Perception of fairness is the critical ingredient that leads people to accept what they consider to be unfavorable decisions and to be willing to advance their views and preferences within the decision-making framework rather than attacking it from the outside.[57]

Of little surprise, the NAS study did not resolve wolf conflict in Alaska (nor did it set out to do such a thing in the first place). Controversy continues to revolve around issues pertaining to the effect of wolves on moose and caribou populations. Disputed biology still characterizes many of these debates. Various value- and ethics-based issues pertaining to wolf management and control, from hunting wolves with snow machines to protecting the famous wolves of Denali, are also still front and center.

What has changed is the way the ADFG is attempting to resolve these sorts of disputes. The Fortymile Caribou Herd Management Plan provides one important example. The Fortymile caribou herd once numbered nearly 500,000 caribou and ranged across eastern interior Alaska and the Yukon Territory. Because of a range of factors, including past overharvest by humans, periodic hard winters, and high predation rates by bears and wolves, the herd declined to about 5 percent of its former size while occupying roughly 25 percent of its former range, mostly in Alaska. Research indicated that wolves were a significant cause of caribou mortality. A significant reduction in the number of wolves on caribou calving grounds was therefore expected to result in less calf predation and subsequent herd growth.

In 1994 the eighteen-member stakeholder-based Fortymile Caribou Herd Management Planning Team was created to identify management goals for the herd. The ADFG pledged to support their plan if it was consensus-based and biologically sound. A number of stakeholders were involved, including the usual assortment of environmental and hunting interests. Also represented, due to the political context of Alaska, were a number of BOG advisory committees, federal land agencies, the ecotourism industry, and native organizations and villages. Canadian interests were also represented on the team, including the Yukon Renewable Resources Department and Dawson (Yukon) First Nation. The planning team spent nearly three years reviewing the biology of the Fortymile ecosystem and considered numerous options for promoting herd recovery.

While there were serious value-based differences among the team members, they worked on an important agreement and common goal: "to restore the abundance and diversity of wildlife in this ecosystem, of which the Fortymile herd is the most important indicator species. To promote healthy wildlife populations for their intrinsic value, as well as consumptive and non-consumptive uses." The team ended up recommending that habitat and range quality be maintained, caribou harvest levels be temporarily reduced, and wolf predation rates on caribou calves be reduced. To accomplish the latter, the team recommended use of nonlethal techniques by the ADFG to control predation by wolves, including a controversial fertility control and relocation program. The alpha pairs in up to fifteen wolf packs would undergo vasectomies or tubal ligations, while subdominant pack members would be translocated to other parts of Alaska. The team also recommended that private trappers redirect their wolf-trapping efforts to caribou calving ranges, the most critical areas for calf survival. Perhaps most important from an outcomes standpoint, stakeholders could only agree on nonlethal wolf control conducted by the state, including no state trapping of wolves. Lethal control meant that the ADFG would be killing wolves, and this was clearly unacceptable to some stakeholders. Nonetheless, important concessions went into these consensus-based recommendations: government agencies gave up control over management decisions, environmental groups accepted resource manipulation, Yukon Natives stopped harvesting caribou, Alaska Natives accepted handling of wolves in culturally unacceptable ways (wolf sterilization), and Alaska hunters reduced their caribou harvest levels.

The Fortymile planning process has been celebrated by many interests in the state as a fair and open process, and the way in which controversial wildlife issues might best be managed in the future. Critical to this perceived success was the way the team and planning process was structured. Existing decision-making processes were not completely abandoned. A number of BOG advisory committees were represented on the team, for example. The BOG was also consulted throughout the process and ended up endorsing the team's recommendations. Furthermore, once the ADFG endorsed the plan, so did Governor Knowles, asserting that the department's action was progressive, professional, and the result of a sound public process. Knowles stated that the team's plan met his three wolf-control criteria, was consistent with NAS recommendations, and "is the most effective and humane way to address this situation and put food on the table for subsistence families in Alaska's interior."[58] The state legislature, including members of the appropriations committee, was also regularly informed about the team's progress. Unlike the Minnesota situation, the Alaska state legislature chose not to get directly involved this time. Some planning team members think that this was due to the well-structured, focused, and relatively quiet nature of this stakeholder process. Unlike the 1990 state wolf management debacle, the Fortymile team was focused on a particular problem and what to do about it, not on how to devise a comprehensive state wolf management plan. The BOG's endorsement of the plan was also an important factor, say others. According to this view, the state legislature wants to defer to the BOG whenever possible. Others believe that legislators, rhetoric to the contrary, also appreciate a stakeholder process that takes the political heat off of them and places it elsewhere.

The stakeholder team, planning process, and management recommendations have also been criticized by some. These groups and individuals contend that the plan fails to meet any of Knowles stated wolf-control criteria. Gordon Haber, a controversial independent wildlife biologist, is especially critical of the "wildlife biology" on which the plan is based. Haber's analysis of wolf politics in Alaska focuses on the poor science being used by the ADFG and now by these questionable stakeholder teams. He believes that these collaborative processes are too often a dangerous and haphazard mishmash of values and science. Haber, including other wildlife biologists in the state, reject the very premise that there even is a Fortymile caribou problem. The plan is based, he says, on the ADFG's misrepresentation of what is known about the peaks and valleys of caribou populations. Haber is also critical of the agency's use of stakeholders in this case. He says, "ADF&G has learned much from the public beatings it has taken from its past wolf-control programs. There is an easier way: Get others to do most of the killing without bloodying your own hands, then sell sterilization and translocation of the survivors as little more than a few harmless snips and a helicopter ride to new hunting grounds."[59]

The Alaska Wildlife Alliance, a one-time team member who later withdrew from the process, is also critical of the team's recommendations. They cite philosophical differences with team members while critiquing both the assumptions of the plan and its implementation methods. They charge that far from being a compromise or an indicator of wildlife reform, the plan merely illustrates the ADFG's "singular determination to manipulate wild predators and ecosystems to favor hunters."[60]

Traditional adversaries of Haber and the Alliance have also been critical of the plan and its process. Some hunting and trapping interests, for example, are suspicious of these stakeholder approaches to wildlife management in general. One explanation, of course, is that they fair well with existing decision-making processes, such as the BOG and its advisory committee system. But for some, it goes beyond simple "venue shopping." One prominent trappers' representative in the state calls stakeholder approaches like the Fortymile process "an abrogation of agency responsibility." He interprets this trend as simply the transfer of responsibilities and accountability from professional wildlife biologists to special interests—the real name of stakeholders.

By 2000, six years after the Fortymile team first met, the caribou herd numbered about 35,000, the high end of the estimate the team had hoped for in 1994. After a long absence, Fortymile caribou traveled to the banks of the Yukon River in the Yukon Territory in fall 2000. Still, evaluating the success of the Fortymile caribou herd recovery effort depends on one's values and political position. Some see this collaborative process as a "powerful tool of democracy, shifting decision making and accountability to the people most affected." Others see it as a threat to their position in the existing decision-making framework. Others believe that while the stakeholding process was commendable, the decisions made by the team (e.g., sterilization and relocation) leave much to be desired. Perhaps most important from a management standpoint, however, is the ADFG's position. They will continue to experiment with stakeholding processes in the future, especially with controversial wildlife issues. At the very least, they are now acutely aware of the political costs associated with the old ways of making wolf and wildlife management decisions.

Policy Lessons

This section analyzes the pervasive themes, questions, and "policy lessons" found in these four stakeholder cases. It examines the political advantages as well as the serious challenges facing stakeholder-based approaches to wolf management.

Stakeholders and the Politics of Place

A participatory and inclusive stakeholder approach can bend and modify to fit particular places with particular players in particular sociopolitical and economic contexts. There are numerous examples of important regional variations that will no doubt affect wolves and other wildlife in the future: the economy of the rural upper Midwest is different from the rural economy of the Southwest, the dairy industry of northern Wisconsin is different from the livestock industry of western Montana, and the interests and beliefs of the Nez Perce in central Idaho are different from those of the Apache near the Blue Range in Arizona. The political context of the Greater Yellowstone Ecosystem (GYE), moreover, is different from that found in New England. Contrast the pervasive federal presence and livestock industry in the GYE with the amount of private land and industrial forestry in New England. In both regions, stakeholders often have a nuanced understanding of the important value-based conflicts and symbol and surrogate issues that are piled onto the wolf debate. They are also able to place wolves in their larger environmental and regional context, including local land-use patterns and trends, unsettled conflicts, and emerging problems and players.

Challenges of Policy and Interest-Based Collaboration

Minnesota's wolf roundtable exemplifies the problems and challenges facing policy and interest-based collaboration. As defined earlier, this type of collaboration involves a large number of interest groups that debate broad policy issues that often transcend both geographic and management boundaries. This was not a case of place-based partners finding common ground on how to manage a local watershed. The roundtable's plan was a major precedent-setting national policy decision that carried serious implications for wolf management throughout the country, especially in neighboring states. Many interests and citizens in Wisconsin and Michigan believed that they had a legitimate stake in the Minnesota wolf management plan because Minnesota wolves are the source for their states' wolf populations. Others questioned what role the national public should have in Minnesota wolf management given the numbers of wolves on public lands and federal wilderness areas. Minnesota wolves, just like Minnesota's Boundary Waters wilderness, they said, are important to the national public, not just to those living in Minnesota.

The roundtable debacle provides another example of the inherent difficulties of policy and interest-based collaboration. Cestero sees these types of collaborations "often becoming mired in controversy, not involving local leaders or residents in a meaningful way and, less frequently, producing on-the-ground conservation benefits." This conclusion, she says, "does not mean that collaboration is an inappropriate approach to resolve broad policy questions, but when a collaborative initiative tackles an issue of regional or national significance, the interests are more numerous and complex, making effective collaboration even more diffi-cult."[61] In a similar vein, Wondolleck and Yaffee ask those interested in exploring collaboration whether the objective is "to set precedent or advance a specific policy objective across a range of sites." If it is, they argue that "action in a different decision-making arena such as the courts or a legislature may be more appropriate."[62]

This type of collaboration becomes even more problematic when it is practiced outside of a larger legislative framework, such as that provided by the National Environmental Policy Act (NEPA). Within an appropri-ate framework, says Cestero, "collaboration can be a tool to implement or adapt, but not circumvent, public land laws such as the National For-est Management Act, Endangered Species Act, or Federal Land Policy Management Act."[63] While the roundtable worked within ESA and FWS guidelines for delisting and state wolf management, members received no vision or mandate from the body most responsible for making pub-lic policy decisions, the state legislature.

Perceptions of Stakeholder Legitimacy

Another problem of interest-based collaboration is that of stakeholder legitimacy. "Communities of interest" often dominate the stakeholder approach to conflict resolution. Organizing agencies seek stakeholders who ostensibly represent large and legitimate interests such as environ-mentalists, ranchers, and hunters. Communication and dialogue are the foundation of these collaborative and consensus-based models. The hope is that conflicting interests can find common ground by acquiring a better understanding of each other's personal values and beliefs. The environmental representative, for example, might learn to better appreci-ate the family-based rancher's precarious economic situation, and thus their apprehension about wolves and other predators. It is doubtful, however, that common ground can be found if stakeholders disagree on whether other stakeholders have a legitimate right to participate in this supposedly public dialogue and debate. Like the important question of standing in a court of law, questions regarding legitimacy are para-mount in the stakeholder approach to wolf policy and management.

While not directing criticism toward the process of collaboration or consensus building, Defenders of Wildlife has questioned the legitimacy of their longtime and formidable adversary the American Farm Bureau Federation (AFBF). Defenders and the Farm Bureau are two of the most influential players in wolf politics throughout the country and are more often lead plaintiff or defendant than collaborative partners.

Conflict between the two groups appears inevitable. Defenders recommends that wolves be reintroduced to all U.S. ecological regions that the animal originally inhabited, and does so for three general reasons: to ensure the long-term recovery and viability of wolves, to restore a measure of ecological integrity to at least some representative examples of native ecosystems, and finally, because of wolves' cultural importance, including the economic, recreational, spiritual, and aesthetic benefits of wild wolf populations.[64] The Farm Bureau, on the other hand, is the largest and most established agricultural interest group in the United States. It has played an important role in the formation of national farm policy and usually advocates free-market approaches and solutions. It has promoted a system "in which property is privately owned, privately managed, and operated for profit...and in which supply and demand are the ultimate determinants of market price."[65] The organization has a strong political ideology and has taken a stand on non-farm policy issues such as civil rights, foreign policy, balanced budgets, and high school textbooks.[66] It has also historically worked with conservative organizations and the Republican party.

The Farm Bureau, represented by the Mountain States Legal Foundation, played the major role in challenging Yellowstone wolf reintroduction. But, according to Defenders, the Farm Bureau's ability to speak on behalf of its "members" is now in question. Rodger Schlickeisen, president of Defenders, proclaims the following:

> From its name, one might suppose that the Farm Bureau exists to serve American family farmers. In reality the Farm Bureau is a gigantic agribusiness and insurance conglomerate. The majority of its "members" are not farmers, but customers of Farm Bureau insurance companies and other business ventures. Yet the organization's nonprofit status allows it to use the U.S. tax code to help build a financial war chest with which it pursues an extreme political agenda, while doing little for—and sometimes working against—America's family farmers.[67]

The basis for Schlickeisen's claim is an extensive white paper and exposé on the Farm Bureau written and researched by Defenders. This report, and a *60 Minutes* exposé as well, alleges that the politically powerful Farm Bureau has more interest in protecting its vast financial holdings than in protecting American family farmers.[68] While the Bureau claims to represent 4.9 million members, Defenders claims that the vast majority of these "members" are either policyholders of one of numerous insurance companies affiliated with state farm bureaus (there are roughly fifty-four farm bureau insurance companies), or are customers of other Farm Bureau business ventures.

Regularly ranked among *Fortune* magazine's top twenty-five most powerful special interests in Washington, the Farm Bureau and its state federations are also a major presence in the states, regularly opposing a spate of environmental and wildlife protection policies. This anti-environmental platform, according to Defenders, has little to do with protecting the small family farm, and everything to do with their morally and ethically questionable financial interests, including agribusinesses, like large hog farms, as well as other corporate stock holdings. "Why would a supposed farmers' organization oppose higher fuel-efficiency standards for automobiles or fight Clean Air Act provisions that apply almost exclusively to urban areas? Why would farmers care about easing restrictions on mining or deregulating telecommunications?" According to Defenders, "seemingly odd policy positions are easier to fathom in the light of the business connections . . . including Farm Bureau links to insurance, oil, chemical, automobile, timber, paper, communications and other industries."[69]

The Farm Bureau, says Defenders, continues its campaign against wolves and other species for sometimes dubious reasons. Not only did the Farm Bureau oppose Yellowstone reintroduction, but the New Mexico Farm and Livestock Bureau, among other groups, actively opposed Mexican wolf reintroduction. In the New Mexico case, Farm Bureau attorneys argued that reintroduced wolves would take food away from spotted owls from which ranchers "derive substantial aesthetic enjoyment." The Defenders' report goes on to quote the New Mexico Bureau's policy manual: "Many predators such as the grizzly bear and some wolf species are contributing very little tangible benefit to the American people, and the extinction of the dinosaur, brontosaurus, pterodactyl, saber-toothed tiger and countless other species is not hindering the occupation of earth by the human race. Therefore be it resolved NMFLB strongly urge that the endangered species act be reworded."[70]

According to Defenders, the real threats posed to family farms and ranches throughout the country are not wolves but rather falling prices and the move toward corporatization. This is perhaps the most important point of the report. The Farm Bureau, according to Defenders, "has pursued a deliberate strategy of fostering enmity between farmers and environmentalists, two groups that could benefit from working together."[71] Questions of legitimacy will prove important with the future use of stakeholders, especially when interests of this size leave the courtroom for the collaborative roundtable. Defenders may want to find common ground with family farmers and ranchers but not via the Farm Bureau—an organization that they believe is more a private corporation than a nonprofit representative body.

The Farm Bureau disagrees with the accusations made by Defenders and tried to reframe the debate as one of environmental extremism and media agendas. "This is not the first time [the] Farm Bureau has been the target of malicious propaganda [and] we doubt that it's the last," says Farm Bureau President Bob Stallman.[72] The Farm Bureau maintains that America's ranch and farm families decide what the Bureau supports and know that the organization supports their interests. The Farm Bureau is especially critical of the role that *60 Minutes* played in publicizing these claims, comparing this story to the "alar scare" story that was run by the program over ten years ago. (This story focused on the use of the supposedly cancer-causing chemical alar on apples.) The Farm Bureau contends that the program was used in the alar case by another environmental group, the Natural Resources Defense Council, to create "a silly scare story that every government agency responsible for food safety refuted."[73] Like the first *60 Minutes* attack, says the Farm Bureau, "this was another carefully orchestrated hit-piece produced hand-in-glove with an extreme environmental group, Defenders of Wildlife. . . . more likely it was just a case of '60 Minutes' being a pawn in a much larger game by environmental extremists to quiet the voice of agriculture, the American Farm Bureau Federation."[74]

Such complaints are not the only ones made regarding stakeholder legitimacy. Some ranching interests, for example, are quick to point out and ridicule the "postcard stakeholder": the proverbial urban college kid who sends in a pre-written public comment postcard to a federal agency, or a handful of "radical" environmentalists who declare themselves some sort of "League," "Association," or "Coalition" and then demand to be invited to the negotiating table. The basic premise underlying this critique is that these "postcard stakeholders" have no economic interests in the area in question, and thus nothing with which to compromise—nothing to lose and everything to gain.

Others make the case that groups like Defenders are simply using the image of the wolf as an effective fund-raising strategy.[75] Wolves and the threats they face are a good way to recruit members and solicit donations. Some critics charge that Defenders and other groups focusing on wolves have a stake in exaggerating and perpetuating this conflict. Once the problem is resolved, the argument goes, the harder it will be to sustain membership and keep the donations flowing.

In sum, questions pertaining to stakeholder legitimacy further complicate policy and interest-based collaborative approaches to wolf policy and management. The question of stakeholder legitimacy could be added to the list of factors challenging this sort of collaboration. These two important political adversaries will likely continue their role in wolf policy and management in the future, and as they do, perceptions of stakeholder legitimacy and representation will likely become even more evident.

The Importance of Early and Continuous Involvement

If wolves never make it to the Adirondacks, it will not be the result of a failure to understand the importance of public participation and citizen outreach. The Adirondack CAC provides a good example of the benefits of getting stakeholders on board early in the decision-making process. It also illustrates the importance of two factors critical for decision-making legitimacy and public acceptance: that stakeholders have a voice in deciding, first, what needs to be decided, and second, who should be responsible for conducting research and gathering information related to such decisions.[76]

Stakeholders will likely want not only a voice in making decisions based on such factors as scientific estimations of impact, but will also want a say in how these estimations are made and how studies are interpreted. Stakeholders should help define not only the issues but also the tools and assumptions used to analyze them, especially when tools of policy analysis, such as CBA (Cost Benefit Analysis), may be inappropriately used to assess what is essentially a value-based issue. If stakeholders are not consulted in some manner during these early stages, a decision-making body is merely postponing conflict. It is also important to keep in mind that "unequivocal policy guidance from biophysical science does not exist," for various reasons, including the fact that often there is no one right description of nature, the difficulty of generating reliable information, and the constantly evolving state of science and scientific concepts.[77] Given this complexity as it pertains to grizzly bear policy, one study notes that "engaging all interests in the development of recovery policies, rather than soliciting comments on agency plans post-development may result in a more stable and equitable product."[78]

Getting Stakeholder Representation Right

Defining *stakeholder* can be one of the most difficult parts of collaborative conservation. The standards and criteria for inclusion must be explicit and generally accepted if the process is to be seen as legitimate. In all four cases except in Wisconsin, where stakeholders had no real decision-making authority, this selection process was time-consuming and laborious. Organizers worked slowly and deliberately to get the right interests and individuals involved, and to make sure that the groups were perceived as fair and balanced. The need for such balance is generally regarded as common sense. The typical stakeholder framework must therefore include not only environmental interests but an assortment of livestock and farming interests as well. The latter are generally thought to represent either an anti-predator position or one advocating as much managerial and landowner flexibility as possible—the ability to kill problem wolves with little to no government interference or bureaucratic hassle.

The question of what *ought* to be the proper stakeholder balance is not so clear, however. Should a stakeholder table be balanced if the general public is not? In other words, should six "pro-wolf" stakeholders always be matched by six "anti-wolf stakeholders" if national, regional, and state public opinion runs 80 percent "pro-wolf" and 20 percent "anti-wolf"? The criteria used to determine who is a legitimate stakeholder are usually straightforward. Is the interest affected by the decision? and Can they block or hinder the decision in another venue? are two questions that are often asked. But those organizing future stakeholder approaches should also be cognizant of the larger public's values and attitudes toward the issue. If there is a general balance on the stakeholder table but no similar balance in the general public, the stakeholder approach may well be seen to be just as unrepresentative as the earlier paradigm. On the other hand, if stakeholder balance is not sought, and those in wolf country feel they have not been adequately represented or heard, what are the chances of successful wolf recovery and long-term persistence? Those advocating balance are also quick to note that not all stakeholders pay the same costs associated with more wolves in more places.

The Importance of Using Local Knowledge and Seeking Rural Perspectives

If a stakeholder approach is to work, both on the ground and in the long-term, incorporating local values and perspectives must be an integral part of the process. While many stakeholder designs are strictly based on "communities of interest," it is essential that they also recognize "communities of place."[79] These communities transcend the pure instrumentality of interest-group politics by being grounded—physically, culturally, and psychologically—in a particular place and context. These communities of place should have a larger and more formalized role in decision-making models.

Often these communities clearly want a bigger role to play. In the Adirondacks, for example, local residents expressed a desire to be involved in "co-management," defined as a decision-making framework in which wildlife management professionals would work in tandem with local stakeholders to make decisions about issues affecting the local area. Moreover, other residents of the state believe that it is of great importance for local residents to be involved in decisions that affect the park. The preliminary study concludes that "community-based discussions will be most useful to the overall decision-making process if discussions are framed within an appropriate context. This context includes an understanding of their community's social and physical characteristics, goals for the future, and linkages with neighboring communities. . . . such a context would allow local residents to discuss questions for which they are best-suited to address."[80] These communities of place may provide new perspectives that are grounded in local situations.[81]

What happens if local citizens in rural communities are not heard when considering wolf management and reintroduction? What happens if environmental interests do not do a better job of listening and outreach? People who want to be heard will find an outlet in one guise or another. The wise-use movement and corporations looking for friends and political symbols will continue to strategically use local resentment and hostility to further their cause—a cause that usually has nothing to do with sustaining the ecological, cultural, and economic integrity of local communities.

While local outreach and reciprocity are of the highest importance—for community building, grassroots democracy, and environmental conservation writ large—it is also essential that we cast clear of romanticizing and mythmaking. This is not a cop-out, but neither is it theoretically pure of heart. Instead, it offers a common-sense approach based on two assumptions: (1) rural cultures and communities will by design or by default play a role in wolf recovery or the lack thereof, and (2) not everything in rural cultures and communities merits protection and safeguarding. This approach means that each case may look somewhat different. Different contexts will call for different approaches in balancing these two assumptions. It could mean that local outreach is taken seriously by management agencies and environmentalists, and that rural ecological knowledge is incorporated into formal decision-making structures. It could also mean, however, that these same agencies and outside communities do not necessarily have to make compromises regarding behavior and "customs" that the national public finds antiquated and inappropriate. Killing wolves and other predators for entertainment may be considered "custom and culture" by some individuals, or at least sold as such, but such practices should not then be open for negotiation in order to be "sensitive to rural interests." It can be too easy to cloak environmentally destructive behavior in the language of rural customs and culture. On the other hand, it is as equally foolish not to utilize a sometimes rich base of local place-based knowledge.

There are various ways in which local stakeholders can be given a new role or bigger voice in wildlife monitoring, policy, or management. One example is community-based habitat monitoring. The "Keeping Track" program founded by Sue Morse in northern Vermont is illustrative.[82] This growing nonprofit organization teaches local citizens, of all types and walks of life, how to effectively monitor and keep track of wildlife in their communities. Morse hopes that citizens can use these important data and information to inform local land-use planning efforts, and thus provide a way to base future policy decisions on sound, scientific, and locally gathered information. The hope is that local officials will use these findings to make smarter and more wildlife-friendly decisions about future growth and development, from subdivisions to strip malls. Morse also believes that community involvement in wildlife monitoring provides an alternative for citizens, something we can do other than lobby government and wring our hands in frustration.

Another successful case of incorporating the local public into wolf management deserves attention. Wisconsin's DNR has instituted a volunteer carnivore tracking program to better monitor Wisconsin's wolf population.[83] For the past twenty years, the WDNR has used traditional ways of monitoring wolves, such as radio telemetry, winter tracks, and howl surveys. These methods are not only expensive but become less effective in detecting abundance and distribution as the wolf population increases. In 1995, the WDNR initiated the innovative carnivore tracking program using local volunteers and professional trackers. After a short training period, local residents assist in the winter tracking of wolves and other forest carnivores, like coyote, fox, and fisher. The WDNR has used the program to determine wolf numbers, pack distribution, and breeding status, as well as to determine the possible existence of rare carnivores, such as the Canada lynx and puma.

According to the WDNR, volunteers have tracked a total of 10,900 miles while putting in 2,160 hours in the most recent four-year study period. While local volunteers had lower encounter rates than professional trackers, the department believes that volunteers play an important role in monitoring the state's wolf population, especially at a time when numbers are so crucial in determining downlisting or delisting. Wisconsin's program provides a positive example of a managing agency going beyond what is required by law and successfully incorporating the local public in state wolf management. While the WDNR sees the program as a useful and cost-effective management tool, it is also an excellent means of creating stewards of the wolf program, building local support, and utilizing their place-based knowledge.

Some conservationists now recognize just how important outreach to rural communities, and ranchers in particular, will be to the future of carnivore conservation in North America. They refuse to accept the "ranchers versus carnivores" framing that dominates so many unproductive debates. The Southern Alberta Conservation Cooperative provides one example. Their primary goal is to reduce conflicts between ranchers and large carnivores. They do so by proactively seeking and using local knowledge in ranching communities, combined with scientific research, to help prevent and solve problems. The cooperative has tried to implement "a community-based conservation approach to ensure that economically sound ranching and viable large carnivore populations remain an integral part of southern Alberta. [The Cooperative] will develop a regional carnivore conservation strategy that combines the traditions and economics of ranching communities with a scientific understanding of carnivore-livestock interactions to sustain large carnivore populations and the working ranch in southern Alberta."[84] Their strategies include, for example, testing and evaluating various depredation avoidance techniques.

Cooperative staff, along with some of the ranchers that participate in the program, also believe that there are fewer regulations in Canada that impede learning by experimental design. Many of these participating ranches are home to an impressive amount of wildlife, including wolves and grizzly bears. These ranchers often have years of place-based knowledge. Some ranchers, for example, like to keep a relatively trouble-free (and territorial) wolf pack on their ranch because they understand that a new pack might present new problems. Remove this pack, the thinking goes, and who knows what will take its place. Such knowledge comes from place-based experience. Some Albertan ranchers also understand that while the political contexts of western Canada and the western United States are similar at times, the legal frameworks for wildlife management are different because there is as yet no comparable endangered species act in Canada. One rancher explains that one of the most important reasons he is comfortable with so many carnivores on his ranch is because there is no top-down federal or provincial government mandating how they are managed. He also makes the familiar assertion that ranchers are often more afraid of proposed government regulation and control than they are of wolves and bears.

Local and rural outreach can be done in various ways, but there is no mistaking how crucial such outreach will be in the future. As witnessed in recent elections, a deep chasm separates the values of urban and rural America. Traditional adversarial approaches to conflict resolution exacerbate these social divisions. Stakeholder-based models hold the promise of offering something more constructive in many of these cases.

The Tribe as Stakeholder

Those involved in collaborative endeavors are well aware that tribal representation is nothing new in natural resource and wildlife management. Tribes are one of several interests regularly invited to the table. What is new, however, is that some of these tribes are beginning to ask why they are being treated as merely another stakeholder when in fact they are a sovereign nation, not merely another community of interest. Finding themselves sitting next to a rancher, animal rights activist, or deer hunter, some tribal representatives are beginning to view being invited solely as a stakeholder by the federal government or the states as a breach of diplomacy.[85]

This concern has been voiced by representatives for the Great Lakes Indian Fish and Wildlife Commission (GLIFWC), an intertribal organization devoted to safeguarding Chippewa (Ojibwe or Anishinabe) hunting and fishing off-reservation treaty rights. GLIFWC representatives are quick to point out that having stakeholder representation is important for communicating Indian concerns, and for hearing the concerns of other stakeholders. But by itself, they say, stakeholding is not sufficient. In addition, they believe that there must also be direct government-to-government dialogue between the federal government, states, and tribes. Regarding wolf policy, for example, such dialogue would occur between the FWS and the tribe before delisting, and with the states after delisting.

Science and Stakeholders

Scientific uncertainty and disagreement are an important theme in these stakeholder cases. As in other environmental policy conflicts, science and biological opinion are often contested by policy participants.[86] Wolf politics is often characterized by an "adversarial" form of analysis in which opposing groups use "their science" to forward their policy objectives. This "dueling scientists" approach often leads to competing knowledge claims and distorted communication. The policy implications are serious, according to policy scientist George Busenberg: "The resulting suspicions make it difficult for any one participant to generate knowledge claims that will be credible to the other participants. Therefore, adversarial analysis creates the risk of delay and deadlock in the policy process, because the participants are denied a common ground of technical knowledge upon which to negotiate policy agreements."[87] Busenberg contrasts this dueling scientists approach to "collaborative analysis":

> In collaborative analysis, the groups involved in a policy debate work together to assemble and direct a joint research team, which then studies the technical aspects of the policy issue in question. Representatives from all the participating groups are given the ability to monitor and adjust the research throughout its evolution. Collaborative analysis aims to overcome suspicions of distorted communication by giving each group in the debate the means to assure that the other groups are not manipulating the analysis. The ultimate goal is to generate a single body of knowledge that will be accepted by all the groups in the debate as a valid basis for policy negotiations and agreements.[88]

The Adirondack CAC proceeded in the spirit of collaborative analysis whereas adversarial analysis has often characterized wolf politics in Alaska. Many environmental groups in Alaska do not trust the assumptions and motivations of what they label "harvest biologists," those agency biologists prioritizing the maximization of game populations for human use and not the regulation of natural systems. Groups seeking wolf control, on the other hand, are just as suspicious of "green biologists," those individuals allowing their personal values to influence their science. Moreover, everyone is suspicious of "barstool biologists" but usually disagree on who these people are. Certainly one of the more frequent statements I heard from a variety of opposing stakeholders was that "the other side was just not using good science."

While scientific disagreement is common, a form of collaborative analysis could be used in some future wolf political conflicts. Stakeholders could assemble and oversee a joint research team that provides them a solid scientific basis for policy negotiation. Stakeholders could work together and select research team members. They could also have input into the assumptions and framing of research questions, the methods of inquiry, and the monitoring of the research as it develops. Of course, scientific agreement may be impossible at times. When it is, stakeholders should be provided with all of the relevant research and an explanation of the basis of the disagreement.

It is important to recognize the limitations of biology as a policy problem-solving tool. As the Alaska case illustrates, science and biology, including that done by the National Academy of Sciences, only goes so far in value-based political conflict. We should expect stakeholders to filter this science using disparate value systems, and in some cases to ignore science and biology altogether. An important theme running throughout wolf politics in Alaska, for example, is the repeated call made for more biological study and research. A number of biologists and wolf advocacy groups have called for more scientific (predatory-prey) study before any wolf control program is initiated. Right or wrong, this request is viewed by some in the debate as being nothing more than a political stalling technique, a way to indefinitely postpone any type of wolf control. They maintain that the biological studies will never be fully complete, and thus wolf control will never be initiated. Even some wolf advocates in the state are skeptical of those calling for more biological study in some cases where the basic research has been done. One wolf advocate even compared them to naysayers doubting the existence of global climate change, always proclaiming that the science remains uncertain. Many wildlife managers are quick to point out the different political pressures facing them than those facing the traditional wildlife researcher. Sooner or later, they say, decisions have to be made.

The Use of Stakeholders and Public Participation in Future Wolf Policymaking and Management

A collaborative and stakeholder-based approach to future wolf conflict is proposed for three general reasons: (1) it can offer a constructive and useful way to work through value-based political conflict, (2) symbol and surrogate issues can be communicated and intelligently discussed, and (3) it can be situated in a particular place and context. Collaborative and consensus-based models of public participation can be legitimate and useful, and offer a promising way to resolve difficult issues and controversies. If assembled and administered in a democratic fashion, these models can foster important dialogue—the type of communication that is not typically found with more adversarial approaches to conflict resolution. The rancher in the Stetson will never really grasp why the animal rights woman in Birkenstocks orders vegan during a stakeholder lunch, but he will know a little more about this person and her position because of the process and its important dialogue.

Future wolf conflict and controversy are certain. Issues pertaining to wolf management will be just as conflictual as those issues related to reintroduction, but more voices and values should now be included in the decision-making process. The policy implications of not doing so are serious, from a loss of public confidence in wildlife management decisions to an increase in wildlife policymaking by the initiative process. From an implementation standpoint, the use of stakeholders will aid managing agencies in making sound and defensible decisions. The approach will expand the manager's understanding of who is affected and what values each stakeholder possesses. It will also likely improve the important flow of communication between managing agencies and affected stakeholders. Agencies will be able to build public understanding and support.[89]

Process is also fundamental to compromise. It is impossible to know just how much common ground exists until stakeholders constructively communicate with one another. While some types of policymaking, like the initiative process, encourage misrepresentation and communication breakdown, a well-structured collaborative approach encourages open and constructive dialogue.

In looking toward the future, we must also address the question of what type of decision-making power these stakeholder-based models might have vis-à-vis a democratically elected and accountable legislative body. We must of course bear in mind that our elected legislators have the same type of diverging values toward wolves as does the general public. There are certainly drawbacks to the legislative process in practice. The Minnesota case, for example, illustrates how "democratic legislative decision making" often entails such features as a rather undemocratic conference committee and a power-based gamesmanship that are certainly not part of the democratic ideal. Moreover, legislative politics can be dangerously slow and acrimonious at times, characteristics that are especially worrisome when a species is on an accelerated course toward extinction. And the interest group imbalance in Washington and the states poses a serious threat to the very nature of a representative democracy.[90]

Problems and shortcomings aside, however, democratically elected political representatives have the right and jurisdiction to get involved in this debate if they choose. While a legislative body can complicate things, it can also offer another layer of accountability. But if a stakeholder model is designed appropriately, seen as legitimate, and enjoys a high degree of agency support and attention, a large number of political representatives will likely endorse its recommendations or at least

choose not to get involved. If they do choose to enter the fray, it is prefer-
able early in the process. Then, stakeholders and organizing agencies
have a legislative foundation on which to base their decisions. Legislative involvement can be obstructionist later in the process, after stakeholders and the managing agency have invested considerable time and
resources.

It is also imperative that stakeholders, managing agencies, and all
policy players recognize the legislative context in which they negotiate,
compromise, and build consensus. The ESA, the National Environmental Policy Act, the National Forest Management Act, and the Federal
Land Policy Management Act provide a few examples. As discussed earlier, some wildlife managers are skeptical of the stakeholder approach
because they see it as a potential threat to legislation that was passed in
a more democratic arena. In other words, they believe the approach
could be used as a way to thwart existing legislation. They contend that
they are already implementing the will of the people as expressed in the
1973 ESA. Stakeholders operating within this legislative context are one
thing, questioning the merit and intent of this law is something quite
different. With the former, collaboration can be used to help formulate
ideas and implement policy, not to circumvent existing public land and
wildlife law. Cestero of the Sonoran Institute sees this larger framework
as a key to constructive collaboration:

> The existing system of public land laws and standards ensures a frame-
> work for accountability in public land management. For many skeptics of
> collaboration, accountability is a central issue. Their questions include:
> "What happens if a collaborative group thinks its plan is a good idea, but
> others don't? Who decides? How do we evaluate the legitimacy of these
> processes?" The current system provides a structured opportunity for
> public input, ensures disclosure of the potential environmental conse-
> quences of an action, and guarantees a process for review of proposals
> and decisions. Lacking a better answer to the skeptics' questions, existing
> laws and standards provide the necessary system of checks and balances.[91]

It is also important to bear in mind that collaboration and stakeholding will not, and should not, preclude politics. Groups and interests
on all sides of this debate will politicize the issues, build coalitions, and
"mobilize bias." This is what happens in a pluralistic democratic society.
Just because a group sits down to collaborate does not mean they forgo
their right to fight for their vision of the public interest. But there is also

a time when groups may want to sit down and deal with the problem at hand.

It is not my intent to offer managing agencies a detailed analysis of what stakeholder processes work and why.[92] Instead, I have stepped back and examined this potential paradigm shift in wildlife management in more general terms. Nevertheless, these four cases do provide a rough conceptual map of where we might go from here. I have focused on process, not the various value-based issues pertaining to wolf recovery and management—issues that cannot be resolved by political or policy analysis. A review of these and other policy lessons follows:

- Recognize wolf politics as a value-based political conflict. This is the most realistic and practical way to proceed with upcoming conflict and controversy. It is realistic because it erases any false hope that the wolf issue can be "solved" once and for all. We will solve the wolf issue only insofar as we solve other contentious policy issues, like abortion and the death penalty. But this framing is also practical in that it points us toward a path of larger public debate and democratic deliberation.
- Recognize the sociopolitical dimensions of wolf politics. A policy-orientation such as this will help wildlife professionals place the wolf issue in its larger sociopolitical context. It makes the reciprocal understanding and mutual comprehension discussed in chapter 2 possible. A meaningful discussion of these issues will present new opportunities for conflict resolution and help find areas of common ground.
- The collaborative "charter" must be carefully structured and written. It must clearly describe legislative and administrative parameters as well as the decision-making authority of the group. The charter will clearly place the team within its larger statutory and constitutional (state) framework. Stakeholders must understand that they are to work within these parameters. If stakeholders want to change laws, they should direct their energies to lobbying Congress or their state legislature, not the stakeholder team.
- Key decision makers and elected representatives must be consulted and kept informed of the group's progress on a regular basis. Consistent consultation with key political representatives, legislative committees, the state wildlife commission, and governor, among other actors, will lessen surprise while providing the group additional layers of legitimacy.
- Use a collaborative approach and public participation early in the decision-making process before a perceived crisis emerges. This timing gives the group the requisite time to come up with a solid and defensible plan. If stakeholders are used in a more limited advisory capacity,

they can help clarify issues and find areas of common ground before these questions go to a state wildlife commission or state legislature for debate. Political timing is also important. A change in executive administration, for example, can present a major threat to a team's planning progress.

- People matter. It is not just the process that is important, but the quality of people doing the collaborating. Stakeholders must be trusted and respected in their community of place or interest. If they are not, the process will be seen as illegitimate. Many stakeholders also emphasize the importance of a good and experienced facilitator. Given the transboundary nature of wolf management, it would also be beneficial in some situations to seek Canadian (interests and agencies) participation. We also should not underestimate the ability of citizens to deal constructively with complicated political and technical issues.
- Agencies matter. A stakeholding process cannot be successful without agency support and buy-in. It is important for wildlife agencies to recognize the human dimensions of wildlife management. Various federal and state wildlife and public land agencies should participate in stakeholder processes. Their participation will encourage interagency communication. This is especially important with a transboundary animal managed on multiple public lands. In some situations it may be more appropriate to have agencies serve in an advisory capacity rather than as full-time voting members of the team.
- Rural citizens must have their voices heard and an opportunity to participate in the decision-making process.
- Tribal stakeholder representation must be sought in addition to more formalized intergovernmental dialogue.
- Use multiple methods of public participation and ways to seek public input (e.g., public meetings, focus groups, public opinion surveys, Internet methods). Other deliberative experiments and innovative ways to include the public in political decision making, like the citizens jury and consensus conference, should also be tested.
- Some stakeholders will refuse to participate or will abandon the process midstream. It is impossible to make all interests perfectly happy with the process or its outcomes. The deep core values of some groups are simply nonnegotiable and not fit for collaboration. These interests may challenge the process using the courts, by lobbying, or by rallying public opposition. Of course, stakeholders choosing not to participate in the process risk not having their voices heard at all.
- Science and wildlife biology should play an important advisory role. Stakeholders may decide to make decisions that go beyond or even run contrary to biological opinion, but they should be provided the best available information on which to base their decisions. Peer-reviewed biology should be given priority, but team managers and facilitators

must make sure that dissenting biological opinion is also presented to stakeholders. If it is not, the agency will be criticized for providing the team slanted and incomplete information and will pay a political price for doing so. Collaborative analysis can also be employed in certain circumstances to avoid the "dueling scientists" problem.

- The history of past collaborative endeavors will influence how people perceive and respond to new stakeholder proposals. If some action or policy implementation did not take place in the past, prospective participants will invariably ask why bother now. Implementation issues should be discussed in the charter. Agency history also matters, in that past decisions and behavior are not quickly forgotten. Rebuilding public confidence in an agency may take time, and the best way to do this is to use a decision-making process that is as open and transparent as possible.

- Recognize that a collaborative process, like all decision-making processes, is not immune from power and politics. Public agencies have been criticized for using stakeholders and public participation as a way to get what they want, and in some cases to support what they are already doing. This approach is no longer accepted. Stakeholders should be willing to question how an issue or problem has been framed by an agency, and what assumptions and tools will be used to analyze it.

- Defend the use of public participation and stakeholding as a way to make wildlife policy and management decisions. A backlash to stakeholding is well under way. Many consumptive-use interests and traditional constituents feel threatened by these new voices and decision-making processes. The number of passed and proposed state constitutional amendments that guarantee some form of hunting rights is evidence of this backlash. Wildlife managers should remind critics of the public interest component of wildlife management and the multiple values Americans have toward wildlife.

Conclusion

Wolves are making their return during interesting times. While we cannot predict how far this shift in wildlife management and the use of stakeholders will proceed—whether it will constitute a full paradigm shift in the field or just a tweaking of old standard practices—wolves will be affected one way or another. They, along with grizzly bears, are the most visible and symbolic animals testing the promise and pitfalls of the stakeholder approach to wildlife management. The use of stakeholders presents a number of challenges, from the question of who is a stakeholder to what power and authority they should be delegated. But as these four cases illustrate, positive benefits are to be had by including a wider spectrum of the public in wolf and wildlife management. "Building bridges" and listening to traditional adversaries are especially important given how vulnerable wolves can be to a public backlash. Stakeholder approaches present a means to deal with value-based political conflict and wolf symbol and surrogate issues in a constructive and educational way. Instead of demonizing opponents (and spending lots of money and resources in the process), a collaborative framework can help find common ground where it exists. Finally, it can situate the decision making and implementation process in its regional and sociopolitical context—the places to which wolves will return and where they will be managed.

Conclusion

Wolf recovery and management are a value-based political conflict that goes beyond biology, economic analysis, and techno-rational approaches to problem solving. Numerous players are involved in this debate, and conflict between them results from competing values and ethics toward wolves, wildlife, and the natural world. Value-based conflict among biologists, wolf advocates, political representatives, ranchers, wildlife managers, hunters, animal rights and welfare interests, and other stakeholders characterizes this debate. These clashes are either conflicts that may preclude compromise, or tensions that may be balanced in the future.

Wolf symbol and surrogate issues further complicate this value-based conflict. Only on the surface is the debate about wolves alone. Deeper are serious conflicts pertaining to land use, government, science, wilderness, biodiversity, compromise, rural communities, and tribal participation. Stakeholders often attempt to define the "wolf problem" in a way that advances other policy goals and objectives. In some cases wolves become an important symbol, and in others a surrogate for more inclusive political and cultural conflicts. These symbol and surrogate issues help answer the question of why the debate over wolf recovery and management has been so controversial and acrimonious. It goes beyond wolves.

These value-based conflicts and symbol and surrogate issues are also taking place against an important backdrop. The politics of place and contextual setting is an important part of this story. The Western frontier's "war on the wolf" places the current debate in its historical context.

Urban-rural value conflict and the transition taking place throughout the intermountain West provide the cultural context. Western ranching and rural economies are other important factors. Debate over their importance and future helps describe the political-economic context. Finally, public opinion, political support, and institutional capacity help explain the management context. These factors are often particular to place and have serious implications for future state wolf management.

The use of stakeholders, collaboration, and public participation is an important trend in wolf policymaking and management. It represents a major shift in the way that wildlife policy decisions are made. There are potential problems and serious challenges to using stakeholders in a fair, effective, and democratic way. Nonetheless, collaborative approaches to future wolf conflict are the way we ought to proceed. A well-structured collaborative approach, embedded within a larger democratic frame-work, is proposed for three general reasons. First, it can offer a useful way to work through some types of value-based political tensions. Second, it can provide a venue in which symbol and surrogate issues can be intelligently communicated and worked through. And third, it can be designed to fit a particular place and varying contexts.

A Policy Orientation to Wolf Conflict

This book embraces an inclusive policy orientation to the debate over wolf reintroduction and management. It follows the important work of others who first recognized the consequential sociopolitical dimensions of large carnivore conservation. As Steven Primm and Tim Clark say, "Carnivore conservation in the Rocky Mountains is more than a bio-logical problem; it is a public policy problem with multiple dimensions. If carnivores are to survive in the wild, scientists, conservationists, land managers, and citizens must develop a broader understanding of the social, cultural, economic, and administrative dimensions of carnivore conservation."[1] A policy orientation can also empower the public—both organized and unorganized—providing them a way to better understand and get involved in their *public* policy.

A policy orientation to wolf recovery and management illustrates the social construction of wolves. The symbol and surrogate issues discussed in chapter 2 show how differently wolf recovery is interpreted by those affected and involved in the debate. Wolves are commonly placed in more inclusive strategies and "policy stories." This approach also places political context front and center. It should be a central part of any wolf policy analysis. From the Western frontier movement and historical war on the wolf to the more rhetorical and contemporary "war on the West," context will shape and influence the future of the wolf. This context often differs in important ways. While there are factors pertaining to wolf recovery that transcend region, some are particular to place and time, whether it is the political economy of northern Minnesota, the "rewilding" of New England, or the timber industry's influence in Maine.

A political approach to wolf recovery and management also illustrates the importance of power and values in the debate. The political, economic, and cultural power of the ranching industry in many areas of the intermountain West provides one prominent example. The industry's power belies its numbers. While the industry and its political representation have not been successful in stopping reintroduction of wolves, they have had a tremendous amount of influence in determining the parameters of the debate and how the ESA will be implemented. The favored position of consumptive users of wildlife in state wildlife management also illustrates how some types of power become institutionalized in formal decision-making bodies and processes. This power is being seriously challenged by new voices and values, however. Some of the many voices in this story have been sidelined in the past but are now becoming more powerful and influential.

The policy process is also an important part of this analysis. From strategically defining the "wolf problem" and setting the agenda to the struggle over political compromise and implementing the ESA, process matters and invariably affects the content of public policy. Process affects outcomes. Wolves are being reintroduced and managed during a period in which existing decision-making processes are being seriously challenged. The use of stakeholders and public participation will likely affect wolves and other wildlife well into the future.

A lot of familiar ground—rehashed and unresolved issues of public policy and administration—is covered in the wolf debate as well. Much of it has to do with enduring turf battles. The sometimes acrimonious relationship between the federal government and the states often characterizes this debate, as it does in dozens of other policy areas. The turf is a bit more perplexing in this case, however. Wolves are challenging old management paradigms and jurisdictional boundaries, but they present new opportunities as well, from the possible new role of reinvigorated tribal management to the largely untested waters of ecosystem management. Other classic issues of public policy and administration have been explored as well, such as sources of agency funding, management incentives, and the case for and against agency flexibility in policy implementation.

Toward a New Wolf Debate

I hope that by now readers would be skeptical of any final, one-size-fits-all, comprehensive policy evaluation and political assessment of the substantive wolf issues discussed in this book. Instead, more useful to readers is a review of what I believe are some of the more difficult value-based and ethical issues that might be addressed or at least acknowledged in future debate. I play the role of democratic facilitator and interpretive mediator.[2] Instead of finishing with the one right answer, from the one right analyst, this role embraces ongoing public deliberation in a democratic context. This approach sees the values on which we base public policy as being part of public inquiry. As argued by Mark Sagoff, "These goals are not known beforehand by a vanguard party of political economists or by an elite corps of philosopher-kings."[3] I conclude, therefore, with a brief review of some of the more difficult questions and issues stakeholders might address in the future.

The politics of problem definition is once again useful here. It not only helps us better understand the political conflict over wolves and the conceptual and rhetorical tools used to gain advantage, but is also a way to define a more democratic approach to wolf politics. Political scientists David Rochefort and Roger Cobb explain: "To restrict participation, issues may be defined in procedural or narrow technical terms. To heighten participation, issues may be connected to sweeping social themes, such as justice, democracy, and liberty."[4] While there are important scientific, biological, and technical dimensions of the wolf debate, we must continually emphasize the public and democratic component of wolves and the future of wildlife. Threats to wilderness, habitat destruction, endangered species, and biodiversity; public land use and management paradigms; perceptions of natural and unnatural; environmental compromise and capitulation; the future of our rural communities; sustainability, stewardship, and a land ethic—these are first and foremost public issues that must be defined as such.

Values and Ethical Dimensions

Veterans of wolf political conflict are often the most adamant in summarizing this debate as being value- and ethics-based. A surprising number of stakeholders in Alaska, for example, compared the wolf debate to the abortion issue. It boils down to competing values, they insist. The difficult and value-laden questions that must be grappled with in the wolf policy debate are similar to ones we ask in other contemporary and divisive policy discussions: Is a fetus a person? When does life end? Who should be allowed to end it? What constitutes a threat to our national interests? In approaching these and other questions, Deborah Stone says,

> There are, to be sure, objective facts underlying all these situations. The fetus could probably be described as consisting of certain kinds of tissues, with a determinable weight, chemical composition, and anatomical formation. But these kinds of facts are simply not the ones that matter in politics. What people care about and fight about are interpretations of fetuses, shootings, wars, and economies. What communities decide about when they make policy is meaning, not matter. And science cannot settle questions of meaning.[5]

Political reason as a process of persuasion is put forth as a way in which participants can search for criteria, justify choices, and forward their vision of the world. Value-based issues such as these and wolf recovery clearly illustrate the limitations of purely scientific and economic political analysis.

The relationship between wolves and wilderness provides but one example of how environmental values will continue to manifest themselves in wolf policy, from setting the agenda through evaluating final outcomes. For some conservationists, the proper order of things should be one of wilderness, then wolves. In other words, we do not deserve wolves if we as a society do not value and protect our wildlands. Wolves require that tough choices be made. They can be stuck wherever. But if wolves are to persist and thrive in a landscape, while becoming more natural and less manipulated, they will require wild country. These voices contend that wolf advocates need to become wilderness advocates first.

There is an ethical component here as well, one that goes well beyond scientific estimations of livestock depredation and economic estimations of impact. The question of whether we should be capturing wild wolves and reintroducing them elsewhere is an important one for many in the debate. For some, the Yellowstone reintroduction made sense and was the right thing to do. But some believe that there are plans that should be reconsidered in terms of ethics, strategy, time, costs, and possible public backlash. In other words, is the argument that bases the case for more wolves on the fact that they can exist in more populated and threatened habitats like those in parts of Europe and India technically correct but morally suspect? Wolves can survive in a Kmart parking lot if shoppers drive carefully, but most people would make the value-based judgment that such an environment is not right for wolves. However one approaches the question, it is not best answered by a spreadsheet but by public debate in an inclusive democratic arena.

The human manipulation and management of wolves and other wildlife are also an important ethical issue in many critiques. The question is not whether we can capture, hold, release, and monitor wolves, but whether we *should* be doing these things in the first place. Biological control is now ubiquitous, according to philosopher and mountaineer Jack Turner: "Biologists control grizzlies, they trap and radio-collar cranes, they have cute little radio backpacks for frogs, they bolt brightly colored plastic buttons to the beaks of harlequin ducks, they even put radio transmitters on minnows. And always for the same reason: more information for a better, healthier ecosystem.... The great need, now, is to begin to imagine an alternative."[6] Many biologists and wildlife managers, on the other hand, interpret management and human manipulation with a different set of organizational and personal values. Some biologists believe we should restore wolves, but only if a concomitant pledge to management and control is made. This ethical discussion will only become more evident in the future as wolves return to more crowded and intensely managed landscapes.

These multifaceted stories of wolves and wilderness, and wolves and control, illustrate how underlying values and environmental ethics will continue to shape the wolf debate. The story will continue to be about more than just wolves. The debate is also far from finished. Wolf recovery efforts in New England, the Pacific Northwest, and the Southern Rockies; ESA delisting and the struggle over state wolf management; and debate over the public hunting and trapping of wolves following delisting are in store for the future. The latter could well be the most controversial and potentially explosive issue in modern wildlife management.

Understanding this, we now need to further examine the critical questions, issues, and general themes presented here and elsewhere. They require more examination and democratic debate by a wider range of citizens and stakeholders. They must also be approached with a better sense of history, culture, politics, and public policy.

The Human Role in Wolf and Wildlife Management

Questions pertaining to wolf management and control will be just as controversial as those regarding reintroduction. Where will wolves be allowed to live, and where will they be prohibited? For what reasons will they be controlled? For whose interests? And how will such control be implemented? These and similar questions will be asked in the future. Stakeholders must be willing to discuss each carefully. As discussed in chapter 1, a philosophical fault line is clearly evident in some wildlife management conflicts.[7] Many stakeholders favoring wolf control emphasize the necessity of hands-on wildlife management. We must "manage the resource," according to this view. Failing to do so is not only foolish and naive, they say, but is also an abrogation of agency responsibility. These stakeholders emphasize the role of humans as part of the natural world. They contend that we must get our hands dirty and make difficult choices. This view often frames the debate in urban versus rural terms. That is, urban wolf advocates are often so out of touch with the natural world that they fail to see themselves as being part of it. While some wolf advocates reject the interventionist paradigm outright, others are simply skeptical of for whom this intervention is being done. More wolf advocates would support control measures if they were certain they were being done to safeguard natural processes, not to make hunting easier or ranching more profitable.

The Public Interest in Wildlife

Future wolf- and wildlife-centered political conflict will likely be related to larger issues regarding state wildlife policymaking, management, and funding. While not a panacea, new stakeholder-based collaborative approaches may help alleviate perceptions of exclusive decision making, unfair treatment, and agency capture. But these criticisms will likely persist until state wildlife commissions become more reflective of the public's values toward wildlife, and these interests are given an opportunity to help pay for the costs associated with wildlife management. In short, no wolf management decision—stakeholder-based or not—will be accepted as completely fair until these inequities of funding and representation are also addressed.

One of the more serious concerns among wolf advocates and the conservation community in general is the disparity between public opinion and those making and implementing public policy. Many believe that the states, especially those in the intermountain West, cannot be trusted with wolf management until the wildlife policymaking process is opened up, becomes more participatory, and most of all, becomes more reflective of public opinion. This divide separating public opinion from state predator policy is seen as one reason why an increasing number of interests are opting for the citizen initiative process as a way to force the public's interest. According to Rob Edward, program director for Sinapu, an organization working to restore wolves to the Southern Rockies, "The chasm between popular will and legislative action will continue to spawn ballot initiatives for years to come." Edward believes that while Colorado legislators at the beginning of the twentieth century may have reflected popular sentiment toward wolves and other predators, present-day legislators do not: "Today's residents of the Rocky Mountain West have a different outlook on wolves and wilderness, seeing the wild as something to be treasured and restored."[8]

A few voices wholeheartedly champion the ballot initiative process as a way to make wildlife policy. The process is an important check on our representative institutions but is also prone to fear mongering, polarization, exaggeration, scientific misrepresentation, and special-interest domination. It is certainly not the type of public deliberation and democratic debate advocated here. Nevertheless, this option will be utilized more in the future, especially with future debate regarding wolf control, unless management decisions become more reflective of the larger public's values and opinions. If key legislative committees, wildlife agencies, and state wildlife commissions fail to adequately represent the multiplicity of values and stakeholders that have a legitimate interest in wolves and wildlife, they should expect a disgruntled public to use whatever means necessary to have their voices heard.

Given the fish- and game-driven sources of state wildlife agency budgets, new stakeholders must also be given a way to contribute to state wildlife agencies. More diverse and equitable sources of funding, such as tax check-offs and other state taxes, would alleviate many fears and apprehensions regarding state wolf management.

If stakeholders from a wider spectrum have a right to participate in wolf policymaking and management, they also have the duty to help pay for some of these costs. In Yellowstone, for example, wolf reintro-duction was framed and defined as a national issue, about which the American public, not just those living near the park, had the right to be heard. Following this logic, many people in communities surrounding Yellowstone are now asking why this national public is not paying for some of the costs associated with this "national interest." If the public decides that livestock compensation programs should continue, the question of who should be doing the compensating should also be up for debate. Many states antagonistic to wolf reintroduction directed as much of their animosity toward the federal government as they did to-ward the reintroduced wolves. Many continue to question the fairness of having to pay for the management of an animal that was strategically framed as being of national interest and concern. If this concern is a le-gitimate one, then pressure should be placed on the federal government to continue their financial support following delisting. We must con-sider a number of different ways, from federal legislation to other types of taxation, to support nongame wildlife management so that the gen-eral public can be asked to shoulder more responsibility.

This issue also brings into focus the distinction between the pub-lic's opinion and the public's behavior. This is why public opinion sur-veys about wolves tell us only part of the story. The public gets a hypo-thetical vote for or against some wolf recovery issue, knowing full well that they will not be expected to do anything in return. Survey re-spondents may want wolves reintroduced someplace, for example, but in no way will they reconsider building their second home in the middle of an important wildlife corridor. Democratic citizens, on the other hand, are given a voice in the debate and are then expected to follow through.

The Management of Public Wildlife for Private Interests

As discussed throughout this book, wolf recovery and management cannot be easily isolated from larger political issues. Wolves are part of a more inclusive debate concerning the management of public wildlife for private interests. The experimental designation of wolves in Yellowstone, central Idaho, and the Southwest provides an important example. In these places, the debate is not only about wolves but about whose interests they should be managed for and at what ecological and economic price. Critics see the designation as a dubious exercise in special interest politics: managing a public "resource" for those with the most squeaky of wheels and the best connections.

In Wisconsin, those hunting black bears with hounds have been compensated by the state when their dogs have been killed in the field by wolves. Game farm operators in northern Wisconsin who are compensated by the state for wolf depredation are yet another example used by critics of the slippery slope of special-interest wildlife management. These are clear examples, say some, of a few special interests wanting to eliminate all natural risks to private profit-making, at the expense of the public and future generations. This important question is increasingly being asked as states write their wolf management plans. One member of Minnesota's wolf roundtable sees it in very value-laden terms of what is "natural." What irked him during roundtable discussions is how a few special interests felt that they had the right to be compensated for wolf depredation. He contends that they are not entitled to public funds and should not be immune from risks we all face in an uncertain world— weather, damage done by deer, geese, and other predators.

It would also be useful to discuss whether wolves should be managed differently on public as opposed to private lands. Some in the debate support more liberal ranching-friendly management on private lands. They believe that landowners raising livestock on private property should be provided as much flexibility as possible in safeguarding their livestock and controlling depredating wolves, and that if depredation does take place, they should receive compensation. Many people also believe, however, that public lands ranching should be treated and evaluated much differently. On the public domain, they say, more conservative wolf management measures should be implemented. Some critics also maintain that if we are to have different management goals and guidelines for wolves on public lands than on private, then some of our most entrenched natural resource laws, such as the 1934 Taylor Grazing Act, must also be up for discussion.

Wolves and Rural Communities

Another option might be to promote a serious dialogue about ecological restoration as well as a rural community restoration. In other words, a two-pronged environmentalism is necessary to achieve long-term wolf and rural community viability. The debate needs to be reframed, and the problem redefined, according to this view. The wise-use movement's framing—wolves versus rural communities—is flawed but largely uncontested by those who care about both. Focusing solely on wolves without thinking carefully about the fate of our rural communities will in the end jeopardize both. This discussion must be honest, open, and critical. It must avoid romanticizing, while at the same time recognize that protecting wolves and rural communities are not mutually exclusive goals. What happens to wolf recovery when yet another ranch becomes subdivided, and another landscape fragmented? Vilifying the local accomplishes as much as stereotyping the urban out-of-touch environmentalist: very little. Some place-based environmental organizations have built on the potential of cooperation, of "turning battlegrounds into common ground."[9] This perspective insists that we often unnecessarily divide some people with a common vision of the future.

Substitutes for a Land Ethic

Rhetoric attacking subsidies is boilerplate political and environmental strategy. Below-cost timber sales, decentralized development that does not pay for itself, western water politics, and finally, public lands ranching are often attacked on economic grounds—the policy story of the unknowing taxpayer being gored by privileged special interests. While such rhetoric is often true and may be fruitful in the short run, it may be detrimental as a long-term and primary environmental strategy. At the very least, it has some serious limitations when it comes to wolves. We, as a society, tax some things and subsidize others. While many of our natural resource and wildlife policies now appear antiquated, governed as they are by the "lords of yesterday," they were a reflection of American frontier values.[10] Government gave away land, water, timber, and minerals, while paying wolf bounties, because developing the arid West was a national goal governed by the ideals of manifest destiny. The issue, then, is not subsidies but in which direction these subsidies should flow and on whose behalf. If environmental values have changed since frontier America, then redirecting subsidies toward policies more in sync with these values is the direction we ought to take.

At its core, the debate over wolves is a debate over public values. But some environmentalists are reluctant these days to argue on openly ethical and political grounds. Environmental goals—from wilderness to wolves—are not just about economic costs, benefits, and trade-offs. Instead, they are about public values: the judgments citizens make about who we are and where we want to go as a nation. They can be historical, ideological, cultural, ethical, aesthetic, or of some other type. There is nothing wrong with this admission, nor is there anything wrong with debating war, abortion, or endangered species using a language of morals and ethics. Aldo Leopold talked of wolves, predators, and "Substitutes for a Land Ethic" in *A Sand County Almanac:*

> A parallel situation exists in respect of predatory mammals, raptorial birds, and fish-eating birds. Time was when biologists somewhat overworked the evidence that these creatures preserve the health of game by killing weaklings, or that they control rodents for the farmer, or that they prey only on "worthless" species. Here again, the evidence had to be economic in order to be valid. It is only in recent years that we hear the more honest argument that predators are members of the community, and that no special interest has the right to exterminate them for the sake of a benefit, real or fancied, to itself.[11]

But where does this leave us? Mark Sagoff is again helpful here: "We may have a policy that is rational in what we may call a deliberative sense, however, if we strive to base law on principles and ideals that reflect our best conception of what we stand for and respect as a nation." Our environmental goals, says Sagoff, "are not to be construed, then, simply as personal wants or preferences; they are not interests to be 'priced' by markets or by cost-benefit analysis, but are views or beliefs that may find their way, as public values, into legislation."[12]

It is dangerously thin ice on which environmentalists expose the economic costs of public lands ranching while at the same time selling wolves as a potential economic boon. This is not to say that the former is not true or important to know about. But wolves have been and will always be about public values, not just economic costs and benefits. Touting wolves as an economic windfall because of increased park visitation, "wolf-jams" in Yellowstone, and the general benefits related to eco-tourism—although all true, significant, and a useful retort in most wolf debates—is an environmental strategy with no heart and no hope. The wolf debate should be centered on values and ecological grounds, not on visitor-days and entrance fees.

This caution will become more important with upcoming state wolf management responsibilities. Wolves in Minnesota provide one example. Minnesota wolves will be controlled and managed to some degree. As the Minnesota wolf population grows, so too will the economic costs borne by the state.[13] Add into this mix a hypothetical (or not so hypothetical) economic downturn with gas prices increasing dramatically. As a result, visitation to northern Minnesota, the International Wolf Center (an eco-tourism facility in northern Minnesota), and our national parks (including trips to Yellowstone) decreases. What now comes of this economic framing? Are wolves no longer worth the economic costs? Furthermore, this scenario says nothing about what this strategy means for species and places lacking such economic value. An honest and constructive political discussion of wolf recovery and management must go *beyond* an economic or scientific framing.

Habitat and Wolves

Future debate over wolf management issues should include a broader discussion about wilderness and wildlife habitat. Focusing on wolves alone is shortsighted and self-defeating. A more inclusive debate might include issues pertaining to roadless areas, rural sprawl, extractive industry, public lands ranching, and industrial forms of recreation. As the case of Alaska illustrates, having extensive wilderness and intact ecosystems does not mean the end of wolf conflict. But it does mean that some biological and ethical conflicts can be avoided or at least minimized. There are serious implications of not addressing wilderness and habitat needs in the future. Possibilities include an increased number of human-wolf conflicts, a political backlash toward wolves perceived to be in inappropriate places, intensive human manipulation, habituation, and the ethical quandaries of managing wolves in unnatural zoolike settings.

Democracy and Wolves

We should strive to make our political institutions more representative, inclusive, fair, deliberative, and, above all, democratic. Humans and wildlife will benefit from such reform. I hope that the themes and questions discussed here will be addressed in the future in a more representative and inclusive democratic framework. What does this mean exactly? It will likely mean different things in different places. Nonetheless, there are a few general components that can be included. First, our elected representatives should provide more vision and guidelines. Despite the serious problems that plague our representative institutions, they are still our representative institutions. There is precedent here as well. Congress once provided the vision and tools necessary to develop the West. Their vision and worldview—however inappropriate in the twenty-first century—are still embodied in our natural resource laws. Strip away the legalese, and these statutes exemplify the values of resourcism. If these laws no longer mirror American values, then these representative bodies should replace them with ones that are more reflective.

Democracy goes beyond our legislative institutions. The state wildlife policymaking and management process should also be examined. Too many interests and values do not have a voice in too many states. If changes are not forthcoming, wildlife policy in the future will be increasingly made via the ballot initiative rather than through a more deliberative process. Grassroots activism and participation are also an essential part of democracy. The number, passion, and sophistication of activists on all sides of this debate provide evidence that grassroots democracy is alive and well. Democracy also happens around kitchen tables, and it is this sort that we desperately need. Meaningful communication needs to take place, not only at some rabble-rousing public comment session but in a less formal way among those who care. And finally, democracy means envisioning a world in which we want to live. Big dreams. It means that we have an opportunity to challenge the sometimes shoddy choices we are given and replace them with a new set of options for the future.

Options, Opportunities, and the Preferred Alternative

Perhaps as a result of reading one too many environmental impact statements, I found it tempting to structure this concluding chapter with a similar framework: alternatives A through D with the author's preferred alternative backed with mountains of supporting evidence. While I chose not to pursue such an ending, there are various future wolf scenarios that may unfold. Alternative A, the preferred alternative, is a best-case scenario (the question "for whom exactly?" illustrates the difficulties inherent in this approach). Wolves are provided secure habitat and wildlands. Preventative measures and better management practices reduce livestock depredation to a marginal problem. State wildlife agencies are able to do what little management is needed with an increase in funds from nongame sources of revenue. There is unprecedented cooperation among the federal government, states, tribes, and private organizations. No longer feared, the ESA becomes a positive instrument of change, replete with economic incentives and a successful private property program. And finally, the use of stakeholders in wolf and wildlife management opens new doors while solving old problems.

Alternative D paints a dramatically different picture of the future. Livestock depredation becomes such a problem that ranchers and anti-wolf interests begin the nation's second war on the wolf, poisons not only killing wolves but other endangered wildlife as well. Wolf recovery begins to be perceived, even among one-time wolf supporters, as a highly unethical mini-industry that has little to do with wilderness and a new land ethic, and everything to do with technology, human manipulation, and unmatched hubris. States, unwilling to channel money from game funds, are unable to afford hands-on intensive state wolf management. Human population growth and decentralized development become such a problem that even the most ardent wolf supporters are no longer certain there are any suitable places left for wolves. And finally, the use of stakeholders does nothing more than complicate an issue that needs no further complicating.

There are, of course, other possible or more likely scenarios. Whatever these may be, I hope that the "preferred alternative" is rigorously debated by the public and their political representatives in a more inclusive and participatory setting, and that it is a democratically and deliberately chosen alternative preferred by the public-at-large. There are serious obstacles and threats to this democratic approach, and it is certainly unfair to place this larger democratic challenge on top of wolves and their recovery. But it will be nothing new.

Notes

Preface

1. Lois Crisler, *Arctic Wild* (1956; New York: Lyons Press, 1999), 92.
2. Rick Bass, *The New Wolves: The Return of the Mexican Wolf to the American Southwest* (New York: Lyons, 1998), 126.

Introduction

The epigraphs are from Rick McIntyre, ed., *War against the Wolf: America's Campaign to Exterminate the Wolf* (Stillwater, Minn.: Voyageur Press, 1995), 30, 10. This book is a compilation of more than one hundred historical documents and modern articles documenting the evolving attitudes toward wolves in America from 1630 to 1995.

1. Several notable case studies address particular wolf reintroduction efforts and the politics behind them, such as Thomas McNamee, *The Return of the Wolf to Yellowstone* (New York: Henry Holt, 1997); and Hank Fischer, *Wolf Wars: The Remarkable Inside Story of the Restoration of Wolves to Yellowstone* (New York: Falcon, 1995). These books tell a gripping story while investigating not only the wolf and its new environs but the Western American culture they are being reintroduced into. The impressive literary works of Rick Bass, for example, *The New Wolves: The Reintroduction of the Mexican Wolf in the American Southwest* (New York: Lyons, 1998); and *The Ninemile Wolves* (New York: Ballantine, 1993), tell similar stories and allow readers to become engaged not only with the fate of these animals but also with their tenuous cultural, political, and legal situations. Several books have been written about wolf history, such as Stanley Paul Young, *The Wolf in North American History* (Caldwell, Idaho: Caxton, 1946); and David E. Brown, ed., *The Wolf in the Southwest: The Making of an Endangered Species* (Tucson: University of Arizona Press, 1983). Bruce Hampton, *The Great American Wolf* (New York: Henry Holt, 1997) is a wonderful historical account. See also Timothy Rawson, *Changing Tracks:*

Predators and Politics in Mount McKinley National Park (Anchorage: University of Alaska Press, 2001). Peter Steinhart, *The Company of Wolves* (New York: Vintage, 1996) provides a popular discussion and analysis of wolf recovery in the United States from a cultural and ecological perspective. Two edited volumes focusing on New England are Virginia A. Sharpe, Bryan Norton, and Strachan Donnelley, eds., *Wolves and Human Communities: Biology, Politics, and Ethics* (Washington, D.C.: Island Press, 2000); and John Elder, ed., *The Return of the Wolf: Reflections on the Future of Wolves in the Northeast* (Hanover, N.H.: University Press of New England, 2000). Recent books covering wolf recovery and management in the Lake Superior region include L. David Mech, ed., *The Wolves of Minnesota: Howling in the Heartland* (Stillwater, Minn.: Voyageur Press, 2000); and Richard P. Thiel, *Keepers of the Wolves: The Early Years of Wolf Recovery in Wisconsin* (Madison: University of Wisconsin Press, 2001).

2. For a critical discussion of these social choices, see Rick Bass, "Vermont as Montana," in *The Return of the Wolf*, ed. Elder, 108–75.

3. Barry Holstrun Lopez, *Of Wolves and Men* (New York: Touchstone, 1978), 4.

4. Ibid., 140.

5. Examples are from the wolves and humans exhibit at the International Wolf Center, Ely, Minnesota.

6. Stephen R. Kellert, Matthew Black, Colleen R. Rush, and Alistair J. Bath, "Human Culture and Large Carnivore Conservation in North America," *Conservation Biology* 10 (1996): 977–90.

7. See David S. Wilcove, *The Condor's Shadow: The Loss and Recovery of Wildlife in America* (New York: Anchor Books, 1999); and David S. Maehr, Reed F. Noss, and Jeffery L. Larkin, eds., *Large Mammal Restoration: Ecological and Sociological Challenges in the 21st Century* (Washington, D.C.: Island Press, 2001).

8. For a general discussion of the policy sciences approach to natural resource policy and management, including the importance of context, see Tim W. Clark, Andrew R. Willard, and Christina M. Cromley, eds., *Foundations of Natural Resources Management* (New Haven: Yale University Press, 2000). Following the work of policy scientist Harold Lasswell, Clark and Willard emphasize the importance of "social process mapping" as a way of better understanding and helping resolve policy problems. The mapping process, among other things, analyzes the participants involved, their various perspectives on the issue, the situations in which they (might) interact, their values and power bases, the strategies they use to achieve their goals, the outcomes they will or might achieve, and possible long-term effects (Clark and Willard, "Learning about Natural Resource Policy and Management," 3–31).

9. See National Research Council, *Wolves, Bears, and Their Prey in Alaska: Biological and Social Challenges in Wildlife Management* (Washington, D.C.: National Academy Press, 1997).

10. Hampton, *The Great American Wolf*, 250.

11. See David J. Mladenoff, Theodore A. Sickley, Robert G. Haight, and Adrian P. Wydeven, "A Regional Landscape Analysis and Prediction of Favorable Gray Wolf Habitat in the Northern Great Lakes Region," *Conservation Biology* 9, 2 (1995): 279–94.

12. U.S. Fish and Wildlife Service, *Recovery Plan for the Eastern Timber Wolf* (Twin Cities, Minn.: USFWS, 1992).

13. Adrian P. Wydeven, Todd K. Fuller, William Weber, and Kristi MacDonald,

"The Potential for Wolf Recovery in the Northeastern United States via Dispersal from Southeastern Canada," *Wildlife Society Bulletin* 26 (1998): 776–84.

14. U.S. Fish and Wildlife Service, *Northern Rocky Mountain Wolf Recovery Plan* (Denver, Colo.: USFWS, 1987).

15. Aldo Leopold, *A Sand County Almanac: With Essays on Conservation from Round River* (New York: Ballantine Books, 1966), 138–39.

16. David R. Parsons, "'Green Fire' Returns to the Southwest: Reintroduction of the Mexican Wolf," *Wildlife Society Bulletin* 26 (1998): 799–807.

17. U.S. Fish and Wildlife Service, *Mexican Wolf Recovery Plan* (Albuquerque, N. Mex.: USFWS, 1982).

18. U.S. Fish and Wildlife Service, *The Reintroduction of the Mexican Wolf within Its Historic Range in the United States: Final Environmental Impact Statement* (Albuquerque, N. Mex.: USFWS, 1996).

19. U.S. Fish and Wildlife Service, *Red Wolf Recovery Plan* (Atlanta, Ga.: USFWS, 1982).

20. Jan DeBlieu, *Meant to Be Wild: The Struggle to Save Endangered Species through Captive Breeding* (Golden, Colo.: Fulcrum, 1991).

21. U.S. Fish and Wildlife Service, *Red Wolf Recovery/Species Survival Plan* (Atlanta, Ga.: USFWS, 1990).

22. Defenders of Wildlife, *Places for Wolves: A Blueprint for Restoration and Long-Term Recovery in the Lower 48 States* (Washington, D.C.: Defenders of Wildlife, 1999).

23. Larry E. Bennett, *Colorado Gray Wolf Recovery: A Biological Feasibility Study* (U.S. Fish and Wildlife Service in cooperation with University of Wyoming Fish and Wildlife Cooperative Unit, 1994).

24. Deborah Stone, *Policy Paradox: The Art of Political Decision Making* (New York: W. W. Norton, 1997). Stone calls her approach to public policy the "polis model." Subsequent page references are given parenthetically in the text.

25. For a discussion of the "postpositive" approach to political and policy analysis, see Randall S. Clemons and Mark K. McBeth, *Public Policy Praxis—Theory and Pragmatism: A Case Approach* (Upper Saddle River, N.J.: Prentice Hall, 2001); Marie Danziger, "Policy Analysis Postmodernized: Some Political and Pedagogical Ramifications," *Policy Studies Journal* 23, 3 (1995): 435–50; Peter deLeon, *Democracy and the Policy Sciences* (Albany: State University of New York Press, 1997); M. E. Hawkesworth, *Theoretical Issues in Policy Analysis* (Albany: State University of New York Press, 1988); and Stone, *Policy Paradox*.

26. Clemons and McBeth, *Public Policy Praxis*, x.

27. Ibid., 178. See also Danziger, "Policy Analysis Postmodernized."

28. See Frank Fischer, *Citizens, Experts and the Environment: The Politics of Local Knowledge* (Durham, N.C.: Duke University Press, 2000); and Frank Fischer, "Citizen Participation and the Democratization of Policy Expertise: From Theoretical Inquiry to Practical Cases," *Policy Sciences* 26 (1993): 165–87.

29. See Barney G. Glaser and Anselm L. Strauss, *The Discovery of Grounded Theory: Strategies for Qualitative Research* (New York: Aldine de Gruyter, 1967); and Norman K. Denzin and Yvonna S. Lincoln, eds., *Strategies of Qualitative Inquiry* (Thousand Oaks, Calif.: Sage, 1998).

30. Ron Westrom, "An Organizational Perspective: Designing Recovery Teams

from the Inside Out," in *Endangered Species Recovery: Finding the Lessons, Improving the Process*, ed. Tim W. Clark, Richard P. Reading, and Alice L. Clarke (Washington, D.C.: Island Press, 1994), 329.

31. Tim W. Clark, *Averting Extinction: Reconstructing Endangered Species Recovery* (New Haven, Conn.: Yale University Press, 1997), 167.

32. Ibid., 1.

33. Paul A. Sabatier and Hank C. Jenkins-Smith, eds., *Policy Change and Learning: An Advocacy Coalition Approach* (Boulder, Colo.: Westview Press, 1993).

34. Stephen R. Kellert, *The Value of Life: Biological Diversity and Human Society* (Washington, D.C.: Island Press, 1996).

1. Wolf Recovery and Management as Value-Based Political Conflict

1. John Hughes, "Wolves Could Adapt in Park, Study Contends," *News Tribune* (Tacoma, Wash.), 6 March 1999, B3.

2. E. E. Schattschneider, *The Semi-Sovereign People: A Realist's View of Democracy in America* (New York: Holt, Rinehart and Winston, 1960), 2.

3. Ibid., 35.

4. The Hrebenar-Thomas project on interest groups, for example, found that many southern and western states have the most powerful interest groups systems in the nation. What determines this interest group power? The authors propose Daniel Elazar's political subculture framework as one possible explanation. They found, for instance, that Minnesota and other "moralistic" states, such as Maine and Vermont, have less powerful group systems than "individualistic" states, such as New Mexico. See Clive S. Thomas and Ronald J. Hrebenar, "Interest Groups in the States," in *Politics in the American States: A Comparative Analysis*, ed. Virginia Gray and R. L. Hanson (Washington, D.C.: CQ Press, 1999), 113–43.

5. See, for example, John Kingdon, *Agendas, Alternatives, and Public Policies*, 2d ed. (New York: HarperCollins, 1995). Kingdon documents numerous players involved in setting the policy agenda.

6. Steven A. Primm and Tim W. Clark, "Making Sense of the Policy Process for Carnivore Conservation," *Conservation Biology* 10 (1996): 1036–45.

7. Paul A. Sabatier, "Policy Change over a Decade or More," in *Policy Change and Learning: An Advocacy Coalition Approach*, ed. Paul A. Sabatier and Hank C. Jenkins-Smith (Boulder, Colo.: Westview Press, 1993), 16.

8. Hank C. Jenkins-Smith and Paul A. Sabatier, "Evaluating the Advocacy Coalition Framework," *Journal of Public Policy* 14, 2 (1994): 181.

9. See James A. Tober, *Wildlife and the Public Interest: Nonprofit Organizations and Federal Wildlife Policy* (New York: Praeger, 1989).

10. Primm and Clark, "Making Sense of the Policy Process for Carnivore Conservation," 1042.

11. Paul Sabatier, "An Advocacy Coalition-Framework of Policy Change and the Role of Policy-Oriented Learning Therein," *Policy Sciences* 21 (1988): 129–68.

12. Primm and Clark, "Making Sense of the Policy Process for Carnivore Conservation," 1042.

13. See Stephen R. Kellert, *The Value of Life: Biological Diversity and Human Society* (Washington, D.C.: Island Press, 1996); subsequent page references are given parenthetically in the text.

14. Stephen R. Kellert, "A Sociological Perspective: Valuational, Socioeconomic, and Organizational Factors," in *Endangered Species Recovery: Finding the Lessons, Improving the Process,* ed. Tim W. Clark, Richard Reading, and Alice L. Clarke (Washington, D.C.: Island Press, 1994), 373.

15. Stephen R. Kellert and Edward O. Wilson, eds., *The Biophilia Hypothesis* (Washington, D.C.: Island Press, 1993).

16. U.S. Fish and Wildlife Service, *The Reintroduction of Gray Wolves to Yellowstone National Park and Central Idaho: Final Environmental Impact Statement* (Helena, Mont.: USFWS, 1994).

17. David T. Schaller, "The Ecocenter as Tourist Attraction: Ely and the International Wolf Center," (Ely, Minn.: International Wolf Center, 1999).

18. See Matthew A. Wilson and Thomas A. Heberlein, "The Wolf, the Tourist, and the Recreational Context: New Opportunity or Uncommon Circumstance?" *Human Dimensions of Wildlife* 1, 4 (winter 1996): 38–53.

19. See, for example, Jim Brandenburg, *Brother Wolf: A Forgotten Promise* (Minocqua, Wis.: Northwood Press, 1993).

20. Barry Lopez, *Of Wolves and Men* (New York: Touchstone, 1978), 138.

21. Ibid., 139.

22. Steven Kellert, *The Public and the Wolf in Minnesota, 1999* (Ely, Minn.: International Wolf Center, 1999).

23. Julia M. Wondolleck and Steven L. Yaffee, *Making Collaboration Work: Lessons from Innovation in Natural Resource Management* (Washington, D.C.: Island Press, 2000), 48.

24. Thomas Prugh, Robert Costanza, and Herman Daly, *The Local Politics of Global Sustainability* (Washington, D.C.: Island Press, 2000), 94.

25. Under the ESA, the secretary of the interior's final decision on listing a species as endangered or threatened must be made "solely on the basis of the best scientific and commercial data available to him." But states have flexibility in how they devise their state wolf management plans insofar as they meet FWS delisting requirements (that these populations are no longer in jeopardy and that the species will not be threatened with endangerment again).

26. L. David Mech, "Estimated Costs of Maintaining a Recovered Wolf Population in Agricultural Regions of Minnesota," *Wildlife Society Bulletin* 26 (1998): 817–22.

27. Dennis Anderson, "Anderson: Mech Says Wolf Plan Is Flawed," *Minneapolis Star Tribune,* 7 March 1999; http://www.nmw.org/wolf/990307_wolf_mech.html (9 August 1999).

28. See Scot J. Williamson, "Origins, History, and Current Use of Ballot Initiatives in Wildlife Management," *Human Dimensions of Wildlife* 3, 2 (1998): 51–59; part of a special issue devoted to ballot initiatives.

29. Donna L. Minnis, "Wildlife Policy-Making by the Electorate: An Overview of Citizen-Sponsored Ballot Measures on Hunting and Trapping," *Wildlife Society Bulletin* 26 (1998): 75–83.

30. L. David Mech, "A New Era for Carnivore Conservation," *Wildlife Society Bulletin* 24 (1996): 400.

31. For an excellent discussion of science and adaptive management in a democratic context, see Kai L. Lee, *Compass and Gyroscope: Integrating Science and Politics for the Environment* (Washington, D.C.: Island Press, 1993).

32. R. McGreggor Cawley and John Freemuth, "Tree Farms, Mother Earth, and

Other Dilemmas: The Politics of Ecosystem Management in Greater Yellowstone," *Society and Natural Resources* 6 (1993): 41–53.

33. Ibid., 48.

34. See L. David Mech, "The Challenge and Opportunity of Recovering Wolf Populations," *Conservation Biology* 9 (1995): 270–78.

35. Todd Wilkinson, *Science under Siege: The Politicians' War on Nature and Truth* (Boulder, Colo.: Johnson Books, 1998), 5.

36. Charles E. Kay, "Wolves in the West," *Peterson's Hunting*, August 1993.

37. Ibid.

38. Ibid.

39. Charles E. Kay, comments made at the Predator-Prey Symposium, Boise, Idaho, 5 January 1999.

40. Paul Rogers and Jennifer LaFleur, "The Giveaway of the West," *San Jose Mercury News* Special Report; reprint of stories originally published 7 November 1999, 2S.

41. Thomas L. Fleischner, "Ecological Costs of Livestock Grazing in Western North America," *Conservation Biology* 8 (1994): 629–44.

42. Charles Davis, "Politics and Public Rangeland Policy," in *Western Public Lands and Environmental Politics,* ed. Charles Davis (Boulder, Colo.: Westview Press, 1997), 74–94.

43. Christopher McGrory Klyza, *Who Controls Public Lands? Mining, Forestry, and Grazing Policies, 1870–1990* (Chapel Hill: University of North Carolina Press, 1996), 115.

44. Debra L. Donahue, *The Western Range Revisited: Removing Livestock from Public Lands to Conserve Native Biodiversity* (Norman: University of Oklahoma Press, 1999), 5.

45. Katharine Collins, "A Prof Takes on the Sacred Cow," *High Country News,* 28 February 2000, 3.

46. Ibid.

47. See, for example, Marion Clawson, *The Western Range Livestock Industry* (New York: McGraw-Hill Book Co., 1950); Phillip Foss, *Politics and Grass* (Seattle: University of Washington Press, 1960); and Paul J. Culhane, *Public Lands Politics: Interest Group Influence on the Forest Service and the Bureau of Land Management* (Baltimore: Johns Hopkins University Press, 1981).

48. David A. Adams, *Renewable Resource Policy: The Legal-Institutional Foundations* (Washington, D.C.: Island Press, 1993).

49. Predator Conservation Alliance, "Wildlife 'Services'? A Presentation and Analysis of the USDA Wildlife Services Program's Expenditures and Kill Figures for Fiscal Year 1998" (Bozeman, Mont., April 2000).

50. Doug J. Swanson, "Despite Name Change, Agency Can't Shed Killer Image," *Washington Post,* 4 November 1998, A23.

51. Rogers and LaFleur, "The Giveaway of the West," 2S.

52. Stephen R. Kellert, *Public Attitudes toward Critical Wildlife and Natural Habitat Issues, Phase I* (Washington, D.C.: U.S. Department of the Interior, Fish and Wildlife Service, 1979); Stephen R. Kellert, *Activities of the American Public Relating to Animals, Phase II* (Washington, D.C.: U.S. Department of the Interior, Fish and Wildlife Service, 1980); Stephen R. Kellert, *Knowledge, Affection and Basic Attitudes toward Animals in American Society, Phase III* (Washington, D.C.: U.S. Department of the Interior, Fish and Wildlife Service, 1980).

53. James J. Kennedy, "Viewing Wildlife Managers as a Unique Professional Culture," *Wildlife Society Bulletin* 13 (1985): 571–79.

54. Thomas D. I. Beck, "Citizen Ballot Initiatives: A Failure of the Wildlife Management Profession," *Human Dimensions of Wildlife* 3, 2 (1998): 21–28.

55. Kennedy, "Viewing Wildlife Managers as a Unique Professional Culture," 571.

56. R. Bruce Gill, "The Wildlife Professional Subculture: The Case of the Crazy Aunt," *Human Dimensions of Wildlife* 1, 1 (1996): 63.

57. Ibid.

58. Kristen G. Mortenson and Richard S. Krannich, *Wildlife Management and the Utah Public: Managers' Attitudes, Beliefs, and Ideas within the Utah Division of Wildlife Resources* (Logan: Institute for Social Science Research on Natural Resources, Utah State University, April 2000).

59. Richard S. Krannich and Tara Teel, *Utah Residents' Views about Selected Wildlife Management Issues: Similarities and Differences across Five Stakeholder Categories* (Logan: Institute for Social Science Research on Natural Resources, Utah State University, 1999).

60. Mortenson and Krannich, *Wildlife Management and the Utah Public*, v.

61. Beck, "Citizen Ballot Initiatives"; see also candid comments made by Beck in David Peterson, *Ghost Grizzlies: Does the Great Bear Still Haunt Colorado?* (Boulder, Colo.: Johnson Books, 1998), 188–98.

62. Beck, "Citizen Ballot Initiatives," 22–23.

63. Ibid., 23.

64. Ibid.

65. Stan Meyer, comments made at Predator Management in Montana Symposium, Billings, Mont., 8 January 2000.

66. Ibid.

67. John F. Reiger, *American Sportsmen and the Origins of Conservation* (New York: Winchester, 1975), 12.

68. Scott Farr, comments made at Predator-Prey Symposium, Boise, Idaho, 5 January 1999.

69. The terms *animal rights* and *animal welfare* should not be used interchangeably. *Animal rights* refers to the belief that animals have rights equal or similar to those of humans. *Animal welfare* refers to the belief that we should strive to reduce the pain and suffering of animals. Thus, an interest in animal welfare does not imply giving rights to animals. See Gary G. Gray, *Wildlife and People: The Human Dimensions of Wildlife Ecology* (Urbana: University of Illinois Press, 1993).

70. Reiger, *American Sportsmen and the Origins of Conservation*, 14.

71. John Myers and Craig Lincoln, "Hunting, Trapping Support Grows If Numbers Increase," *Duluth News Tribune*, 14 April 1999, 1.

72. Kellert, *The Value of Life*, 65–79.

73. See Bruce Hampton, *The Great American Wolf* (New York: Henry Holt, 1997), for an excellent history of wolf politics in Alaska. See also National Research Council, *Wolves, Bears, and Their Prey in Alaska: Biological and Social Challenges in Wildlife Management* (Washington, D.C.: National Academy Press, 1997).

74. Mech, "The Challenge and Opportunity of Recovering Wolf Populations," 270–78.

75. Gordon C. Haber, "Biological, Conservation, and Ethical Implications of Exploiting and Controlling Wolves," *Conservation Biology* 10, 4 (1996): 1076.

76. Ibid.

77. Wayne Pacelle, "Forging a New Wildlife Paradigm: Integrating Animal Protection Values," *Human Dimensions of Wildlife* 3, 2 (1998): 49.

78. Ibid., 42–50.

79. Ibid., 49.

80. Jan E. Dizard, *Going Wild: Hunting, Animal Rights, and the Contested Meaning of Nature* (Amherst: University of Massachusetts Press, 1999).

81. Ibid., 49.

82. Ibid., 171.

83. Ibid., 166.

84. L. David Mech, "Managing Minnesota's Recovered Wolves," *Wildlife Society Bulletin* 29, 1 (2001): 70–77.

85. L. David Mech, "Historical Overview of Minnesota Wolf Recovery," in *The Wolves of Minnesota: Howl in the Heartland*, ed. L. David Mech (Stillwater, Minn.: Voyageur Press, 2000), 15–27.

86. Robert R. Ream, "Minnesota Wolf Range: Past, Present, and Future," in *The Wolves of Minnesota*, ed. Mech, 34.

87. See William Lynn, "With Predatory Intent: Ethics and the Recovery of Large Predators in the New Millennium," paper presented at Defenders of Wildlife's Carnivores 2000: A Conference on Carnivore Conservation in the 21st Century, 12–15 November 2000.

2. The Wolf as Symbol, Surrogate, and Policy Problem

1. "Simpson Authors Bill Introducing Wolves into New York State," http://www.gop.gov/item-news.asp?N=20000519133311 (13 September 2000).

2. Steven A. Primm and Tim W. Clark, "Making Sense of the Policy Process for Carnivore Conservation," *Conservation Biology* 10, 4 (1996): 1037.

3. Steven L. Yaffee, "The Northern Spotted Owl: An Indicator of the Importance of Sociopolitical Context," in *Endangered Species Recovery: Finding the Lessons, Improving the Process*, ed. Tim W. Clark, Richard P. Reading, and Alice L. Clarke (Washington, D.C.: Island Press, 1994), 53.

4. Ibid., 59.

5. Danny Westneat, "Wolves Could Survive Here—Olympic Park Studied as Potential Home," *Seattle Times*, 2 March 1999, A1.

6. L. David Mech, "Estimated Costs of Maintaining a Recovered Wolf Population in Agricultural Regions of Minnesota," *Wildlife Society Bulletin* 26, 4 (1998): 818.

7. Peter Steinhart, *The Company of Wolves* (New York: Vintage Books, 1995), 344.

8. Deborah Stone, *Policy Paradox: The Art of Political Decision Making* (New York: W. W. Norton and Company, 1997), 137; subsequent page references are given parenthetically in the text.

9. Two important books examining the role that symbols play in politics and public policy are Murray Edelman, *The Symbolic Uses of Politics* (Urbana: University of Illinois Press, 1964); and Charles D. Elder and Roger W. Cobb, *The Political Uses of Symbols* (New York: Longman, 1983).

10. For a fascinating discussion of the social construction of fish and wildlife, see Rik Scarce, *Fishy Business: Salmon, Biology, and the Social Construction of Nature*

(Philadelphia: Temple University Press, 2000). Also see Rik Scarce, "What Do Wolves Mean? Conflicting Constructions of *Canis Lupus* in 'Bordertown,'" *Human Dimensions of Wildlife* 3, 3 (1998): 26–45.

11. E. E. Schattschneider, *The Semisovereign People* (Hinsdale, Ill.: Dryden Press, 1960), 68.

12. David A. Rochefort and Roger W. Cobb, "Problem Definition: An Emerging Perspective," in *The Politics of Problem Definition: Shaping the Policy Agenda* (Lawrence: University Press of Kansas, 1994), 3.

13. Janet A. Weiss, "The Powers of Problem-Definition: The Case of Government Paperwork," *Policy Sciences* 22 (1989): 116.

14. Tim W. Clark, A. Peyton Curlee, and Richard P. Reading, "Crafting Effective Solutions to the Large Carnivore Conservation Problem," *Conservation Biology* 10, 4 (1996): 947.

15. Tim W. Clark, *Averting Extinction: Reconstructing Endangered Species Recovery* (New Haven, Conn.: Yale University Press, 1997), 141; subsequent page references are given parenthetically in the text.

16. Robert B. Keiter, "An Introduction to the Ecosystem Management Debate," in *The Greater Yellowstone Ecosystem: Redefining America's Wilderness Heritage*, ed. Robert B. Keiter and Mark S. Boyce (New Haven, Conn.: Yale University Press, 1991), 3–18.

17. Matthew A. Wilson, "The Wolf in Yellowstone: Science, Symbol, or Politics? Deconstructing the Conflict between Environmentalism and Wise Use," *Society & Natural Resources* 10 (1997): 454.

18. Patrick C. Jobes, "Population and Social Characteristics in the Greater Yellowstone Ecosystem," *Society & Natural Resources* 6 (1993): 149–63.

19. See, for example, Richard L. Knight and Sarah F. Bates, eds., *A New Century for Natural Resources Management* (Washington, D.C.: Island Press, 1995).

20. Hanna J. Cortner and Margaret A. Moote, *The Politics of Ecosystem Management* (Washington, D.C.: Island Press, 1999), 37.

21. Robert B. Keiter and Patrick T. Holscher, "Wolf Recovery under the Endangered Species Act: A Study in Contemporary Federalism," *Public Land Law Review* 11 (spring 1990): 34.

22. Tim W. Clark, Steven C. Minta, A. Peyton Curlee, and Peter M. Kareiva, *Carnivores in Ecosystems: The Yellowstone Experience* (New Haven, Conn.: Yale University Press, 2000), 4.

23. Richard P. Reading, Tim W. Clark, and Stephen R. Kellert, "Attitudes and Knowledge of People Living in the Greater Yellowstone Ecosystem," *Society & Natural Resources* 7 (1994): 349–65.

24. Senator Larry Craig, "My, What Big Eyes You Have! Central Idaho Peers into the Eyes of the Gray Wolf," 24 September 1999; http://www.senate.gov/~craig/releases/COLbigeyes.htm (13 September 2000).

25. Senator Larry Craig, "Lynx, Bears, and Wolves—Oh My!! 31 March 2000; http://www.senate.gov/~craig/releases/COLlynxprotect.htm (13 September 2000).

26. Ibid.

27. See Thomas F. Weise, William L. Robinson, Richard A. Hook, and L. David Mech, *An Experimental Translocation of the Eastern Timber Wolf.* Audubon Conservation Report No. 5 in cooperation with U.S. Department of the Interior Fish and Wildlife Service, Region 3, 1975.

28. Ibid., foreword.

29. R. Edward Grumbine, *Ghost Bears: Exploring the Biodiversity Crisis* (Washington, D.C.: Island Press, 1992), 29.

30. Gary K. Meffe, C. Ronald Carroll, and contributors, *Principles of Conservation Biology*, 2d ed. (Sunderland, Mass.: Sinauer Associates, 1997), 6.

31. See Grumbine, *Ghost Bears*; Meffe, Carroll, and contributors, *Principles of Conservation Biology*; and Reed F. Noss, Howard B. Quigley, Maurice G. Hornocker, Troy Merrill, and Paul C. Paquet, "Conservation Biology and Carnivore Conservation in the Rocky Mountains," *Conservation Biology* 10 (1996): 949–63.

32. Robert MacArthur and Edward O. Wilson, *The Theory of Island Biogeography* (Princeton, N.J.: Princeton University Press, 1967).

33. Jan DeBlieu, *Meant to Be Wild: The Struggle to Save Endangered Species through Captive Breeding* (Golden, Colo.: Fulcrum Publishing, 1991), 15.

34. Noss et al., "Conservation Biology and Carnivore Conservation in the Rocky Mountains," 950.

35. Bruce McClellan and David Shackleton, "Grizzly Bears and Resource Extraction Industries: Effects of Roads on Behavior, Habitat Use, and Demography," *Journal of Applied Ecology* 25 (1988): 457–60.

36. Paul Paquet, "The Road to Environmental Degradation Is Paved with Governments' Bad Intentions," paper presented at Defenders of Wildlife's Carnivores 2000: A Conference on Carnivore Conservation in the 21st Century, Denver, Colo., 12–15 November 2000.

37. Paul Paquet, James R. Stittholt, and Nancy L. Staus, "Wolf Reintroduction Feasibility in the Adirondack Park," prepared for the Adirondack Citizens Advisory Committee on the Feasibility of Wolf Reintroduction (Corvallis, Oreg.: Conservation Biology Institute, 1999), 40–41.

38. The institute also helps answer the question of how wolves can be flourishing in places such as the upper Midwest while their future is in doubt in the Northeast. While part of the answer may be social (they conclude that the ultimate factor determining population viability for wolves is human attitude), the ecological characteristics of the two regions are also significant. The lack of connectivity with wolves in Canada is not the only important difference. In the Adirondack Park, wolf habitat is more condensed than in the upper Midwest. In less physiographically complex environments such as northern Minnesota there are multiple travel routes linking blocks of wolf habitat. In contrast, wolves in the more mountainous Adirondacks may not be able to avoid some travel routes such as often-used valley bottoms. As a result, destruction (by development, for example) of one route in Minnesota may be less important to overall wolf viability than destruction of one route in the Adirondacks.

39. Clark, Curlee, and Reading, "Crafting Effective Solutions to the Large Carnivore Conservation Problem," 942.

40. See L. David Mech, "The Challenge and Opportunity of Recovering Wolf Populations," *Conservation Biology* 9 (1995): 270–78.

41. Sigurd F. Olson, *Open Horizons* (Minneapolis: University of Minnesota Press, 1969), 153.

42. Lois Crisler, *Arctic Wild* (1956; New York: Lyons Press, 1999), 92.

43. It is important to note the role that literature has played in the wolf policy debate, often shaping perceptions and public opinion in important ways. Although

based more on fiction than wolf biology and science, Farley Mowat's *Never Cry Wolf* (Toronto: Seal Books, 1963) is thought to have had a remarkable effect on how people think about the human-wolf relationship. For a more general discussion of literature and environmental policy, see Daniel G. Payne, "Talking Freely around the Campfire: The Influence of Nature Writing on American Environmental Policy," *Society & Natural Resources* 11 (1999): 39–48.

44. Rick Bass, *The New Wolves: The Return of the Mexican Wolf to the American Southwest* (New York: Lyons, 1998), 126.

45. James G. MacCracken and Jay O' Laughlin, "Recovery Policy on Grizzly Bears: An Analysis of Two Positions," *Wildlife Society Bulletin* 26, 4 (1998): 905.

46. Nicholas Lemann, "No People Allowed," *New Yorker,* November 22, 1999, 98.

47. Center for Biological Diversity, "Wolf Safe Haven Plan: Creating a Safe Haven for Mexican Gray Wolf Recovery," 1998.

48. Kristin DeBoer, "Dreams of Wolves," in *The Return of the Wolf: Reflections on the Future of Wolves in the Northeast,* ed. John Elder (Hanover, N.H.: Middlebury College Press, 2000), 71.

49. Quoted in DeBoer, "Dreams of Wolves," 71.

50. "The Wildlands Project," special issue, *Wild Earth* 10, 1 (2000): 4.

51. Edward O. Wilson, "A Personal Brief for The Wildlands Project," *Wild Earth* 10, 1 (2000): 1.

52. Michael E. Soulé and John Terborgh, eds., *Continental Conservation: Scientific Foundations of Regional Reserve Networks* (Washington, D.C.: Island Press, 1999).

53. Michael E. Soulé and Reed F. Noss, "Rewilding and Biodiversity as Complementary Goals for Continental Conservation," *Wild Earth* 8, 3 (1998): 18–28.

54. Dave Foreman, Barbara Dugelby, Jack Humphrey, Bob Howard, and Andy Holdsworth, "The Elements of Wildlands Network Conservation Plan: An Example from the Sky Islands," *Wild Earth* 10, 1 (2000): 20.

55. Mark Pearson, "Wild San Juans," *Wild Earth* 10, 1 (2000): 78–83.

56. Quoted in Charles C. Mann and Mark L. Plummer, "The High Cost of Biodiversity," *Science* 260, 5116 (June 25, 1993): 1870.

57. Congressional Research Service, Endangered Species List Revisions: A Summary of Delisting and Downlisting (Washington, D.C.: 1998).

58. Mark Sagoff, "On the Value of Endangered and Other Species," *Environmental Management* 20 (1996): 897–911.

59. See, for example, Clark, Reading, and Clarke, eds., *Endangered Species Recovery*; Grumbine, *Ghost Bears*; and Daniel J. Rohlf, "Six Biological Reasons Why the Endangered Species Act Doesn't Work—And What to Do About It," *Conservation Biology* 5, 3 (1991): 273–82.

60. See Rocky Barker, *Saving All the Parts: Reconciling Economics and the Endangered Species Act* (Washington, D.C.: Island Press, 1993).

61. Dale D. Goble, "Of Wolves and Welfare Ranching," *Harvard Environmental Law Review* 16 (1992): 101.

62. Tim W. Clark, Richard P. Reading, and Alice L. Clarke, introduction to *Endangered Species Recovery,* 4.

63. Michael O'Connell, "Response to: 'Six Biological Reasons Why the Endangered Species Act Doesn't Work and What to Do About It,'" *Conservation Biology* 6, 1 (1992): 140–43.

64. Edward E. Bangs, Steven H. Fritts, Joseph A. Fontaine, Douglas W. Smith, Kerry M. Murphy, Curtis M. Mack, and Carter C. Niemeyer, "Status of Gray Wolf Restoration in Montana, Idaho, and Wyoming," *Wildlife Society Bulletin* 26, 4 (1998): 785–98.

65. Christopher McGrory Klyza and David J. Sousa, "Creating Chaos: The Endangered Species Act and the Politics of Institutional Disruption," paper presented at the Annual Meeting of the Western Political Science Association, 15–17 March 2001, Las Vegas, Nev.

66. U.S. Fish and Wildlife Service, Great Lakes–Big Rivers Region, "Gray Wolves Rebound; U.S. Fish and Wildlife Service Proposes to Reclassify, Delist Wolves throughout Midwest," news release, 11 July 2000.

67. U.S. General Accounting Office, *Endangered Species Act: Information on Species Protection on Nonfederal Lands.* GAOIRCED-95-16 (Washington, D.C.: 1994).

68. See Steven L. Yaffee, *Prohibitive Policy: Implementing the Federal Endangered Species Act* (Cambridge, Mass.: MIT Press, 1982); Philip D. Brick and R. McGreggor Cawley, eds., *A Wolf in the Garden: The Land Rights Movement and the New Environmental Debate* (Lanham, Md.: Rowman and Littlefield, 1996); and Bruce Yandle, ed., *Land Rights: The 1990s' Property Rights Rebellion* (Lanham, Md.: Rowman and Littlefield, 1995).

69. Statement of Representative Helen Chenoweth-Hage, House Committee on Resources, Hearing on H.R. 3160, "Common Sense Protections for Endangered Species Act," 2 February 2000; http://www.house.gov/chenoweth (13 September 2000).

70. U.S. General Accounting Office, *Endangered Species Act: Information on Species Protection on Nonfederal Lands.*

71. Michael J. Bean, *The Evolution of National Wildlife Law,* 3d ed. (New York: Praeger, 1997).

72. The Defenders of Wildlife court brief made the case that the red wolf regulation is valid under the Constitution's Commerce Clause because it substantially affects interstate commerce by preserving a documented ongoing commerce in wildlife-related study and tourism generated by the reintroduced wolves.

73. Michael J. Bean, foreword to *Saving a Place: Endangered Species in the 21st Century,* ed. John A. Baden and Pete Geddes (Burlington, Vt.: Ashgate, 2000), xxi.

74. Andrew J. Hoffman, Max H. Bazerman, and Steven L. Yaffee, "Balancing Business Interests and Endangered Species Protection," in *Saving a Place,* ed. Baden and Geddes, 173–98.

75. For a comprehensive review of predator compensation programs, see Jessica Montag, *Predator Compensation Programs: An Annotated Bibliography* (Missoula: University of Montana, School of Forestry, 2001).

76. See L. David Mech, "Returning the Wolf to Yellowstone," in *The Greater Yellowstone Ecosystem,* ed. Keiter and Boyce, 309–22.

77. Ibid., 314–15.

78. Despite the Tenth Circuit's reading, the ambiguity of this clause—that animal populations are to be deemed experimental "only when, and at such times as, the population is wholly separate geographically from non-experimental populations of the same species"—will likely continue to be interpreted by other courts for recovery efforts in other regions. See Daniel R. Dinger, "Throwing *Canis lupus* to

the Wolves: *United States v. McKittrick* and the Existence of the Yellowstone and Central Idaho Experimental Wolf Populations under a Flawed Provision of the Endangered Species Act," *Brigham Young University Law Review* 2000, 1 (2000): 377–425.

79. Dale D. Goble, "Of Wolves and Welfare Ranching," *Harvard Environmental Law Review* 16 (1992): 112.

80. Jeanne Nienaber Clarke and Daniel McCool, *Staking Out the Terrain: Power Differentials among Natural Resource Management Agencies* (Albany: State University of New York Press, 1985), 78.

81. Ibid., 83–84.

82. Hank Fischer, *Wolf Wars* (Helena, Mont.: Falcon, 1995), 155.

83. Thomas McNamee, *The Return of the Wolf to Yellowstone* (New York: Henry Holt and Company, 1997), 220.

84. David Gaillard, "Wolves Here to Stay!" *The Home Range* 10, 2 (spring 2000): 6.

85. Sara Folger, "Decisions, Decisions . . . ," *The Home Range* 10, 2 (spring 2000): 4.

86. Michael Robinson, "Jaguar and Wolf Recovery in the American Southwest: Politics and Problems," *Wild Earth* 9, 4 (1999–2000): 67.

87. Legislature of the State of Idaho, Fifty-sixth Legislature, First Regular Session 2001, House Joint Memorial No. 5 by Resources and Conservation Committee; http://www3.state.id.us/oasis/HJM005.html (10 April 2001).

88. See, for example, Mark D. Duda and Kira C. Young, *New Mexico Residents' Opinions toward Mexican Wolf Reintroduction* (Harrisonburg, Va.: Responsive Management, 1995); and Kellert, *The Public and the Wolf in Minnesota* (Ely, Minn.: International Wolf Center, 1999). The debate over reintroducing wolves should not be framed as one pitting a national environmental constituency versus an antagonistic and environmentally hostile regional one. Public attitude surveys regarding Yellowstone wolf restoration prior to their release (1989), for instance, document the existence of a broad middle that falls neither in the "love'em group" or "hate'em group." Survey work by Alistair Bath shows that between the strong wolf support by members of Defenders of Wildlife and the strong opposition by members of the Wyoming Stock Growers Association is a more moderate middle. Similar to findings about public opinion regarding wolves in other regions of the country, respondents closer to potential wolf range have a more negative attitude toward the animal than those farther away. While a majority of the countywide public opposed Yellowstone reintroduction (51.7 percent opposing, 38.8 percent favoring), a plurality of the statewide public favored reintroduction (48.5 percent favoring, 34.5 percent opposing). Despite fears among some local residents that wolves would ruin hunting outside Yellowstone, a majority of members in the hunting-based Wyoming Wildlife Federation (66.8 percent) favored reintroduction. See Alistair J. Bath, "Public Attitudes about Wolf Restoration in Yellowstone National Park," in *The Greater Yellowstone Ecosystem*, ed. Keiter and Boyce, 367–76. See also A. J. Bath and T. Buchanan, "Attitudes of Interest Groups in Wyoming toward Wolf Restoration in Yellowstone National Park," *Wildlife Society Bulletin* 17 (1989): 519–25.

89. Renee Askins, "Releasing Wolves from Symbolism," *Harpers* 290 (1995): 15.

90. Hank Fischer, comments made at Predator Management in Montana Symposium, Billings, Mont., 8 January 2000.

91. William J. Paul, "Wolf Depredation on Livestock in Minnesota, Annual Update of Statistics—1999" (Grand Rapids, Minn.: U.S. Department of Agriculture, Animal and Plant Health Inspection Service, Wildlife Services, 2000).

92. U.S. Fish and Wildlife Service, *Reintroduction of the Mexican Wolf within Its Historic Range in the Southwestern United States: Final Environmental Impact Statement* (Albuquerque, N. Mex.: U.S. Fish and Wildlife Service, 1996). For a more recent assessment, including the new tribal role, see Ray Ring, "Wolf at the Door," *High Country News* 34, 10 (2002): 1, 10–14.

93. Ibid.

94. Quoted in Patrick I. Wilson, "Wolves, Politics, and the Nez Perce: Wolf Recovery in Central Idaho and the Role of Native Tribes," *Natural Resources Journal* 39 (1999): 553.

95. Ibid., 554.

96. Ibid., 558.

97. Jaime Pinkham, comments made at Predator-Prey Symposium, Boise, Idaho, 5 January 1999.

98. Quoted in Michelle Nijhuis, "Return of the Natives," *High Country News*, 26 February 2001, 12.

99. Ibid., 11.

100. Tim W. Clark, Richard P. Reading, and Alice L. Clarke, "Synthesis," in *Endangered Species Recovery*, 420, 419.

101. Bangs et al., "Status of Gray Wolf Restoration in Montana, Idaho, and Wyoming," 797.

102. Wilson, "The Wolf in Yellowstone," 465.

103. See Clark, *Averting Extinction*; and Tim W. Clark and Steven R. Kellert, "Toward a Policy Paradigm of the Wildlife Sciences," *Renewable Resources Journal* 6, 1 (1988): 7–16.

104. Susan L. Carpenter and W. J. P. Kennedy, *Managing Public Disputes: A Practical Guide to Handling Conflict and Reaching Agreements* (San Francisco: Jossey-Bass, 1988).

105. Michael K. Briand, *Practical Politics: Five Principles for a Community That Works* (Urbana: University of Illinois Press, 1999), 125.

3. Wolves and the Politics of Place

1. U.S. Fish and Wildlife Service, *Recovery Plan for the Eastern Timber Wolf* (Twin Cities, Minn.: U.S. Fish and Wildlife Service, 1992).

2. Minnesota Department of Natural Resources, *Minnesota Wolf Management Plan* (St. Paul: Minnesota Department of Natural Resources, 1999).

3. Minnesota Department of Natural Resources, *Minnesota Wolf Management Plan* (St. Paul: Minnesota Department of Natural Resources, 2001).

4. Kimberly Byrd, "The Great Minnesota Wolf Debate," *International Wolf* 10, 3 (fall 2000): 22–24.

5. U.S. Fish and Wildlife Service, *Northern Rocky Mountain Wolf Recovery Plan* (Denver: U.S. Fish and Wildlife Service, 1987), v.

6. Edward E. Bangs, Steven H. Fritts, Joseph A. Fontaine, Douglas W. Smith, Kerry M. Murphy, Curtis M. Mack, and Carter C. Niemeyer, "Status of Gray Wolf Restoration in Montana, Idaho, and Wyoming," *Wildlife Society Bulletin* 26 (1998): 785–98.

7. Robert B. Keiter, "An Introduction to the Ecosystem Management Debate," in *The Greater Yellowstone Ecosystem: Redefining America's Wilderness Heritage,* ed. Robert B. Keiter and Mark S. Boyce (New Haven: Yale University Press, 1991), 3–18.

8. David E. Brown, *The Wolf in the Southwest: The Making of an Endangered Species* (Tucson: University of Arizona Press, 1983).

9. U.S. Fish and Wildlife Service, *Mexican Wolf Recovery Plan* (Albuquerque, N. Mex.: U.S. Fish and Wildlife Service, 1982).

10. David R. Parsons, "'Green Fire' Returns to the Southwest: Reintroduction of the Mexican Wolf," *Wildlife Society Bulletin* 26 (1998): 799–807.

11. U.S. Fish and Wildlife Service, *The Reintroduction of the Mexican Wolf within Its Historic Range in the United States: Final Environmental Impact Statement* (Albuquerque, N. Mex.: U.S. Fish and Wildlife Service, 1996).

12. James P. Lester, "Federalism and State Environmental Policy," in *Environmental Politics and Policy: Theories and Evidence,* 2d ed. (Durham, N.C.: Duke University Press, 1995), 39–60; subsequent page references are given in the text.

13. See Barry G. Rabe, "The Promise and Pitfalls of Decentralization," in *Environmental Policy: New Directions for the Twenty-First Century,* ed. Norman J. Vig and Michael E. Kraft (Washington, D.C.: CQ Press, 2000), 32–54; and Lester, "Federalism and State Environmental Policy," 39–60.

14. See Robert B. Keiter and Patrick T. Holscher, "Wolf Recovery under the Endangered Species Act: A Study in Contemporary Federalism," *Public Land Law Review* 11 (spring 1990): 19–52; and Patrick Impero Wilson, "Wolves, Politics, and the Nez Perce: Wolf Recovery in Central Idaho and the Role of Native Tribes," *Natural Resources Journal* 39 (summer 1999): 543–64.

15. See Peter Matthiessen, *Wildlife in America* (New York: Viking, 1987); Rick McIntyre, ed., *War against the Wolf: America's Campaign to Exterminate the Wolf* (Stillwater, Minn.: Voyageur Press, 1995); Richard Thiel, *The Timber Wolf in Wisconsin: The Death and Life of a Majestic Predator* (Madison: University of Wisconsin Press, 1993); and Stanley Paul Young, *The Wolf in North American History* (Caldwell, Idaho: Caxton Printers, 1946).

16. Keiter and Holscher, "Wolf Recovery under the Endangered Species Act," 23.

17. Lester, "Federalism and State Environmental Policy."

18. William R. Mangun and Jean C. Mangun, "An Intergovernmental Dilemma in Policy Implementation," in *Public Policy Issues in Wildlife Management,* ed. William R. Mangun (New York: Greenwood Press, 1991), 3–16; William R. Mangun and Jean C. Mangun, "Implementing Wildlife Policy across Political Jurisdictions," *Policy Studies Journal* 19 (1991): 519–26.

19. See Michael J. Bean and Melanie J. Rowland, *The Evolution of National Wildlife Law,* 3d ed. (Westport, Conn.: Praeger, 1997).

20. Defenders of Wildlife, *Saving Biodiversity: A Status Report on State Laws, Policies and Programs* (Washington, D.C.: Defenders of Wildlife, 1996).

21. See Mangun and Mangun, "An Intergovernmental Dilemma in Policy Implementation," 3–16.

22. William R. Mangun, "Fish and Wildlife Policy Issues," in *American Fish and Wildlife Policy: The Human Dimension* (Carbondale, Ill.: Southern Illinois University Press, 1992), 3–32.

23. James A. Tober, *Wildlife and the Public Interest: Nonprofit Organizations and Federal Wildlife Policy* (New York: Praeger, 1989).

24. Bob Ream, "A History of Wolf Restoration Policy and Politics in the Northern Rocky Mountains, U.S.," paper presented at Beyond 2000: Realities of Global Wolf Restoration Symposium, Duluth, Minn., 23–26 February 2000.

25. See, for example, Daniel J. Elazar, Virginia Gray, and Wyman Spano, *Minnesota Politics and Government* (Lincoln: University of Nebraska Press, 1999); and Neal Peirce, "Minnesota: The Successful Society," in *The Great Plains States of America: People, Politics, and Power in the Nine Great Plains States* (New York: W. W. Norton, 1973).

26. Elazar, Gray, and Spano, *Minnesota Politics and Government*, 19, 206, 171.

27. See Congressional Research Service, *Major Federal Land Management Agencies: Management of Our Nation's Lands and Resources* (Washington, D.C.: Congressional Research Service, 1995). Wilderness statistics also available at http://www.wilderness.net/nwps/ (30 January 2001).

28. Kevin Proescholdt, Rip Rapson, and Miron L. Heinselman, *Troubled Waters: The Fight for the Boundary Waters Canoe Area Wilderness* (St. Cloud, Minn.: North Star Press, 1995).

29. Charles F. Wilkinson, *Crossing the Next Meridian: Land, Water, and the Future of the West* (Washington, D.C.: Island Press, 1992), 17.

30. Roderick Nash, *Wilderness and the American Mind* (New Haven: Yale University Press, 1967), 24–25.

31. Young, *The Wolf in North American History*, 111, 146.

32. Keiter, "An Introduction to the Ecosystem Management Debate," 13.

33. Renee Askins, "Releasing Wolves from Symbolism (excerpts from testimony before the House Committee on Resources)," *Harper's* 290 (April 1995): 15.

34. Michael J. Manfredo and Harry C. Zinn, "Population Change and Its Implications for Wildlife Management in the New West: A Case Study of Colorado," *Human Dimensions of Wildlife* 1, 3 (fall 1996): 62–74.

35. Ibid.

36. Ibid., 70.

37. Ray Rasker and Ben Alexander, *The New Challenge: People, Commerce, and the Environment in the Yellowstone to Yukon Region* (The Wilderness Society, 1997).

38. Jim Howe, Ed McMahon, and Luther Probst, *Balancing Nature and Commerce in Gateway Communities* (Washington, D.C.: Island Press, 1997).

39. Vanessa K. Johnson, *Rural Residential Development Trends in the Greater Yellowstone Ecosystem since the Listing of the Grizzly Bear, 1975–1998* (Bozeman, Mont.: Sierra Club Grizzly Bear Ecosystems Project, 2000).

40. Richard L. Knight, "Private Lands: The Neglected Geography," *Conservation Biology* 13 (1999): 223–24.

41. See, for example, Debra L. Donahue, *The Western Range Revisited: Removing Livestock from Public Lands to Conserve Native Biodiversity* (Norman: University of Oklahoma Press, 1999); Denzel Ferguson and Nancy Ferguson, *Sacred Cows at the Public Trough* (Bend, Oreg.: Maverick, 1984); and George Wuerthner, "Subdivisions versus Agriculture," *Conservation Biology* 8 (1994): 905–8.

42. Hank Fischer, *Wolf Wars: The Remarkable Inside Story of the Restoration of Wolves to Yellowstone* (Helena, Mont.: Falcon, 1995).

43. Paul H. Templet, "The Positive Relationship between Jobs, Environment, and the Economy: An Empirical Analysis and Review," *Spectrum: The Journal of State Government* 68, 2 (1995): 37–50.

44. Stephen M. Meyer, *Environmentalism and Economic Prosperity: Testing the Environmental Impact Hypothesis,* Massachusetts Institute of Technology, Project on Environmental Politics and Policy, 1992.

45. Thomas Michael Power, *Lost Landscapes and Failed Economies: The Search for a Value of Place* (Washington, D.C.: Island Press, 1996).

46. Thomas Michael Power, "Ecosystem Preservation and the Economy in the Greater Yellowstone Area," *Conservation Biology* 5 (1991): 395–404.

47. Ibid., 395.

48. Stephen M. Meyer, *Endangered Species Listings and State Economic Performance,* Working Paper No. 4., Massachusetts Institute of Technology, Project on Environmental Politics and Policy, March 1995.

49. Jane Brisset and Craig Lincoln, "Economic Diversity Eludes Northland," *Duluth News Tribune,* 29 August 1999, A1. Economic data from Minnesota Department of Economic Security and Minnesota Department of Revenue.

50. For depredation statistics and associated monetary costs, see L. David Mech, "Estimated Costs of Maintaining a Recovered Wolf Population in Agricultural Regions of Minnesota," *Wildlife Society Bulletin* 26 (1998): 817–22; and William J. Paul, *Wolf Depredation on Livestock in Minnesota, Annual Update of Statistics, 1999* (Grand Rapids, Minn.: USDA, Wildlife Services, 1999).

51. U.S. Fish and Wildlife Service, *The Reintroduction of the Mexican Wolf within Its Historic Range in the United States: Final Environmental Impact Statement.*

52. Ad in *New York Times,* 3 May 1999; http://www.sw-center.org (13 December 1999).

53. Patricia Wolff, *The Taxpayers Guide to Subsidized Ranching in the Southwest,* produced by the Center for Biological Diversity and New West Research, September 1999, 3.

54. George Wuerthner, "Why Wolf Recovery Is a Failure," *High Country News,* 19 June 2000, 16.

55. Joel Carson, "Reintroducing the Mexican Wolf: Will the Public Share the Costs, or Will the Burden Be Borne by a Few?" *Natural Resources Journal* 38 (spring 1998): 297–326.

56. See, for example, Willett Kempton, James S. Boster, and Jennifer A. Hartley, *Environmental Values in American Culture* (Cambridge, Mass.: MIT Press, 1995).

57. Robert S. Erikson, Gerald C. Wright, and John P. McIver, *Statehouse Democracy: Public Opinion and Policy in the American States* (Cambridge: Cambridge University Press, 1993); and James A. Stimson, Michael B. MacKuen, and Robert S. Erikson, "Dynamic Representation," *American Political Science Review* 89, 3 (1995): 543–64.

58. Stephen R. Kellert, *The Public and the Wolf in Minnesota, 1999* (Ely, Minn.: International Wolf Center, 1999).

59. Stephen R. Kellert, *The Value of Life: Biological Diversity and Human Society* (Washington, D.C.: Island Press, 1996), 106–7.

60. See Stephen R. Kellert, "The Public and the Timber Wolf in Minnesota," *Transactions of the North American Wildlife and Natural Resources Conference* 51 (1986): 193–200; and Kellert, *The Public and the Wolf in Minnesota, 1999.*

61. Kellert, *The Public and the Wolf in Minnesota, 1999*, 400.

62. Ibid.

63. Support for the MDNR in other policy areas has been found by other public opinion surveys as well. Minnesotans appear satisfied with the agency, even during a time of changing demographic patterns and management priorities. See John Myers, "Minnesotans Happy with DNR," *Duluth News Tribune*, 26 September 2000, A1.

64. Kathryn A. Schoenecker and William W. Shaw, "Attitudes toward a Proposed Reintroduction of Mexican Gray Wolves in Arizona," *Human Dimensions of Wildlife* 2 (1997): 42–55.

65. Mark D. Duda and Kira C. Young, *New Mexico Residents' Opinions toward Mexican Wolf Reintroduction* (Harrisonburg, Va.: Responsive Management, 1995).

66. Terry B. Johnson, *Preliminary Results of a Public Opinion Survey of Arizona Residents and Interest Groups about the Mexican Wolf* (Phoenix: Arizona Game and Fish Department, 1990).

67. Responsive Management, *Wildlife and the American Mind: Public Opinion on and Attitudes toward Fish and Wildlife Management* (Harrisonburg, Va.: Responsive Management, 1998), 154.

68. See reproduced comment letters on the Draft Environmental Impact Statement from federal, state, and tribal agencies, members of Congress, state legislators, and local governments in U.S. Fish and Wildlife Service, *The Reintroduction of the Mexican Wolf within Its Historic Range in the United States: Final Environmental Impact Statement.*

69. Rob Breeding, "Questions for Feds about Wolf Recovery," *Arizona Daily Sun*, 18 May 2001, D1.

70. Minnesota Department of Natural Resources, *Minnesota Wolf Management Plan.*

71. Jerry Maracchini, Director, State of New Mexico, Department of Game and Fish, letter to Nancy Kaufman concerning DEIS, October 27, 1995, in U.S. Fish and Wildlife Service, *The Reintroduction of the Mexican Wolf within Its Historic Range in the United States: Final Environmental Impact Statement.*

72. See Ruth S. Musgrave and Mary Anne Stein, *State Wildlife Laws Handbook* (Rockville, Md.: Government Institutes, 1993). Minnesota's DNR has no fish and game commission. Instead, a commissioner of Natural Resources is appointed by the governor, and each division director is subject to the supervision of this commissioner.

73. Humane Society of the United States, "State Wildlife Management: The Pervasive Influence of Hunters, Hunting, Culture and Money"; http://www.hsus.org/programs/wildlife/factsheets/swmfact.html (6 September 2000).

74. Humane Society of the United States, "It's Time to Fight for Minnesota's Gray Wolves," 16 February 2000; http://www.hsus.org/whatnew/graywolves021600. html (6 September 2000).

75. William R. Mangun, "Fiscal Constraints to Nongame Management Programs," in *Management of Nongame Wildlife in the Midwest: A Developing Art*, ed. James B. Hale, Louis B. Best, and Richard L. Clawson (Chelsea, Mich.: Bookcrafters, North Central Section of the Wildlife Society, 1986), 23–32.

76. Mangun and Mangun, "An Intergovernmental Dilemma in Policy Implementation," 5.

77. Ted Williams, "Who's Managing the Wildlife Managers?" *Orion Nature Quarterly* 5, 4 (1986): 20.

78. Minnesota Department of Natural Resources, *Who Pays for the DNR?* (St. Paul: Minnesota Department of Natural Resources, 1998).

79. John Myers, "Who's Guarding the Outdoors?" *Duluth News Tribune*, 16 January 2000, 4D.

80. Ibid.

81. Arizona Game and Fish Department, *2000–2001 Annual Report* (Phoenix: Arizona Game and Fish Department, 2001).

82. New Mexico Game and Fish Department, *1999 Annual Report* (Albuquerque: New Mexico Game and Fish Department, 1999).

83. Deborah Stone, *Policy Paradox: The Art of Political Decision Making* (New York: W. W. Norton & Company, 1997).

84. Statement of Representative Helen Chenoweth-Hage, Hearing on S. 2123, the "Conservation and Reinvestment Act," Senate Committee on Environment and Public Works, May 24, 2000; http://www.House.gov/chenoweth/ (13 September 2000).

85. See Jon Margolis, "CARA's Not Quite the Girl She Used to Be," *High Country News*, 6 November 2000.

86. Quoted in Ruth S. Musgrave and Mary Anne Stein, *State Wildlife Laws Handbook* (Rockville, Md.: Government Institutes, 1993), 382.

87. L. David Mech, "A New Era for Carnivore Conservation," *Wildlife Society Bulletin* 24, 3 (1996): 397–401.

88. The important factors related to successful wolf recovery in the Upper Peninsula, at least according to one veteran wildlife manager in the state, include the following: (1) favorable wolf habitat: over 90 percent of the Upper Peninsula is forested, roughly half is comprised of public land, and the remainder is mostly owned by timber companies or is private woodland; (2) geography: unlike Isle Royale, the Upper Peninsula is no island, and it has benefited from healthy wolf populations in Ontario, Minnesota, and Wisconsin; (3) deer: the white-tailed deer population has made a striking recovery since the 1970s. This rebound has provided an opportunity for wolves to recolonize the area, while alleviating (at least for the moment) fears of unacceptable wolf-caused losses; (4) no significant public lands ranching: little ranching is practiced in the area, and what ranching and farming there are remain isolated and are more monitored than in the West; (5) public opinion: the Michigan DNR took a pro-active role and commissioned a public attitude survey regarding wolves at the right time and in the right way. Like placing a toe in unknown water, the department found that Upper Peninsula residents as well as hunters were generally pro-wolf and positive about *natural* wolf recovery in the state; (6) environmental awareness, information, and education: this is generally harder to isolate, but according to this manager, it is no less important than these other factors. He believes that compared to 1974, the amount and quality of information regarding predators in larger ecosystems has improved noticeably.

4. The Use of Stakeholders and Public Participation in Wolf Policymaking and Management

1. See Douglas J. Amy, *The Politics of Environmental Mediation* (New York: Columbia University Press, 1987); James E. Crowfoot and Julia M. Wondolleck, *Environmental Disputes: Community Involvement in Conflict Resolution* (Washington,

D.C.: Island Press, 1990); and Julia M. Wondolleck, *Public Lands Conflict and Reso-lution: Managing National Forest Disputes* (New York: Plenum, 1988).

2. Quoted in Donald Snow, "Coming Home: An Introduction to Collaborative Conservation," in *Across the Great Divide: Explorations in Collaborative Conservation and the American West,* ed. Philip Brick, Donald Snow, and Sarah Van de Wetering (Washington, D.C.: Island Press, 2000), 2.

3. Margaret A. Moote, Mitchell P. McClaran, and Donna K. Chickering, "Theory in Practice: Applying Participatory Democracy Theory to Public Land Planning," *Environmental Management* 21 (1997): 877–89. Also see Toddi A. Steelman and William Ascher, "Public Involvement Methods in Natural Resource Policy Making: Advantages, Disadvantages and Trade-Offs," *Policy Sciences* 30 (1997): 71–90.

4. Barb Cestero, *Beyond the Hundredth Meeting: A Field Guide to Collaborative Conservation on the West's Public Lands* (Tucson, Ariz.: Sonoran Institute, 1999), 9.

5. Julia M. Wondolleck and Steven L. Yaffee, *Making Collaboration Work: Lessons from Innovation in Natural Resource Management* (Washington, D.C.: Island Press, 2000), 21.

6. In Susan L. Flader, *Thinking Like a Mountain: Aldo Leopold and the Evolution of an Ecological Attitude toward Deer, Wolves, and Forests* (Columbia: University of Missouri Press, 1974).

7. U.S. Fish and Wildlife Service, *Grizzly Bear Recovery in the Bitterroot Ecosystem: Final Environmental Impact Statement* (Missoula, Mont.: U.S. Fish and Wildlife Service, 2000).

8. Ibid., xix.

9. For an informative discussion of the paradigm shift in the field of wildlife management, see Daniel J. Decker, Charles C. Krueger, Richard A. Baer Jr., Barbara A. Knuth, and Milo E. Richmond, "From Clients to Stakeholders: A Philosophical Shift for Fish and Wildlife Management," *Human Dimensions of Wildlife* 1, 1 (1996): 70–82.

10. Ibid.

11. Ibid., 71.

12. Ibid., 80.

13. Lisa C. Chase, Tania M. Schusler, and Daniel J. Decker, "Innovations in Stake-holder Involvement: What's the Next Step?" *Wildlife Society Bulletin* 28 (2000): 208–17. Also see Daniel J. Decker and Lisa C. Chase, "Human Dimensions of Living with Wildlife—Management Challenges for the 21st Century," *Wildlife Society Bulletin* 25 (1997): 788–95.

14. Steven A. Primm, "A Pragmatic Approach to Grizzly Bear Conservation," *Conservation Biology* 10 (1996): 1026–35.

15. Ibid., 1033.

16. Congressional Research Service, *Endangered Species List Revisions: A Summary of Delisting and Downlisting,* Washington, D.C., 5 January 1998.

17. Julia M. Wondolleck, Steven L. Yaffee, and James E. Crowfoot, "A Conflict Management Perspective: Applying the Principles of Alternative Dispute Resolution," in *Endangered Species Recovery: Finding the Lessons, Improving the Process* ed. Tim W. Clark, Richard Reading, and Alice L. Clarke (Washington, D.C.: Island Press, 1994), 306.

18. Cestero, *Beyond the Hundredth Meeting,* 4.

19. Garret Hardin, "The Tragedy of the Commons," *Science* 162 (1968): 1243–48.

20. Elinor Ostrom, *Governing the Commons: The Evolution of Institutions for Collective Action* (Cambridge: Cambridge University Press, 1990); and Elinor Ostrom et al., "Revisiting the Commons: Local Lessons, Global Challenges," *Science* 284 (1999): 278–82.

21. See Jeanne Nienaber Clarke and Daniel McCool, *Staking Out the Terrain: Power Differentials among Natural Resource Management Agencies* (Albany: State University of New York Press, 1985); and Phillip Foss, *Politics and Grass* (Seattle: University of Washington Press, 1960).

22. Ed Marston, "Bringing Back Grizzlies Splits Environmentalists," *High Country News*, 13 May 1996, 15; special issue devoted to collaboration in the American West.

23. Sherry Arnstein, "A Ladder of Citizen Participation," *Journal of the American Institute of Planners* 35 (1969): 216–24.

24. Daniel Kemmis, *Community and the Politics of Place* (Norman: University of Oklahoma Press, 1990), 116.

25. Ibid., 126–27.

26. See Benjamin Barber, *Strong Democracy: Participatory Politics for a New Age* (Berkeley: University of California Press, 1984); Carole Pateman, *Participation and Democratic Theory* (Cambridge: Cambridge University Press, 1970); and Robert Putnam, "Bowling Alone: America's Declining Social Capital," *Journal of Democracy* 6 (1995): 65–78.

27. Hanna J. Cortner and Margaret A. Moote, *The Politics of Ecosystem Management* (Washington, D.C.: Island Press, 1999).

28. Thomas Prugh, Robert Costanza, and Herman Daly, *The Local Politics of Global Sustainability* (Washington, D.C.: Island Press, 2000).

29. See George C. Coggins, "Regulating Federal Natural Resources: A Summary Case against Devolved Collaboration," *Ecology Law Quarterly* 25, 4 (1998): 602–10.

30. Senator Larry Craig, "Lynx, Bears, and Wolves—Oh My!!" March 31, 2000; http: www.senate.gov/~craig/releases/COLlynxprotect.htm (13 September 2000).

31. For a good discussion of this issue, see Jan E. Dizard, *Going Wild: Hunting, Animal Rights, and the Contested Meaning of Nature* (Amherst: University of Massachusetts Press, 1999).

32. See Edward P. Weber, "The Question of Accountability in Historical Perspective: From Jackson to Contemporary Grassroots Ecosystem Management," *Administration & Society* 31, 4 (1999): 451–94.

33. Sarah B. Pralle, "Issue Containment in Forestry Politics: A Case Study of the Quincy Library Group," paper presented at the 2001 Annual Meeting of the Western Political Science Association, 15–17 March 2001, Las Vegas, Nev.

34. Michael McCloskey, "The Skeptic: Collaboration Has Its Limits," *High Country News*, 13 May 1996, 7. Also see Michael McCloskey, "Local Communities and the Management of Public Forests," *Ecology Law Quarterly* 25, 4 (1999): 624–29.

35. McCloskey, "The Skeptic," 7.

36. Amy, *The Politics of Environmental Mediation*, 161.

37. Ibid., 134.

38. Minnesota Department of Natural Resources, *Minnesota Wolf Management Plan*, February 1999.

39. Allen Garber, comments made at Beyond 2000: Realities of Global Wolf Restoration, Duluth, Minn., 25 February 2000.

40. Martiga Lohn, "Wolf Plan Rejected by Senate," *Duluth News Tribune*, 14 April 2000, 1A.

41. Defenders of Wildlife, "Action Alert: Minnesota Wolf Needs Your Help."

42. Wisconsin Department of Natural Resources, *Wisconsin Wolf Management Plan* (Madison: Wisconsin Department of Natural Resources, 1999).

43. Legislative approval is required if the department recommends public hunting with a zone and quota system.

44. Christine L. Thomas, "The Policy/Administration Continuum: Wisconsin Natural Resource Board Decisions," *Public Administration Review* 50 (1990): 446–49.

45. Wisconsin Department of Natural Resources, Natural Resources Board; http://www.dnr.state.wi.us/org/nrboard/ (16 January 2002).

46. The stakeholder team, illustrating the types of interests and values of this approach, includes some of the following organizations: Wisconsin Trappers Association, the Wisconsin Cattlemen's Association, the Timber Wolf Alliance, the Timber Wolf Information Network, Sierra Club, Defenders of Wildlife, Audubon Society, Izaak Walton League, Wisconsin Bowhunter's Association, Dairy Farmer's Association, Wisconsin Poultry Growers Association, Wisconsin Humane Society, Alliance for Animals, Wisconsin Farm Bureau, and a representative of each Wisconsin Native American tribe.

47. U.S. Fish and Wildlife Service, *Recovery Plan for the Eastern Timber Wolf* (Twin Cities, Minn.: U.S. Fish and Wildlife Service, 1992).

48. For polling information, see Responsive Management, *Wildlife and the American Mind: Public Opinion on and Attitudes toward Fish and Wildlife Management* (Harrisonburg, Va.: Responsive Management, 1998), 207–21.

49. Bill Weber, "Way of the Wolf," *Wildlife Conservation* 102 (1999): 41.

50. Nina Fascione and Stephen Kendrot, "Wolves for the Adirondacks?" *Adirondack Journal of Environmental Studies* spring/summer (1998): 7–10.

51. See Timothy Rawson, *Changing Tracks: Predators and Politics in Mt. McKinley National Park* (Anchorage: University of Alaska Press, 2001).

52. See Samuel J. Harbo Jr. and Frederick C. Dean, "Historical and Current Perspectives on Wolf Management in Alaska," in *Wolves in Canada and Alaska: Their Status, Biology and Management*, ed. Ludwig N. Carbyn (Edmonton, Alberta: Canadian Wildlife Service Report Series Number 45, 1981).

53. Dale A. Haggstrom, Anne K. Ruggles, Catherine M. Harms, and Robert O. Stephenson, "Citizen Participation in Developing a Wolf Management Plan for Alaska: An Attempt to Resolve Conflicting Human Values and Perceptions," in *Ecology and Conservation of Wolves in a Changing World*, ed. Ludwig N. Carbyn, Steven H. Fritts, and Dale R. Seip (Edmonton, Alberta: Canadian Circumpolar Institute, 1995), 482.

54. Ibid., 483.

55. Ibid., 485.

56. National Research Council, *Wolves, Bears, and Their Prey in Alaska: Biological and Social Challenges in Wildlife Management* (Washington, D.C.: National Academy Press, 1997), 15.

57. Ibid., 176.

58. Alaska Department of Fish and Game, press release, "State Adopts Non-Lethal Wolf Management Program," 18 November 1997.

59. Gordon C. Haber, "State's 'Nonlethal' Wolf Control Is a Snow Job," *Anchorage Daily News*, 29 November 1997, B8.

60. Stephen Wells, "Assault on Fortymile Wolves Begins," *The Spirit* 17, 1 (1998): 5.

61. Cestero, *Beyond the Hundredth Meeting*, 71.

62. Wondolleck and Yaffee, *Making Collaboration Work*, 250.

63. Cestero, *Beyond the Hundredth Meeting*, 74.

64. Defenders of Wildlife, *Places for Wolves: A Blueprint for Restoration and Long-Term Recovery in the Lower 48 States* (Washington, D.C.: Defenders of Wildlife, 1999).

65. William P. Browne and Allan J. Cigler, eds., *U.S. Agricultural Groups: Institutional Profiles* (New York: Greenwood Press, 1990), 24.

66. Ibid.

67. Rodger Schlickeisen, foreword to *Amber Waves of Gain: How the Farm Bureau Is Reaping Profits at the Expense of America's Family Farmers, Taxpayers and the Environment*, by Defenders of Wildlife (April 2000).

68. Defenders of Wildlife, *Amber Waves of Gain*. The report attempts to build on an earlier investigation by the late Joseph Y. Resnick, a two-term congressman from New York, and his former aide Samuel R. Berger (later to become National Security Advisor to President Clinton). See Samuel R. Berger, *Dollar Harvest: The Story of the Farm Bureau* (Lexington, Mass.: Heath Lexington Books, 1971).

69. Defenders of Wildlife, *Amber Waves of Gain*, 46.

70. Ibid., 61, 57.

71. Ibid., 84.

72. "Statement by AFBF President Bob Stallman Regarding the April 9-'60 Minutes' Attack on Farm Bureau"; http://www.fb.org/news/ (25 September 2000).

73. Stewart Truelsen, "60 Minutes Déjà Vu"; http://www.fb.org/views/ (September 25, 2000).

74. Ibid.

75. See, for example, Tom Knudson, "Green Machine: Mission Adrift in a Frenzy of Fund Raising," *Sacramento Bee*, 23 April 2001, A1; part of a controversial special report on the current state of American environmentalism ("Environment, Inc").

76. For a discussion of this issue as it pertains to Yellowstone, see James G. Thompson, "Addressing the Human Dimensions of Wolf Reintroduction: An Example Using Estimates of Livestock Depredation and Costs of Compensation," *Society and Natural Resources* 6 (1993): 165–79.

77. James G. MacCracken and Jay O' Laughlin, "Recovery Policy on Grizzly Bears: An Analysis of Two Positions," *Wildlife Society Bulletin* 26, 4 (1998): 905.

78. Ibid.

79. See Kemmis, *Community and the Politics of Place*; and Wendell Berry, *Sex, Economy, Freedom, and Community* (New York: Pantheon Books, 1993).

80. Jody W. Enck and Tommy L. Brown, *Preliminary Assessment of Social Feasibility for Reintroducing Gray Wolves to the Adirondack Park in Northern New York*, Human Dimensions Research Unit Series No. 00-3, Department of Natural Resources, Cornell University, Ithaca, N.Y., 2000, 46.

81. Catherine Henshaw Knott explores the importance of "communities of place" in *Living with the Adirondack Forest: Local Perspectives on Land Use Conflicts* (Ithaca, N.Y.: Cornell University Press, 1998). Knott, an anthropologist, argues that

locals in the Adirondacks, especially those with expert knowledge, should play a greater role in land-use decisions than they currently do now. Many of the values and concerns of rural citizens given voice in Knott's book were echoed time and again in my interviews and fieldwork in rural parts of the country. She sees many local "woodspeople" not as ignorant knee-jerk anti-environmentalists but as important yet largely untapped storehouses of indigenous knowledge and information. Knott sees these marginalized and largely powerless local citizens as able to provide one source of important information and ecological knowledge on which land-use decisions should be based. She says, "It is crucial that the woodspeople themselves make their voices heard above the battle, in the desolate pauses between confrontations, because in the end they are a part of the Adirondack land community. Because of their membership in this community and their role as the bearers of indigenous knowledge of the land, they are among the best potential mediators of the conflict—people who value the land and their deep connections to it" (278).

82. See David Dobbs, "On the Track of Something Good," *Audubon* 101, 3 (May–June 1999): 36–39; and Steve Lerner, "A Walk on the Wild Side," *Amicus Journal* 21, 2 (summer 1999): 22–25.

83. Jane E. Wiedenhoeft, Sarah Boles, Alexia Sabor, and Pam Troxell, "A Volunteer Carnivore Tracking Program and Its Potential Use in Monitoring the Timber Wolf *(Canis lupus)* Population in Northern and Central Wisconsin" (Park Falls: Wisconsin Department of Natural Resources, 2000).

84. Carolyn Callaghan, Timothy Kaminski, Charles Mamo, and Michael Gong, "The Southern Alberta Conservation Cooperative: Community Conservation for Wolves, Grizzly Bears and Ranchers," paper presented at Defenders of Wildlife's Carnivores 2000: A Conference on Carnivore Conservation in the 21st Century, 12–15 November 2000, Denver.

85. For an important discussion of this issue as it pertains to Canadian forest management, see National Aboriginal Forestry Association, "Aboriginal Participation in Forest Management: Not Just Another Stakeholder," Ottawa, Ontario, 1995.

86. See Daniel Sarewitz, Roger A. Pielke Jr., and Radford Byerly Jr., eds., *Prediction: Science, Decision Making, and the Future of Nature* (Washington, D.C.: Island Press, 2000).

87. George J. Busenberg, "Collaborative and Adversarial Analysis in Environmental Policy," *Policy Sciences* 32 (1999): 1.

88. Ibid.

89. Decker et al., "From Clients to Stakeholders."

90. A surprise amendment in the U.S. Senate seeking to legislate wolves out of Oregon provides an important example of how the democratic approach to policymaking is sometimes not so democratic. A few wolves had made their way from Idaho to eastern Oregon, much to the dismay of the Oregon Cattlemen's Association. An amendment was added to the FY 2001 Department of the Interior appropriations funding bill that would disallow any future wolf migration while also calling for the removal of any wolves already in the area. This type of policymaking is becoming increasingly popular in Washington. Idaho State University political scientist Ralph Maughan, a specialist in the predator politics of the Northern Rockies region, is not surprised by this legislative behavior. Congress, he says, has taken to all sorts of methods that can be used to avoid having to achieve a majority to pass legislation or to even know who is behind it. Members bring legislation to the floor

that has not had a hearing, they add major provisions to bills in conference committee that were never discussed on the House or Senate floor, and they are blatantly legislating in an appropriations bill.

91. Cestero, *Beyond the Hundredth Meeting*, 74–75.

92. For a more detailed analysis, see Susan Todd, *Designing Effective Negotiating Teams for Environmental Disputes: An Analysis of Three Wolf Management Plans* (Ph.D. diss., University of Michigan, 1995). Todd, an experienced facilitator who facilitated the Fortymile Caribou Management Team, examines the British Columbia Wolf Working Group, the Alaska Wolf Management Team, and the Yukon Wolf Management Team.

Conclusion

1. Steven A. Primm and Tim W. Clark, "Making Sense of the Policy Process for Carnivore Conservation," *Conservation Biology* 10, 4 (1996): 1037.

2. According to Harold D. Lasswell, "the policy sciences of democracy" were "directed toward knowledge to improve the practice of democracy." See Harold D. Lasswell, "The Policy Orientation," in *The Policy Sciences*, ed. Daniel Lerner and Harold D. Lasswell (Palo Alto, Calif.: Stanford University Press, 1951), 15. For more contemporary discussions of this democratic approach, see Peter deLeon, *Democracy and the Policy Sciences* (Albany: State University of New York Press, 1997); Frank Fischer, *Citizens, Experts, and the Environment: The Politics of Local Knowledge* (Durham, N.C.: Duke University Press, 2000); Frank Fischer, "Citizen Participation and the Democratization of Policy Expertise: From Theoretical Inquiry to Practical Cases," *Policy Sciences* 26 (1993): 165–87; and Lawrence C. Walters, James Aydelotte, and Jessica Miller, "Putting More Public in Policy Analysis," *Public Administration Review* 60, 4 (2000): 349–59.

3. Mark Sagoff, *The Economy of the Earth: Philosophy, Law, and the Environment* (Cambridge: Cambridge University Press, 1988), 70.

4. David A. Rochefort and Roger W. Cobb, "Problem Definition: An Emerging Perspective," in *The Politics of Problem Definition: Shaping the Policy Agenda* (Lawrence: University Press of Kansas, 1994), 5.

5. Deborah Stone, *Policy Paradox: The Art of Political Decision Making* (New York: W. W. Norton, 1997), 376.

6. Jack Turner, *The Abstract Wild* (Tucson: University of Arizona Press, 1996), 119.

7. See Jan E. Dizard, *Going Wild: Hunting, Animal Rights, and the Contested Meaning of Nature* (Amherst: University of Massachusetts Press, 1999).

8. Rob Edward, "Government for the Few," *Southern Rockies Wolf Tracks* 7, 2 (winter 1999): 3.

9. Dan Dagget, *Beyond the Rangeland Conflict: Toward a West That Works* (Layton, Utah: Gibbs Smith, 1995).

10. Charles F. Wilkinson, *Crossing the Next Meridian: Land, Water, and the Future of the West* (Washington, D.C.: Island Press, 1992).

11. Aldo Leopold, *A Sand County Almanac* (Oxford: Oxford University Press, 1966), 247.

12. Sagoff, *The Economy of the Earth*, 70, 28.

13. L. David Mech, "Estimated Costs of Maintaining a Recovered Wolf Population in Agricultural Regions of Minnesota," *Wildlife Society Bulletin* 26 (1998): 817–22.

Index

Martin A. Nie is assistant professor of natural resource policy in the School of Forestry at the University of Montana.